The Modernist House

The Modernist House presents a global survey of 100 iconic houses. Organized chronologically, this exciting collection begins in the early twentieth century and traces the development of architecture's response to living in an industrialized world. The selection includes key works from the 1920s and 1930s, and goes on to explore the International Style they inspired. Later works are influenced by architectural debates about regional influences and responses to globalization. Every aspect of the Modernist house is explored: the concern for new materials and technology, the rejection of ornament and a predilection for plain surfaces and open-plan living. Here is the chance to compare the work of the world's best-known Modern architects, through their most significant houses. Exemplary buildings such as Le Corbusier's Villa Savoye, Walter Gropius's Double House and Ludwig Mies van der Rohe's Farnsworth House are presented alongside buildings by lesser-known architects. ***The Modernist House*** is an essential guide to this fascinating period of architectural history.

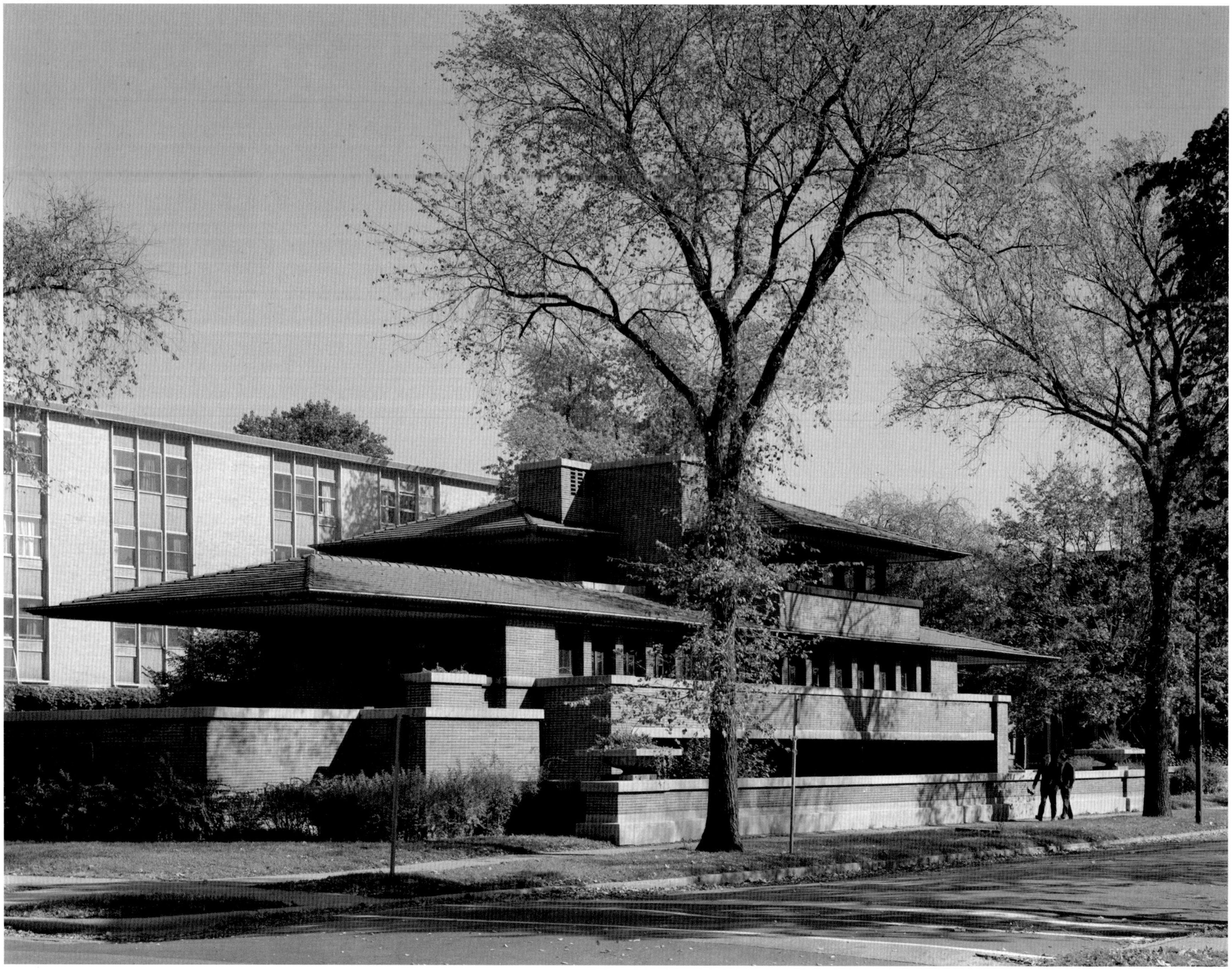

Robie House Frank Lloyd Wright

Inspired by the flat, expansive landscape of the American Midwest, Robie House is the quintessential expression of the Prairie Style of architecture that typified Frank Lloyd Wright's early career. Wright was reacting against the historical revivalism prevalent in American building at the time and sought to create a new form of domestic design that combined functionality with beauty. The house is characterized by its linearity, emphasized by low proportions and long bands of windows. A gently sloping, hipped roof overhangs dramatically to shelter the house from the elements. Inside, the open-plan space radiates from a sturdy central fireplace and the light fittings, furniture and carpets are part of the integral design. Considered to be one of the most influential buildings in the architectural history of the United States, Robie House inspired a revolution in design and was a precursor to European movements such as Modernism, Constructivism, the Bauhaus and minimalism.

Robie House, Chicago, IL, USA, 1908–10. **Frank Lloyd Wright**. **b** Richland Center, WI, USA, 1867. **d** Phoenix, AZ, USA, 1959.

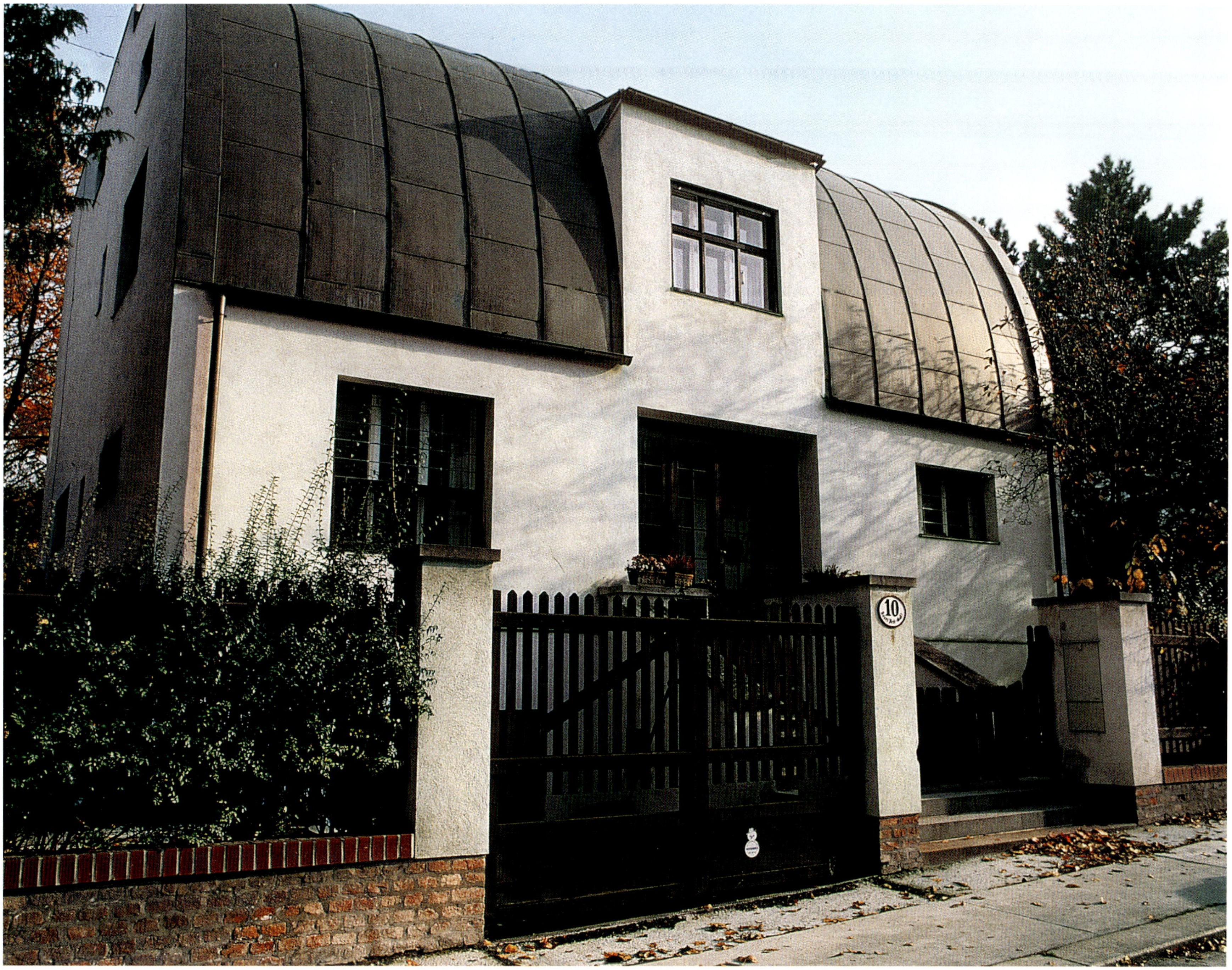

Steiner House Adolf Loos

The curved metal roofline of the street front of this house masks its scale and the fact that it is built on three levels; more importantly, that the rear facade is rectilinear and flat-roofed, evidence of Adolf Loos's perception of architecture as spatial sequences, or *Raumplan*. One of the first houses to be constructed of reinforced concrete, the Steiner House is also one of the few built works by Loos, a famous polemicist against the elaborate decoration of the Art Nouveau and Vienna Secessionist movements. Apart from the curved roof, the geometric form and rear garden facade of the house anticipate later Modern characteristics, such as functional interior spaces, solid white cubic forms and horizontal fenestration. Loos, influenced by a visit to the United States where he encountered the severity of Louis Sullivan's work, fought against ornamentation; his famous essay 'Ornament and Crime' was published in 1908.

Steiner House, Vienna, Austria, 1910. **Adolf Loos**. **b** Brno, Czech Republic, 1870. **d** Vienna, Austria, 1933.

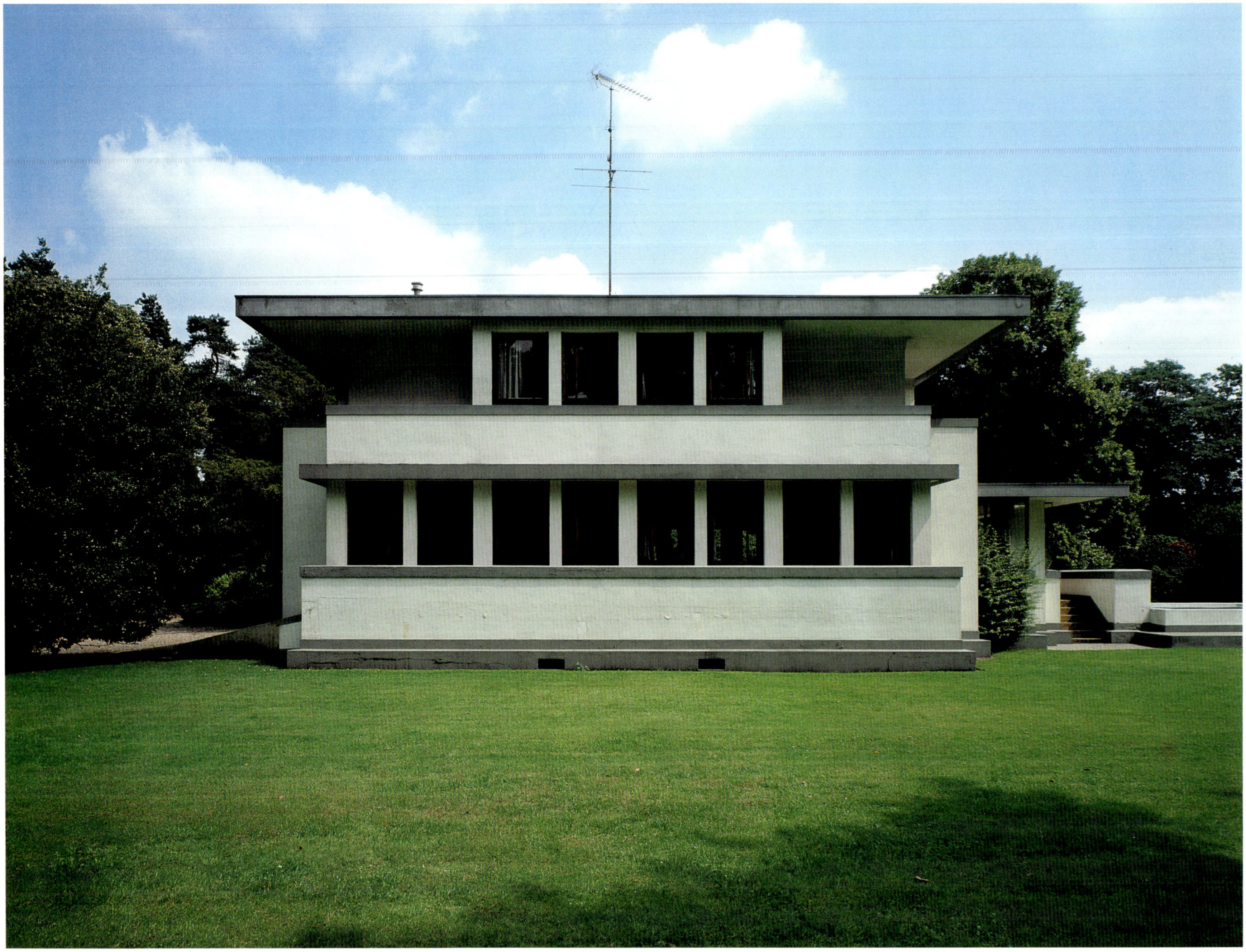

Villa Nora Robert van't Hoff

The horizontality of this flat-roofed house is emphasized by the grey lines painted around the edges of the concrete slabs. Designed just after Robert van't Hoff had returned from a trip to meet Frank Lloyd Wright in Chicago, the house alludes to Wrightian overhangs, extended horizontals and sliding volumes, but here expressed in smooth reinforced concrete. The symmetrical plan is animated by a skylight that admits light to the interior of the house and a terrace that overlooks an artificial pond to the south. Publicity about the house brought van't Hoff to the attention of Theo van Doesburg, who invited him to contribute to the publication of the first issue of *De Stijl* (The Style), the magazine produced by the highly influential Dutch group of Modern artists and architects of the same name. Although van't Hoff stayed with the group for two years, his interest in architecture waned and he built the last of his nine buildings at the young age of thirty-four.

Villa Nora (Villa Henny), Huis ter Heide, The Netherlands, 1914–16. **Robert van't Hoff**. **b** Rotterdam, The Netherlands, 1887. **d** New Milton, UK, 1979.

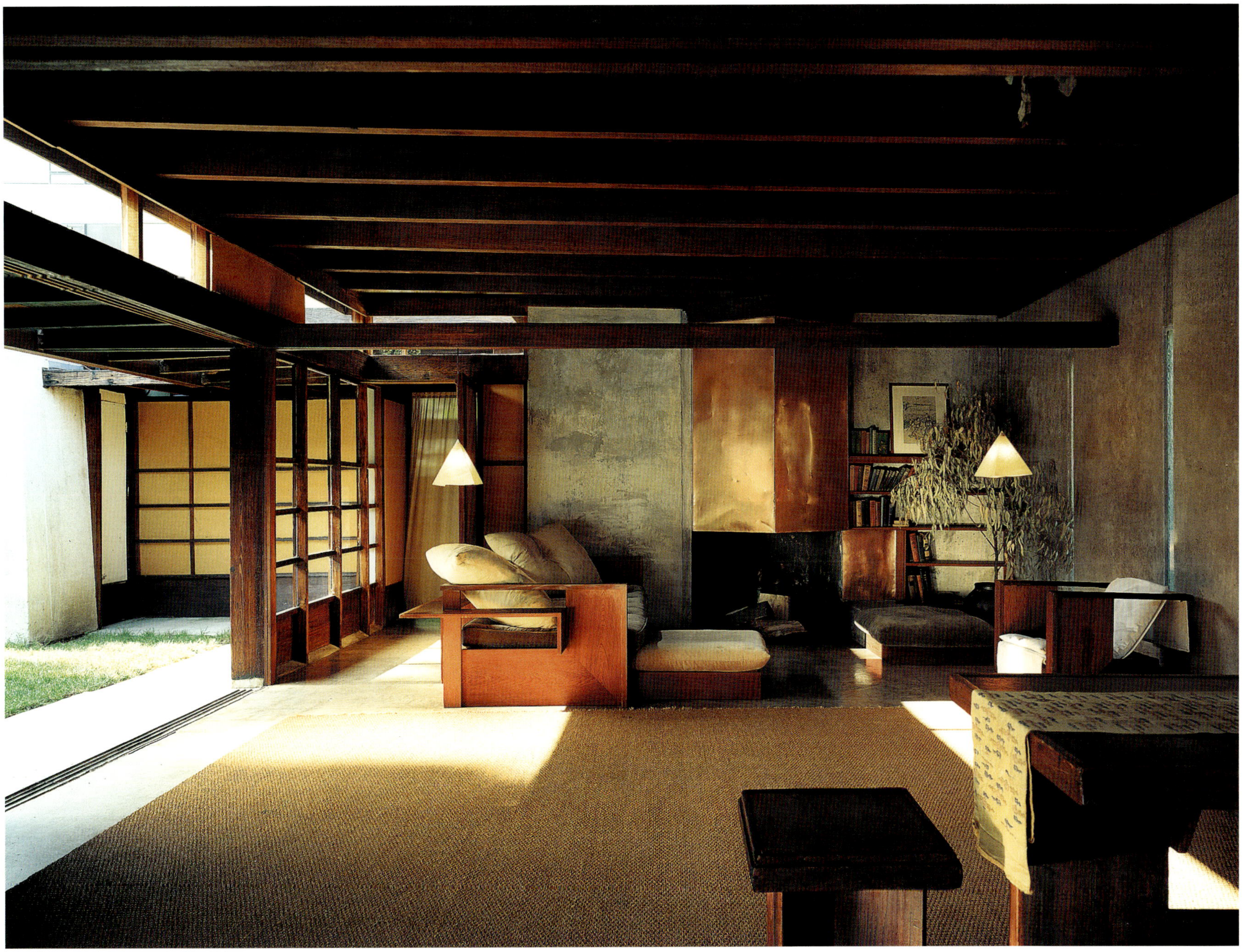

Kings Road Studios Rudolph Schindler

The soothing palette of this experimental house reflected the independent lifestyle chosen by its adventurous inhabitants. Designed by Rudolph Schindler for himself, his wife and another couple, this unusual architectural composition consisted of four individual studios and a shared kitchen. Arranged in pairs, each L-shaped set of studios framed a private outdoor patio with a fireplace that served as a traditional living room in the warm climate of southern California. The couples slept on the roof in open-air sleeping lofts and ate food grown in their own garden. A student of Otto Wagner's in Vienna, Schindler began working for Frank Lloyd Wright in Chicago in 1917. While in California on a project, he became captivated with the warm climate, lifestyle and the many opportunities he found there, so he and his wife settled in Los Angeles. They sponsored fellow Austrian architect, Richard Neutra, to join them, and their families shared the Kings Road Studios from 1925 to 1928.

Kings Road Studios, Los Angeles, CA, USA, 1921–2. **Rudolph Michael Schindler**. **b** Vienna, Austria, 1887. **d** Los Angeles, CA, USA, 1953.

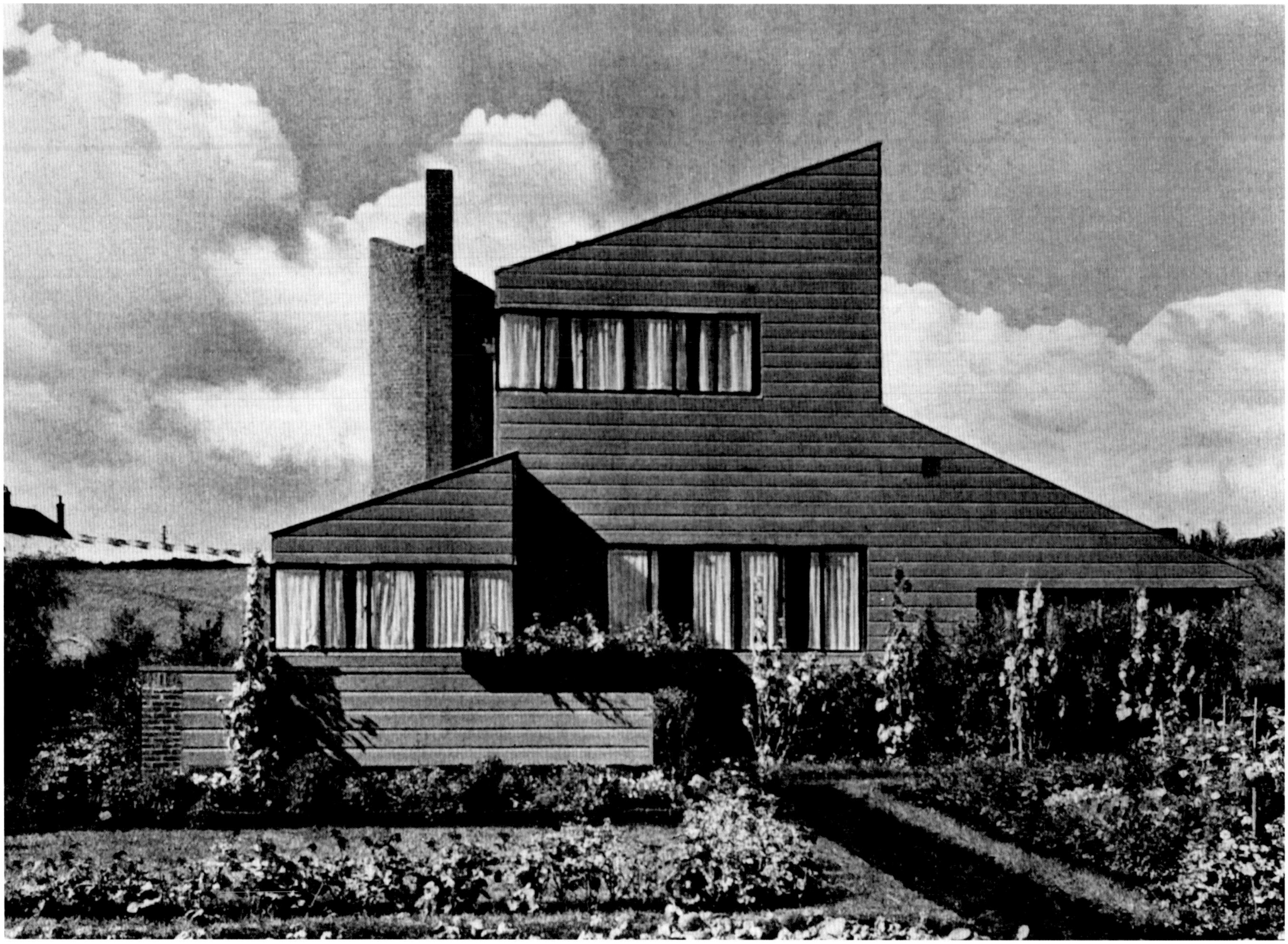

Aalsmeer House Bijvoet & Duiker

The asymmetrical, single-pitched roofs of the Aalsmeer House, although antithetical to the then contemporary trend of flat roofs, exemplify the peculiar economical approach of the Dutch Modern Movement. The timber-frame construction, with exterior wood cladding, is also inconsistent with the acknowledged Modern building materials, although it does enable an open plan and a free facade, both hallmarks of early Modern architecture. The architects exploited the building method of column construction to full effect, particularly in the use of corner windows. In plan, the house is a simple square with the addition of a garden shed and a circular stairwell along one side. Both of these features are clearly delineated on the elevations, form following function. The seemingly aberrant materials and dynamic composition, although unusual at the time it was built, became prominent features in the later seminal architecture of 1950s and 1960s California.

Aalsmeer House, Aalsmeer, The Netherlands, 1924. **Bernard Bijvoet**. **b** Amsterdam, The Netherlands, 1889. **d** Haarlem, The Netherlands, 1979.
Johannes Duiker. **b** The Hague, The Netherlands, 1890. **d** Amsterdam, The Netherlands, 1935.

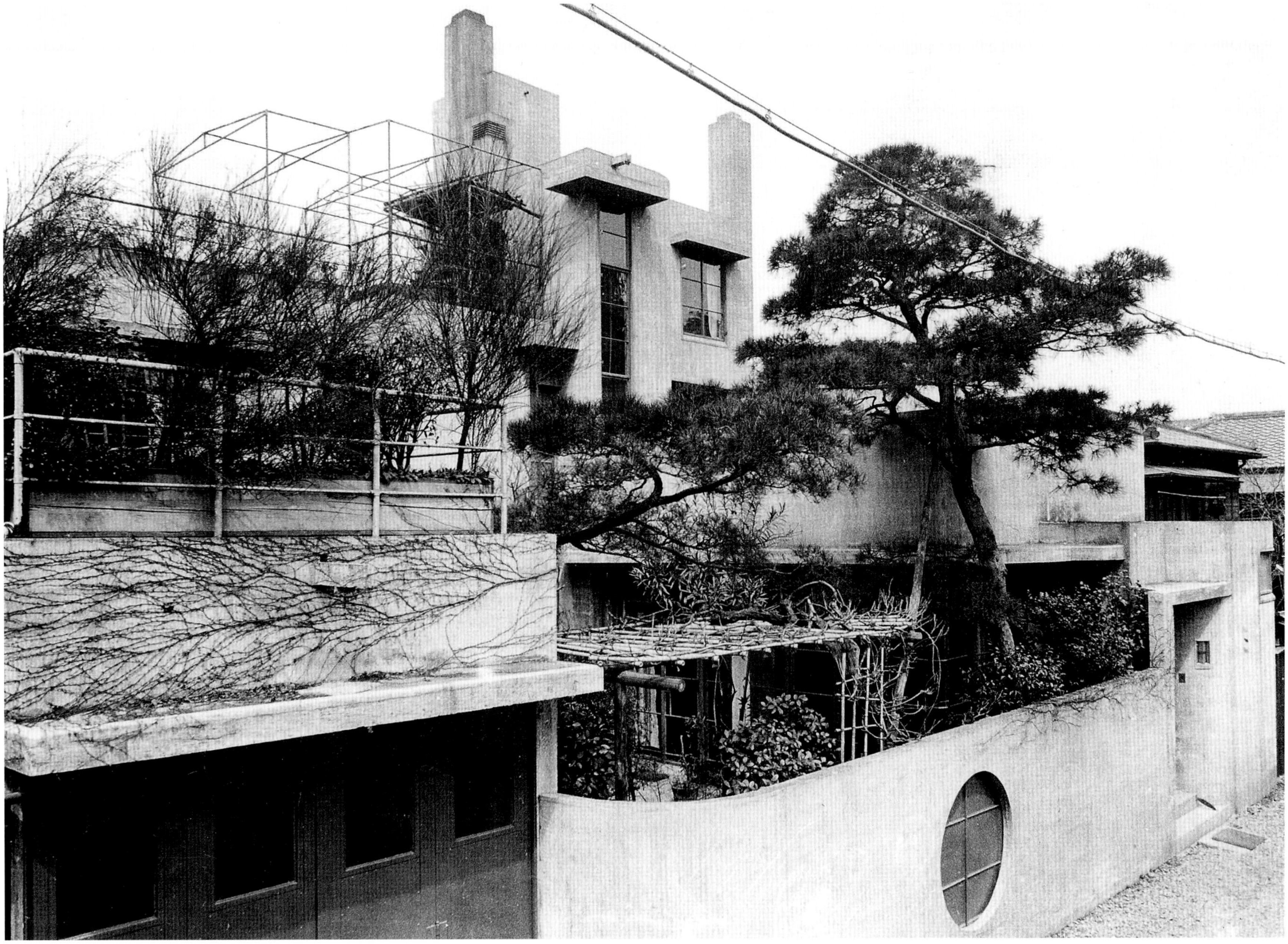

Reinanzaka House Antonin Raymond

This exposed reinforced concrete house was the first of its kind in Japan. Antonin Raymond was a Czech-born architect, educated in America, who was sent to Japan by Frank Lloyd Wright to work on the Imperial Hotel in 1919. On completion, he and his wife, the designer Noémi Pernessin, decided to stay in Tokyo and build this house. It was Raymond's first break with the Wrightian style, choosing plain surfaces and cubic forms to draw out the similarities between Modern architectural concepts and those of traditional Japanese architecture. Both the interior and exterior walls are exposed concrete and all of the rooms are orientated towards the south, opening onto a private garden. The Raymonds also developed an interest in local artefacts, which was reflected in their integration of traditional Japanese objects, such as rice paper lanterns, with modern furniture and textiles to achieve stylish compositions that were sensitive to their settings.

Reinanzaka House, Tokyo, Japan, 1924. **Antonin Raymond**. **b** Kladno, Czech Republic, 1888. **d** New Hope, PA, USA, 1976.

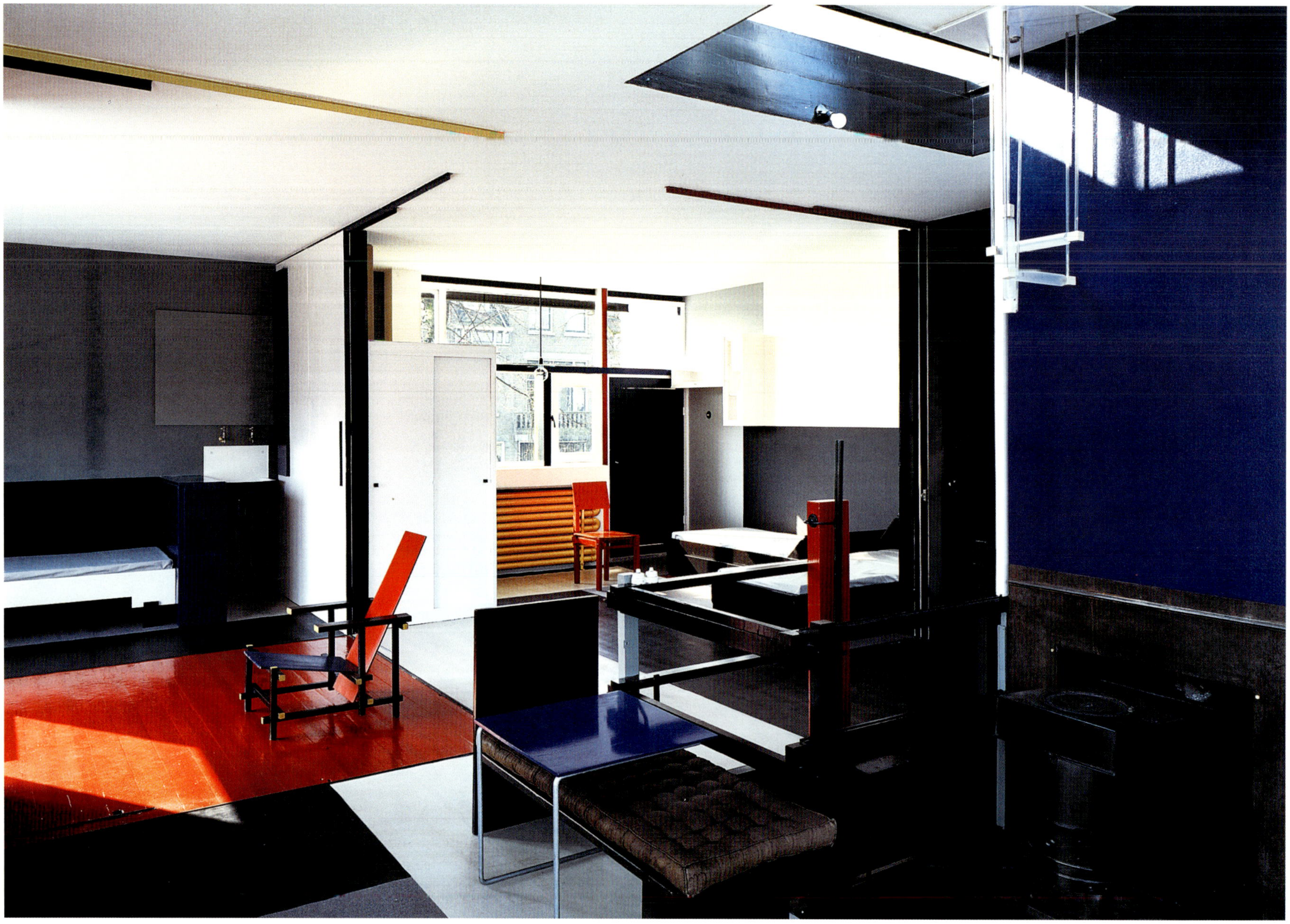

Rietveld Schröder House Rietveld & Schröder

The open-plan spatial organization of this 1924 house was remarkable for its time. The first floor was occupied by a large living and dining area, with sliding panels for partitioning off smaller rooms arranged around it. It was also innovative in its use of huge windows, strong blocks of colour and built-in furniture. The design programme was developed by the client, Truus Schröder, in collaboration with Gerrit Rietveld, as an expression of her desire for a house where she could live closely with her children and entertain a constant flow of visitors and encourage liberal ideas. Rietveld started his career as a furniture designer with links to the radical Dutch De Stijl movement. The Rietveld Schröder house is celebrated as the first architectural embodiment of De Stijl principles of colour and abstraction, with its white and grey intersecting planar walls and coloured windows and railings, and is a landmark in the history of Modern house design.

Rietveld Schröder House, Utrecht, The Netherlands, 1924. **Gerrit Thomas Rietveld**. **b** Utrecht, The Netherlands, 1888. **d** Utrecht, The Netherlands, 1964.
Truus Schröder. **b** Deventer, The Netherlands, 1900. **d** Utrecht, The Netherlands, 1985.

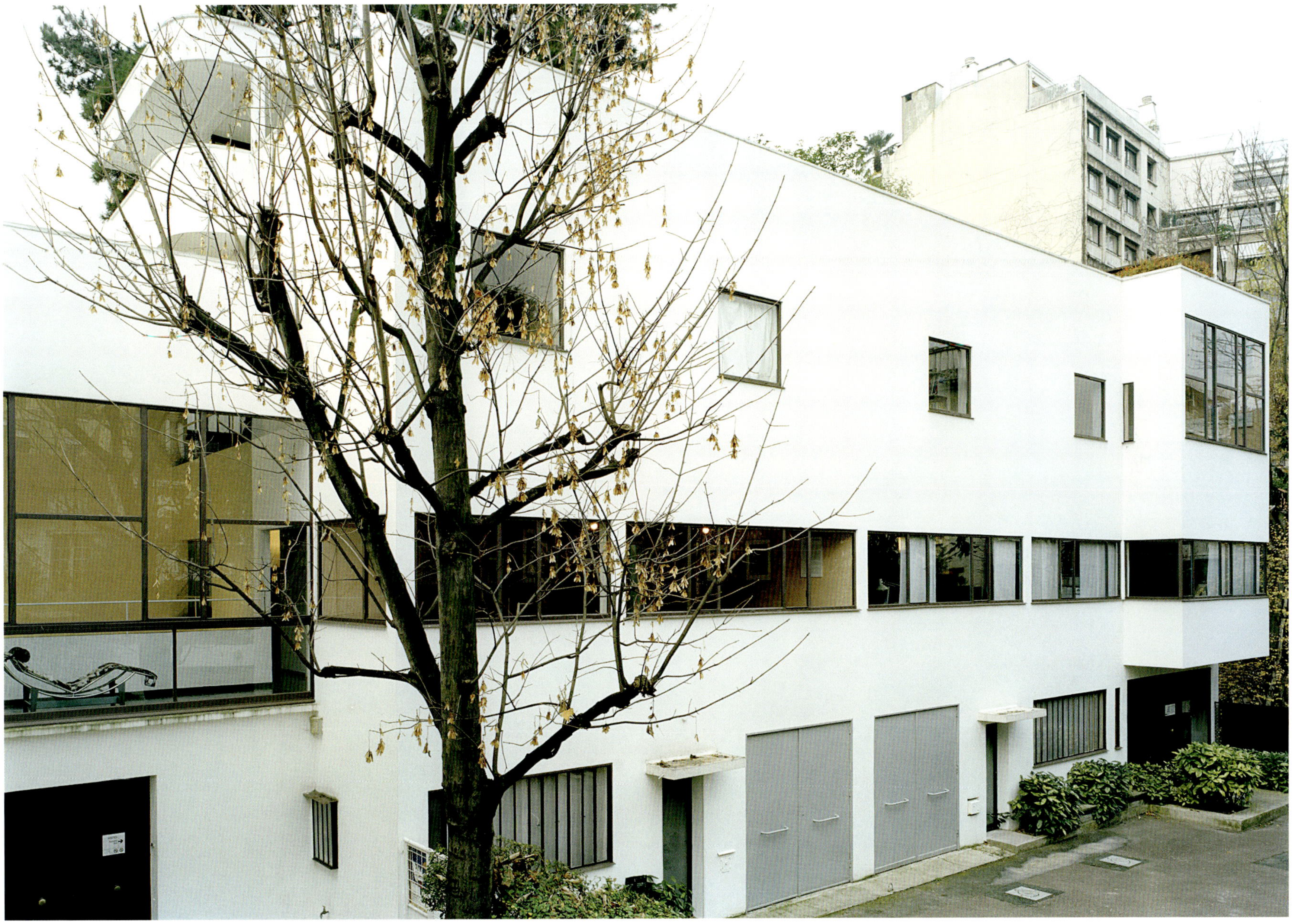

Maisons La Roche-Jeanneret Le Corbusier

Consisting of two adjoining dwellings in one reinforced concrete structure, the Maisons La Roche-Jeanneret are founding icons of Modernist architecture. The volumes are placed at right angles to one another on an awkward L-shaped site, facing onto a forecourt that maximizes the amount of light penetrating the frontage. The more conventional, cubic portion of the building contains a practical family home for Le Corbusier's brother, Albert Jeanneret, while the creative focus is concentrated on the house for the banker and art collector, Raoul La Roche. Here, a curving vertical gallery interrupts the strong horizontal lines of the facade. Inside, the space is more dramatic than functional, including an imposing triple-height entrance hall with a cantilevered first-floor balcony. The complex spatial interplay within embodies Le Corbusier's theory of the 'promenade architecturale' in which a building is designed as a carefully considered progression through a variety of spaces.

Maisons La Roche-Jeanneret, Paris, France, 1923–5. **Le Corbusier (Charles-Edouard Jeanneret)**. **b** La Chaux-de-Fonds, Switzerland, 1887. **d** Cap Martin, France, 1965.

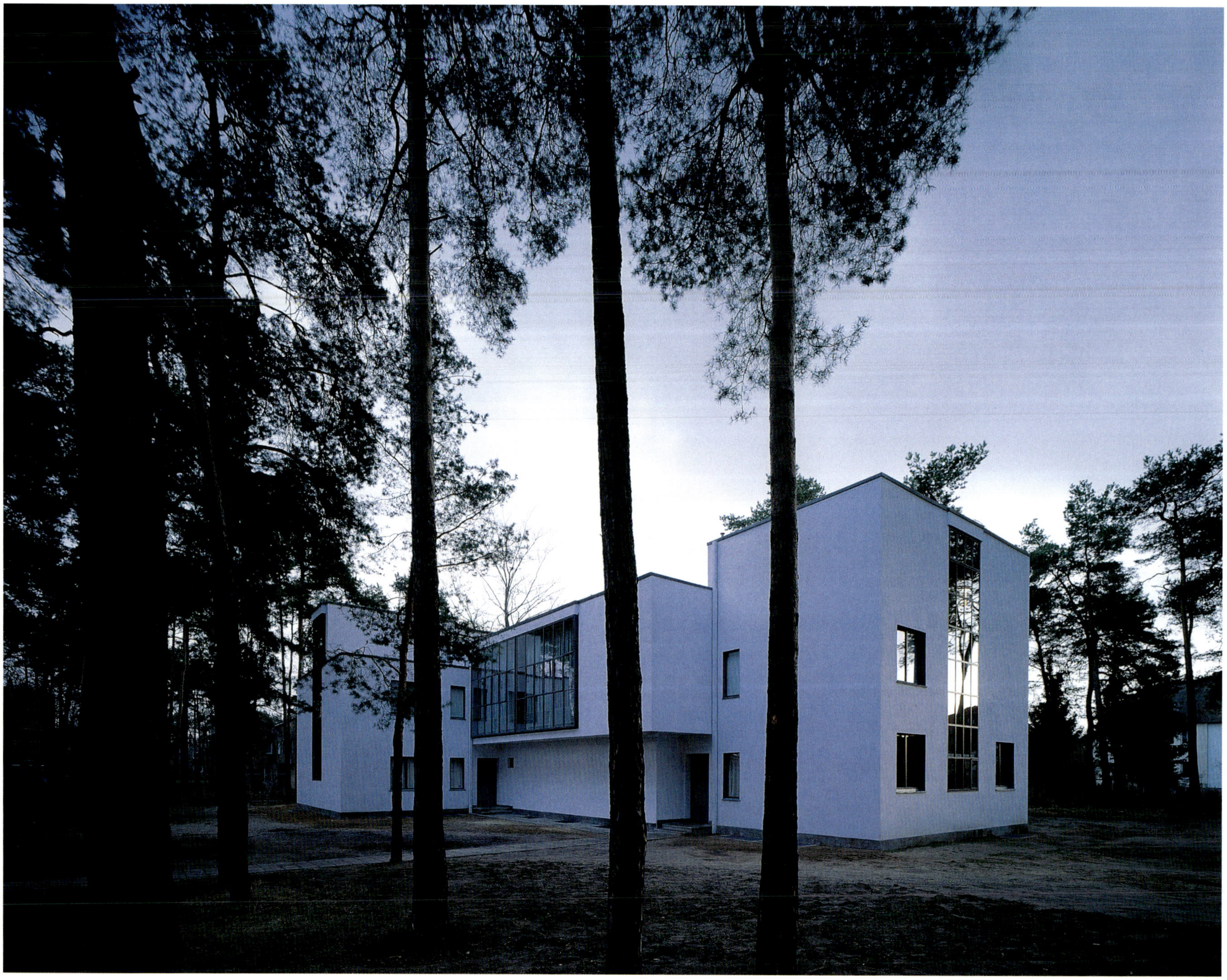

Double House Walter Gropius

White, cuboid forms, asymmetrical composition and fenestration that elevates function to expression — the tall windows light and denote stairwells, the large window an artist's studio — are hallmarks of European Modernism. And this 'double house', one of three pairs designed by Walter Gropius for staff at the Bauhaus, comes from the heart of that movement. Like the school itself, the form suggests equilibrium between dynamic forces rather than symmetrical balance; the two large blocks at either end almost strain to rotate around the central arm. Large, first-floor studios are the principal spaces, a device that shows its ancestry in late nineteenth-century artists' houses, such as those by Norman Shaw. Despite its artistic intentions, there is also a room in the house for servants. Gropius had to meet the demands of bourgeois occupants — though they be artists — as Bauhaus staff included the likes of Wassily Kandinsky, Paul Klee and Oskar Schlemmer.

Double House, Dessau, Germany, 1926. **Walter Gropius**. **b** Berlin, Germany, 1883. **d** Boston, MA, USA, 1969.

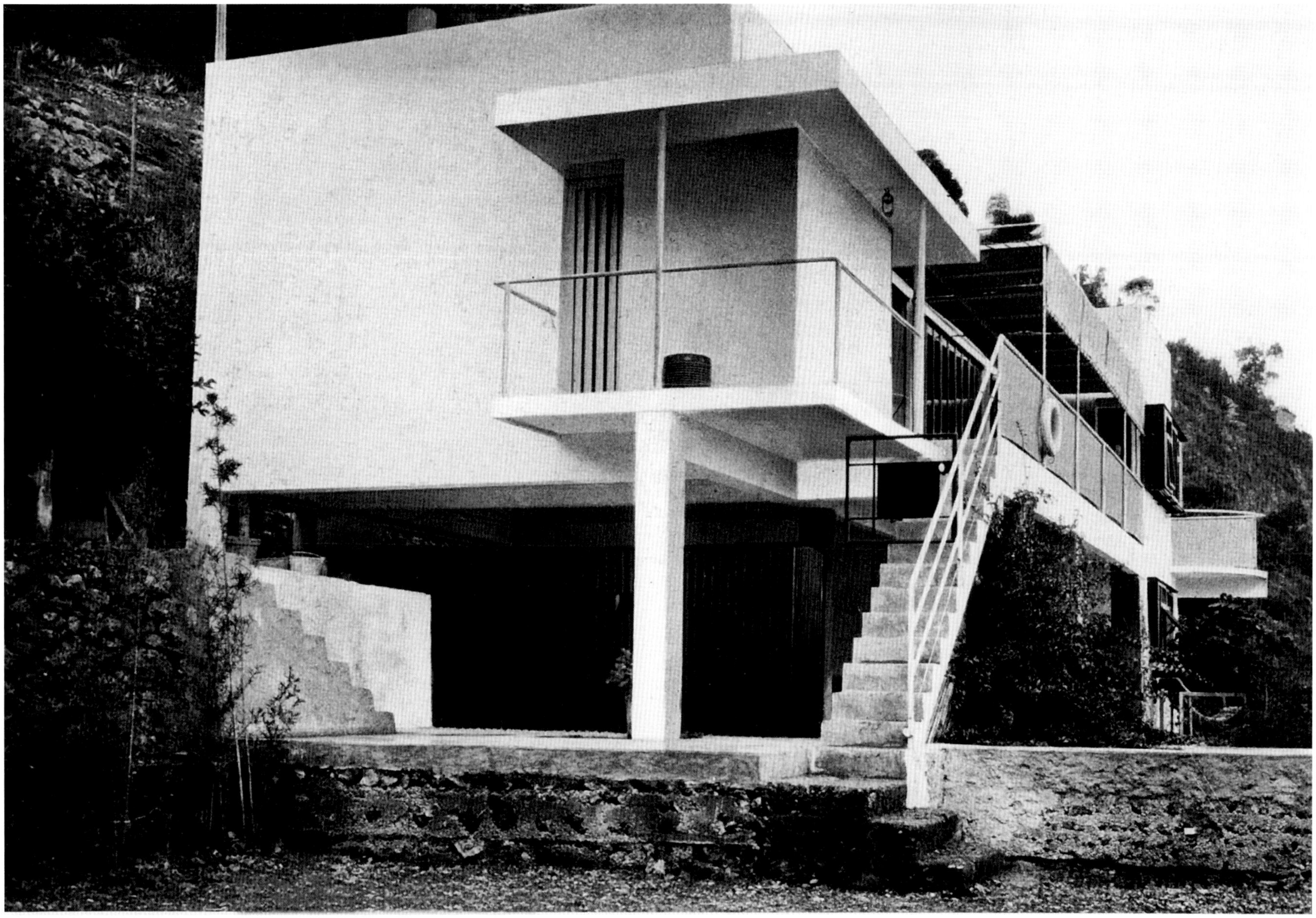

Villa E-1027 Gray & Badovici

Built as a small vacation house on a spectacular, isolated site overlooking the Mediterranean, this house was designed with a 'minimum of space, maximum of comfort' in collaboration with its occupant, Jean Badovici. Its name corresponds to the coded initials of its creators: E=Eileen, 10=J, 2=B and 7=G. Composed of a regular, rectangular volume and adjoining terrace, the house — Eileen Gray's most famous work and an important example of Modernist architecture — is subdivided according to functional demands, and its sensuous yet practical furnishings contributed to its sense of intimacy. Le Corbusier also painted murals on the walls and built his own cabin nearby. As the designers wrote in a 1929 edition of *L'Architecture vivante*: 'This very small house thus has, concentrated in a very small space, all that might be useful for comfort and to help indulge in *joie de vivre*.' Gray built little and is today mainly known for her highly innovative furniture and interior design.

Villa E-1027, Roquebrune, France, 1926–9. **Eileen Gray**. **b** Enniscorthy, Ireland, 1878. **d** Paris, France, 1976.
Jean Badovici. **b** Bucharest, Romania, 1893. **d** Monaco, Principality of Monaco, 1956.

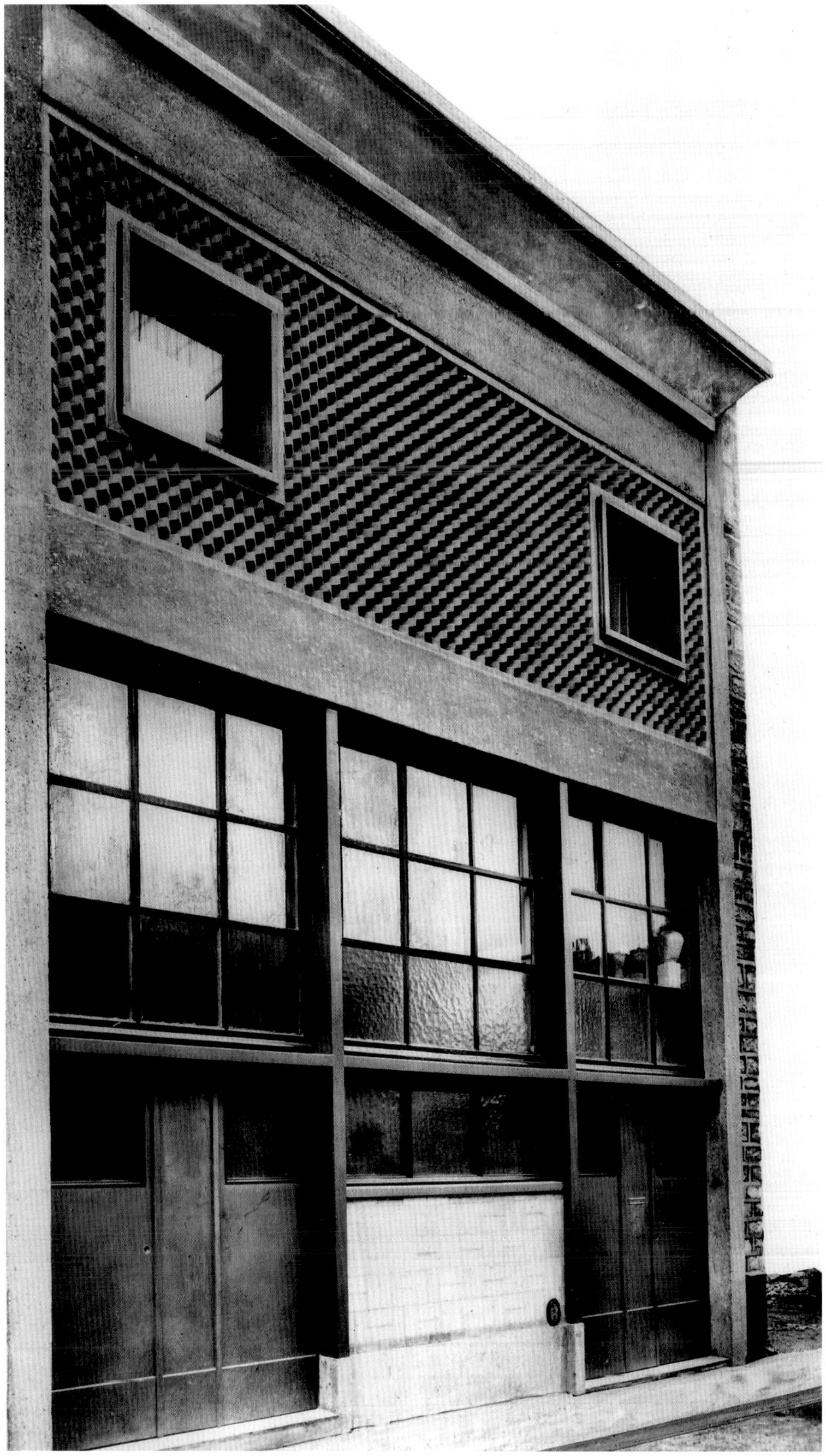

Residence and Studio for Chana Orloff Auguste Perret

The facade of this residence and studio, designed for the Cubist sculptress Chana Orloff, abstractly suggests a face — eyes, brow, nose and mouth. Located in an intimate Parisian street expressly built for artists, the house stands in contrast to its neighbours, the white, purist studios by André Lurçat. Its internal organization is expressed externally by the use of a reinforced concrete frame, infilled with glass and entrance doors at the ground-floor studio level, and bricks laid in a rough, rhythmical chevron pattern at the first-floor apartment level. Containing two studios (one serving as a gallery), the house is one of several that Auguste Perret designed for artistic clients, including the painters Marc Chagall, Georges Braque and Maurice Denis. The use of concrete (which Perret helped pioneer), the unique handling of materials and the precision of the finish (such as the fine line of the cornice), are all characteristic of Perret's attentive craftsmanship.

Residence and Studio for Chana Orloff, Paris, France, 1926–9. **Auguste Perret**. **b** Brussels, Belgium, 1874. **d** Paris, France, 1954.

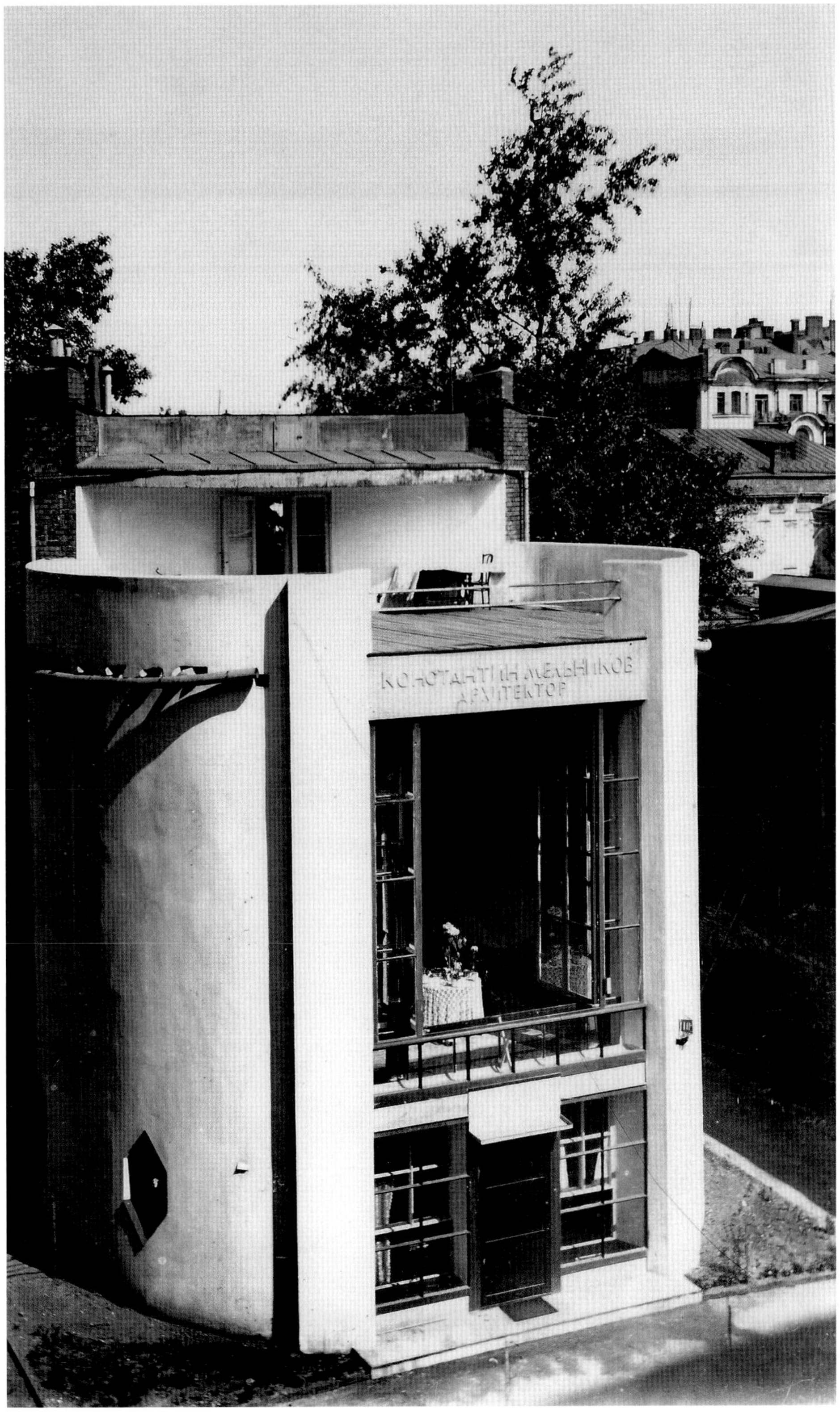

Melnikov House Konstantin Melnikov

A remarkable fusion of two masonry cylinders, Konstantin Melnikov's house and studio, in its traditional street setting, is a strong statement recalling formal Constructivist experiments. Its interior arrangements, however, show how awkward such forms are to adapt for occupancy, even for the bohemian lifestyle of a revolutionary artist. The spaces are most successful on the upper floor, when the whole form is incorporated, or where freestanding screens do not compromise the volume. Below are irregularly shaped storage rooms with hexagonal windows, a visual incongruence from the mystic components of Russian Constructivism, alongside the revolutionary and *sachlich* elements. Somehow, during the New Economic Policy, Melnikov procured this site in Moscow in the once lively district around the Arbat, an area that had attracted artists under the tsars. He managed to build this extraordinary house and remain in it throughout the Stalinist terror, for almost fifty years.

Melnikov House, Moscow, Russia, 1927–9. **Konstantin Stepanovich Melnikov**. **b** Moscow, Russia, 1890. **d** Moscow, Russia, 1974.

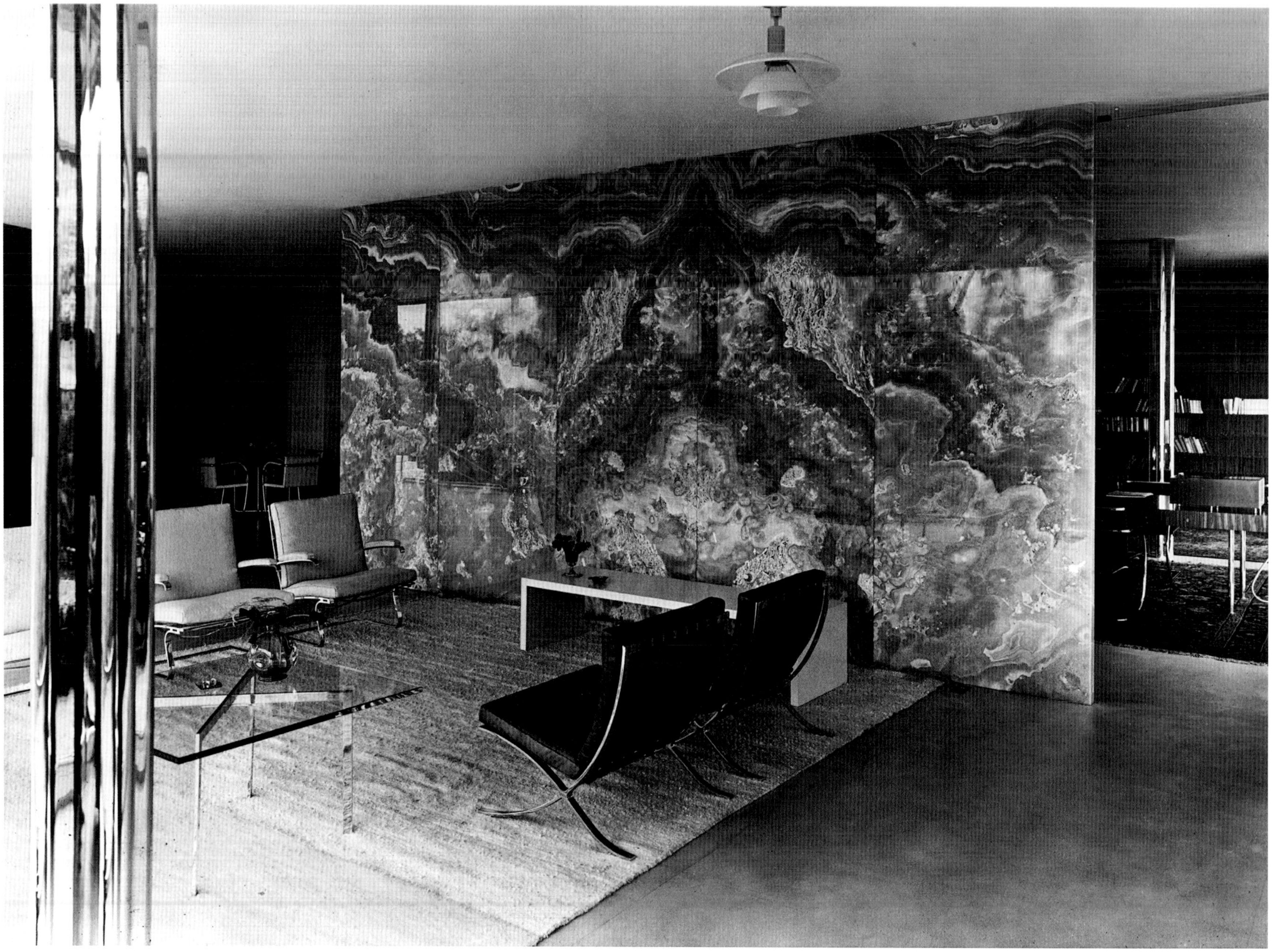

Tugendhat House Ludwig Mies van der Rohe

Arguably Mies's finest European residence, the Tugendhat House is the archetypal Modern villa. Designed concurrently, the house is a domesticated version of the German Pavilion in Barcelona and utilizes the same stylistic concepts: a travertine floor, the use of luxurious materials such as chrome and onyx, and the cruciform steel column structure topped with a slab roof. The sloping site allowed for a revolutionary arrangement internally. The house is accessed from the top floor while the main living quarters are below, where uninterrupted glass walls face onto the garden and emulate the openness of the Pavilion. The flat roof, open-plan layout and restrained white facade combined with innovative technologies that take advantage of new industrial techniques, make this one of the landmark buildings of early Modernism. However, while Modern design could be austerely functional, Mies uses high quality finishes to endow this house with an unusual warmth and elegance.

Tugendhat House, Brno, Czech Republic, 1928–30. **Ludwig Mies van der Rohe (Ludwig Mies)**. **b** Aachen, Germany, 1886. **d** Chicago, IL, USA, 1969.

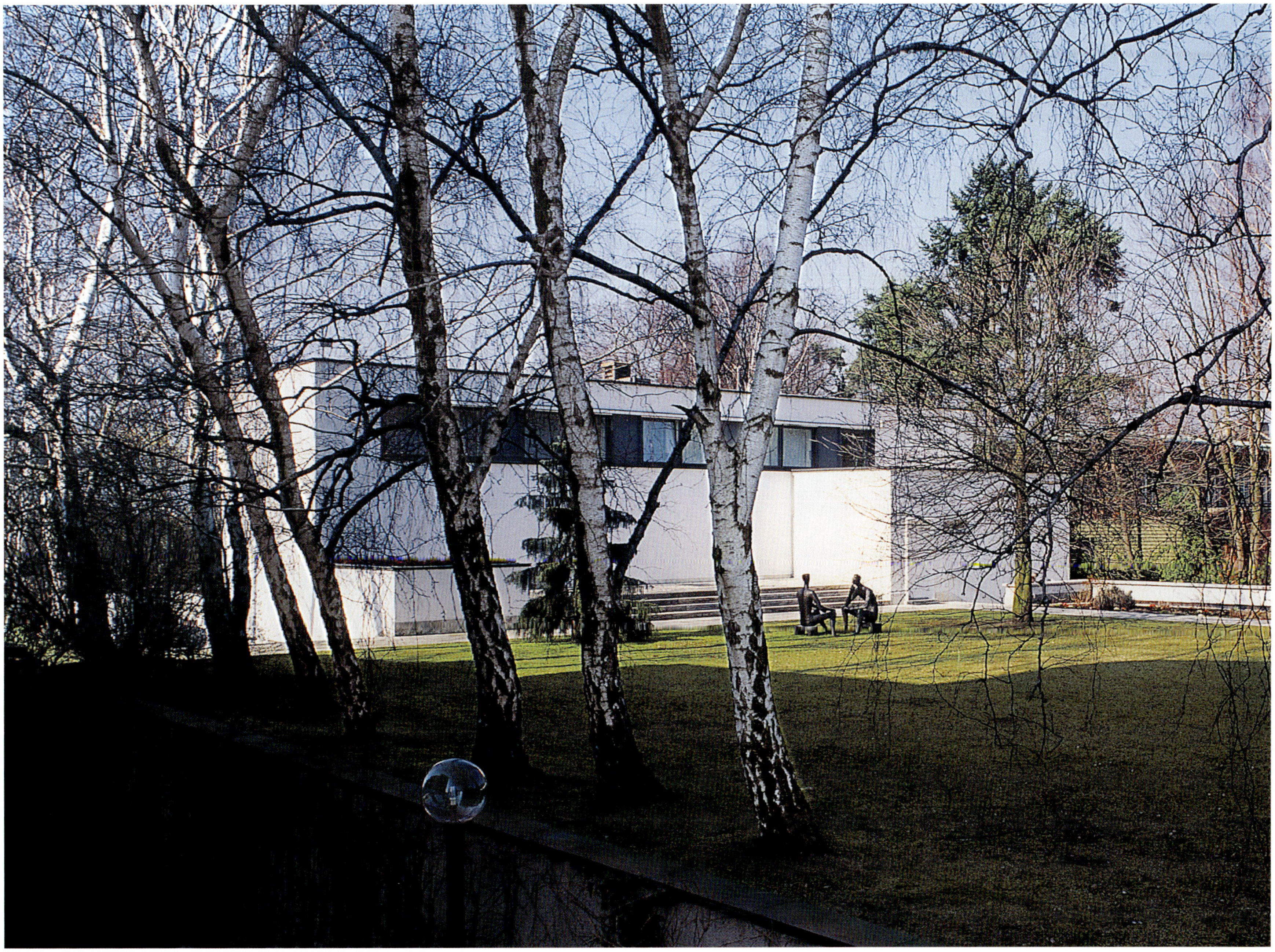

Mendelsohn House Erich Mendelsohn

A composition of simple white boxes, ribbon windows, flat roofs and abstract white walls places this house as decidedly Modern, but in a quieter, less histrionic fashion than many of its contemporaries. Built at the height of his fame, the architect's own house was a surprising retreat from the exhilarating, Expressionist architecture of the 1920s that had made him so famous. The entrance is approached along a meandering path through the woods, which reaches a series of outdoor terraces. The interiors are surprisingly cosy and relaxed, opening up at the rear to views of Lake Havel. But the Jewish Erich Mendelsohn's success — and even his life — was threatened by the rise of the Nazis in Germany. The day after Hitler's accession to power, less than three years after having completed this house, Mendelsohn emigrated to England, before moving to Palestine in 1936, where he designed many buildings. He eventually settled in the United States.

Mendelsohn House, Berlin, Germany, 1929–30. **Erich Mendelsohn**. **b** Allenstein, Germany, 1887. **d** San Francisco, CA, USA, 1953.

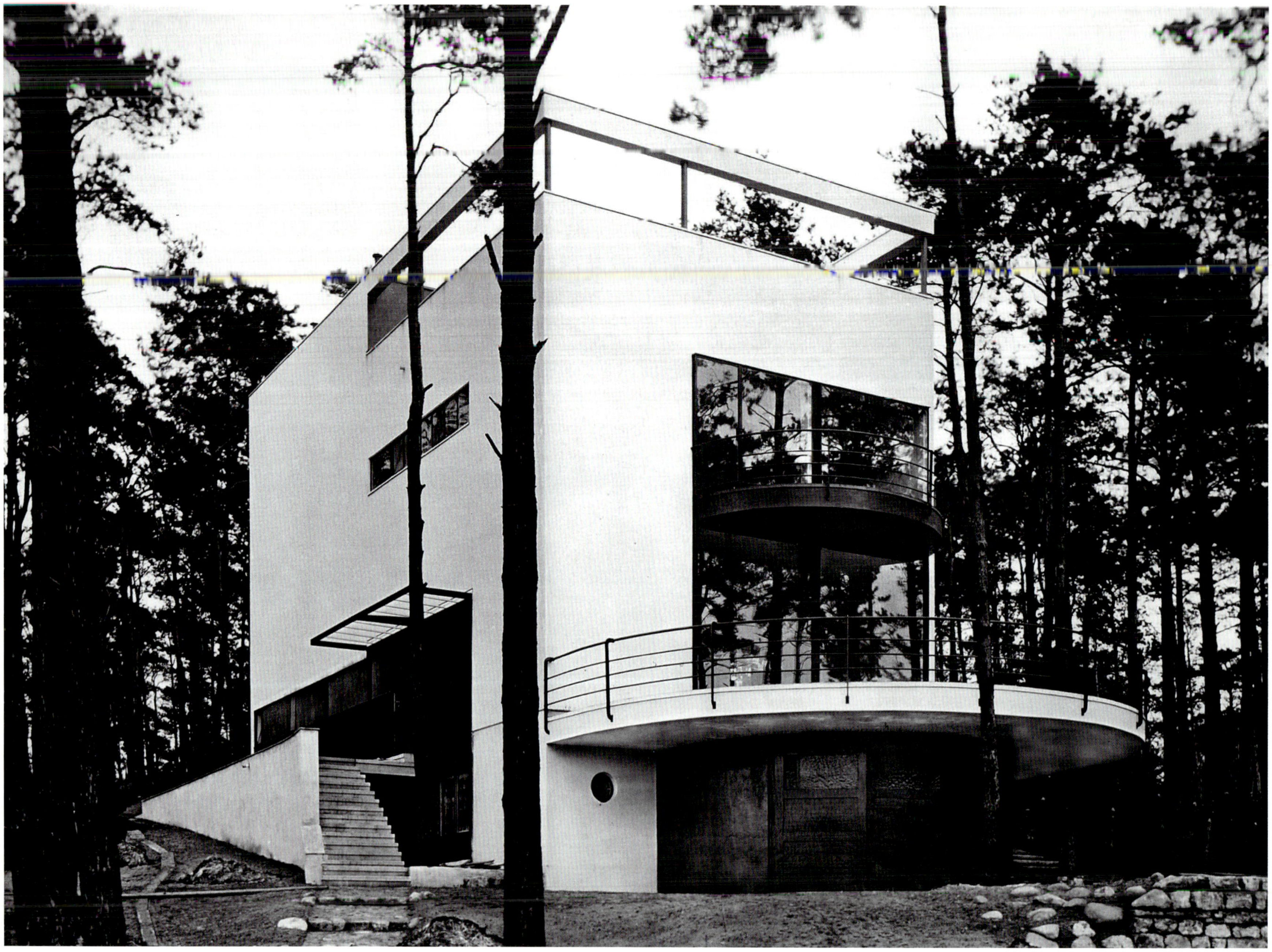

House II at Rupenhorn Hans & Wassili Luckhardt

Flat-roofed and essentially regular cuboid forms with traces of Corbusian influences, the Luckhardt brothers' three houses at Rupenhorn are archetypal Modernist images. Using a similar design language and identical construction, the houses mark the triumph of *Neue Sachlichkeit* (New Objectivity) over the Expressionism which characterized their earlier work. Objectivity becomes an aesthetic, achieving that elusive goal of uniting art and everyday life. Internal details proclaim these values, with plain polished stone walls, radiators treated as sculptural objects, books as decorative patterns. Pragmatic things like cars, servants and cooking are banished from the principal floor. The billowing terrace of House II perhaps shows the merest hint of the architects' Expressionist heritage but it also establishes a clear, abstract plane from which the living and sleeping quarters of the house arise; being *sachlich* did not necessarily mean *Existenzminimum*.

House II at Rupenhorn, Berlin, Germany, 1929–30. **Hans Luckhardt**. **b** Berlin, Germany, 1890. **d** Bad Wiessee, Germany, 1954. **Wassili Luckhardt**. **b** Berlin, Germany, 1889. **d** Berlin, Germany, 1972.

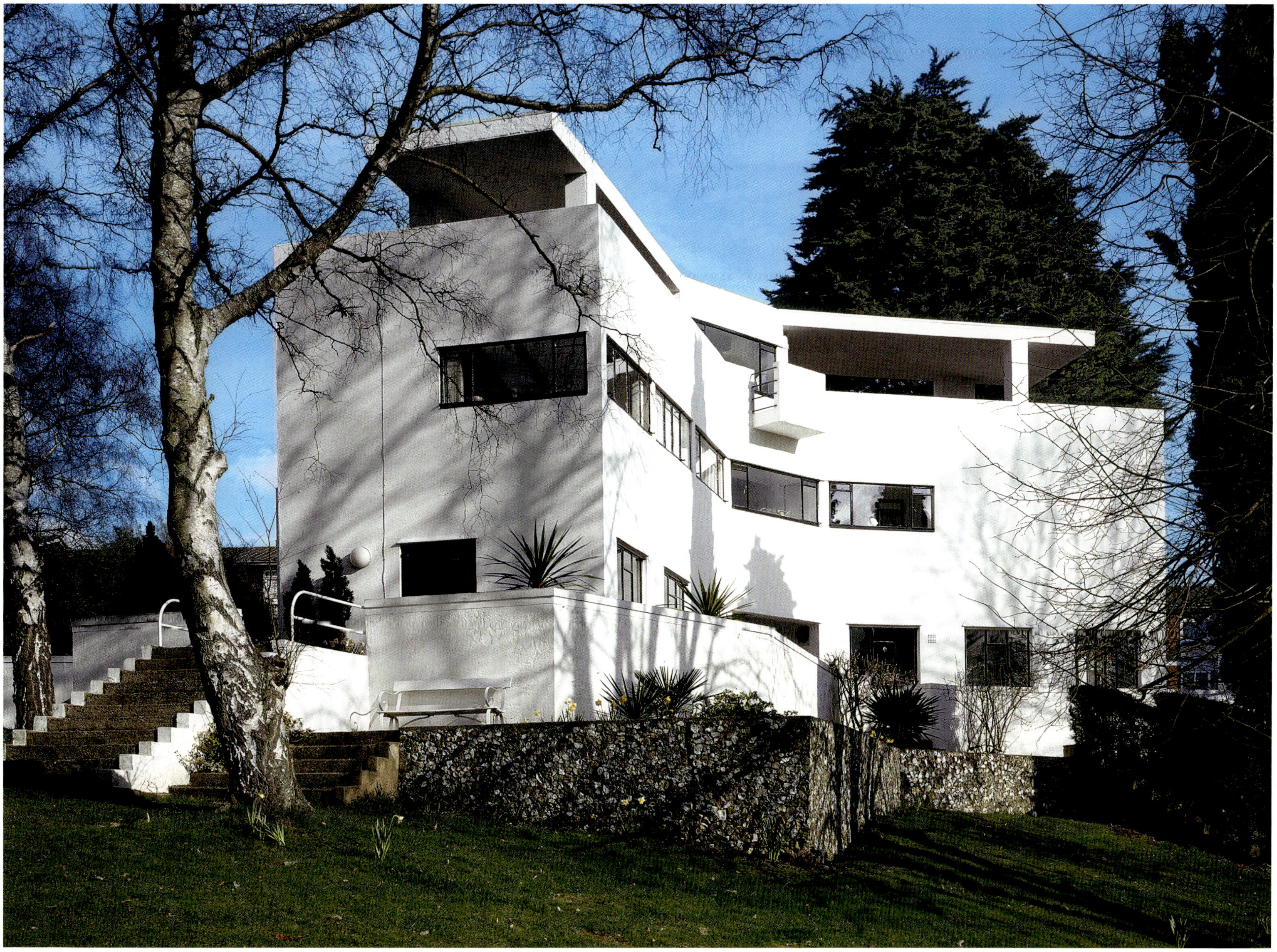

High and Over Amyas Connell

Perched on the hillside above Amersham, Amyas Connell's first major commission has three cubic wings forming a Y-shaped plan around a hexagonal hall, and is orientated to make the most of spectacular views. Corridors are almost completely eliminated and spaces flow elegantly yet informally into one another, while still clearly segregating different areas. The long bands of windows and roof-top sun terrace show the influence of Le Corbusier, but the house also reflects the interest in Classical proportion of both the architect and the client, Bernard Ashmole, director of the British School in Rome, where Connell studied. High and Over has been viewed both as the last great British country house and as the first Modern house in the English countryside. In 1933, Connell formed a partnership with fellow New Zealander, Basil Ward, and English architect, Colin Lucas; as Connell Ward Lucas they built what are considered by many to be the best inter-war Modern houses in Britain.

High and Over, Amersham, UK, 1928–31. **Amyas Douglas Connell**. **b** Eltham, New Zealand, 1901. **d** London, UK, 1980.

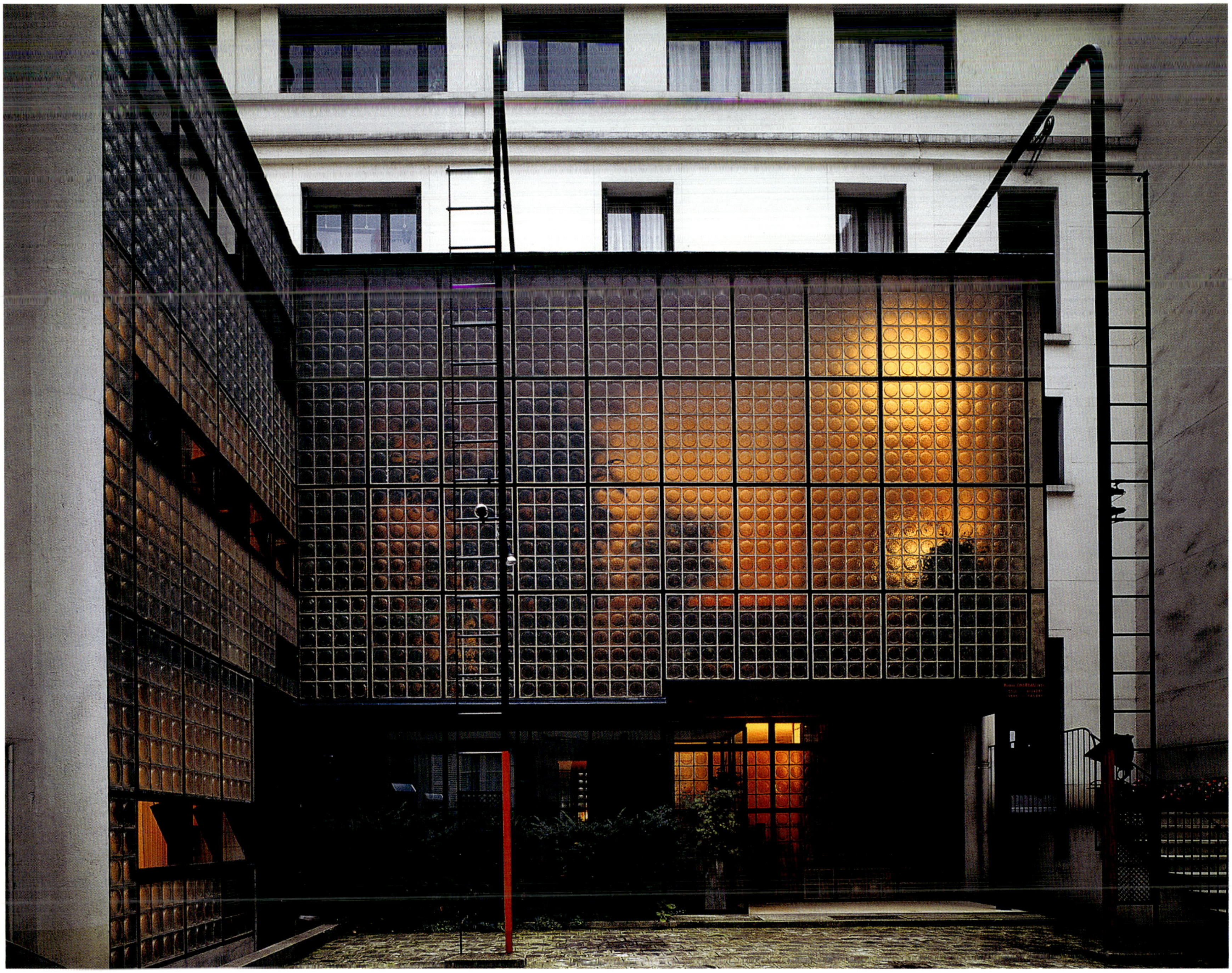

Maison de Verre Pierre Chareau

The translucence of the Maison de Verre's glass blocks, and the precision of its black steel framing and red oxide accents, are reminiscent of an inlaid black-lacquered Japanese box. This three-storey house, built as a doctor's residence with a surgery at ground-floor level, is inserted into the void of an eighteenth-century courtyard, and is one of the canonical works of the twentieth century. Diffused light filters into the open-plan interior via the two glass facades, and the framing device of the exterior steel ladder is continued inside in the slender, black steel vertical forms that punctuate the constantly shifting horizontals of the floor plan. Collaborating with the Dutch architect Bernard Bijvoet, Pierre Chareau created a house with a sensual urbanity, unique for its inventive handling of standard ready-made materials, its deployment of suspended and sliding components, and a density of form and refinement of details.

Maison de Verre, Paris, France, 1928–31. **Pierre Chareau**. **b** Bordeaux, France, 1883. **d** East Hampton, NY, USA, 1950.

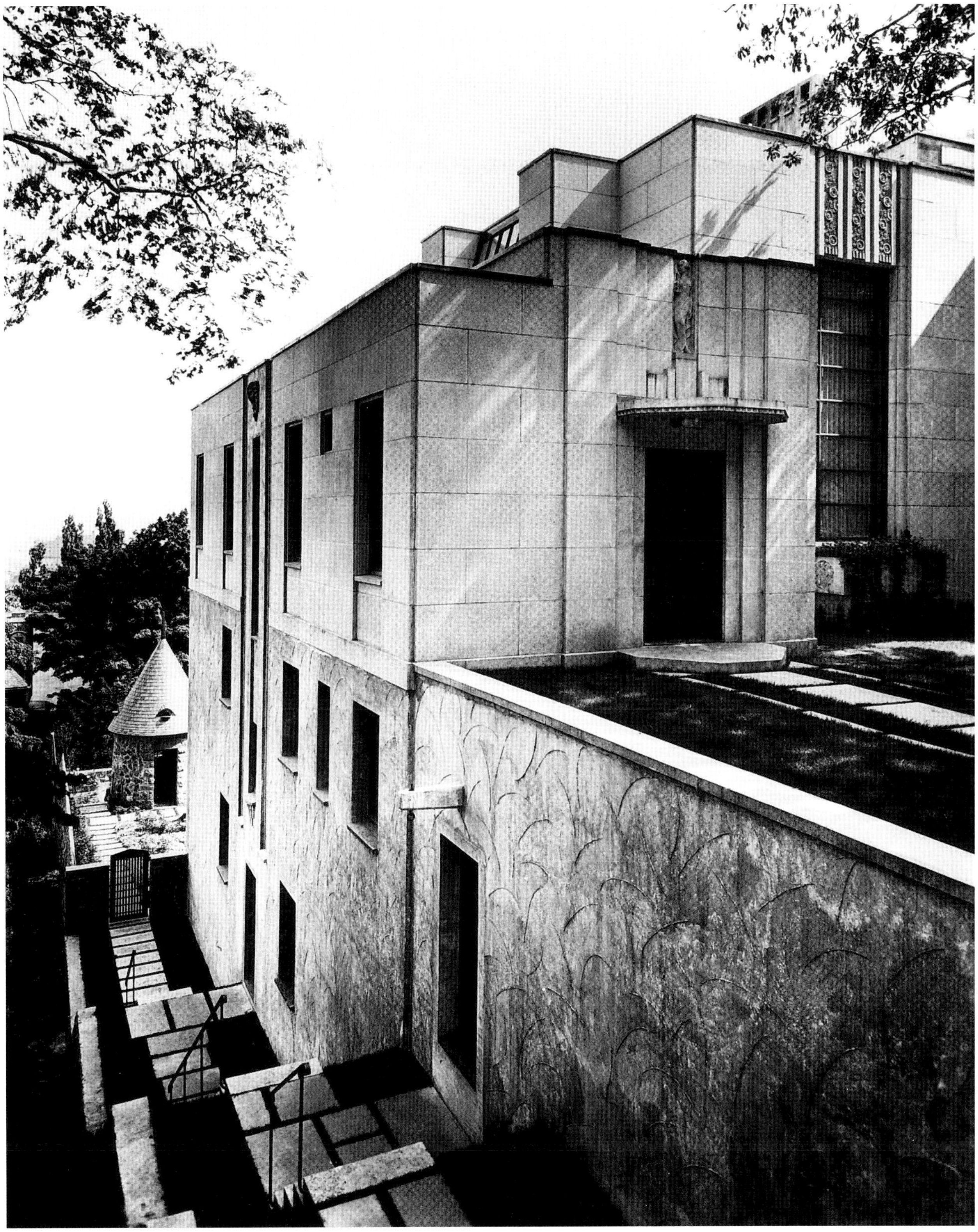

Maison Cormier Ernest Cormier

Amid the strong concrete volumes and rich play of light and shadow lie the seductive sculptural details that invite the visitor into the house and world of architect Ernest Cormier. The Muse of Artistic Inspiration, sculpted by the architect himself, serenely guards the entrance to this Art Deco house, whose five storeys cascade down the southern slope of Mont Royal. With an interior as opulent as its exterior is refined, the house is quite fitting for an architect who was as much an artist as he was an engineer. While studying at the École des Beaux-Arts in Paris, Cormier mingled and worked with those who were to become the pioneers of the Modern Movement, such as Le Corbusier. The influence of these two schools of thought — seen here in the use of Beaux-Arts ordered proportions and Modernist volumes — can be found in all of Cormier's works and became a definitive characteristic of the Art Deco style he brought back to eastern Canada.

Maison Cormier, Montreal, QC, Canada, 1930–1. **Ernest Cormier**. **b** Montreal, QC, Canada, 1885. **d** Montreal, QC, Canada, 1980.

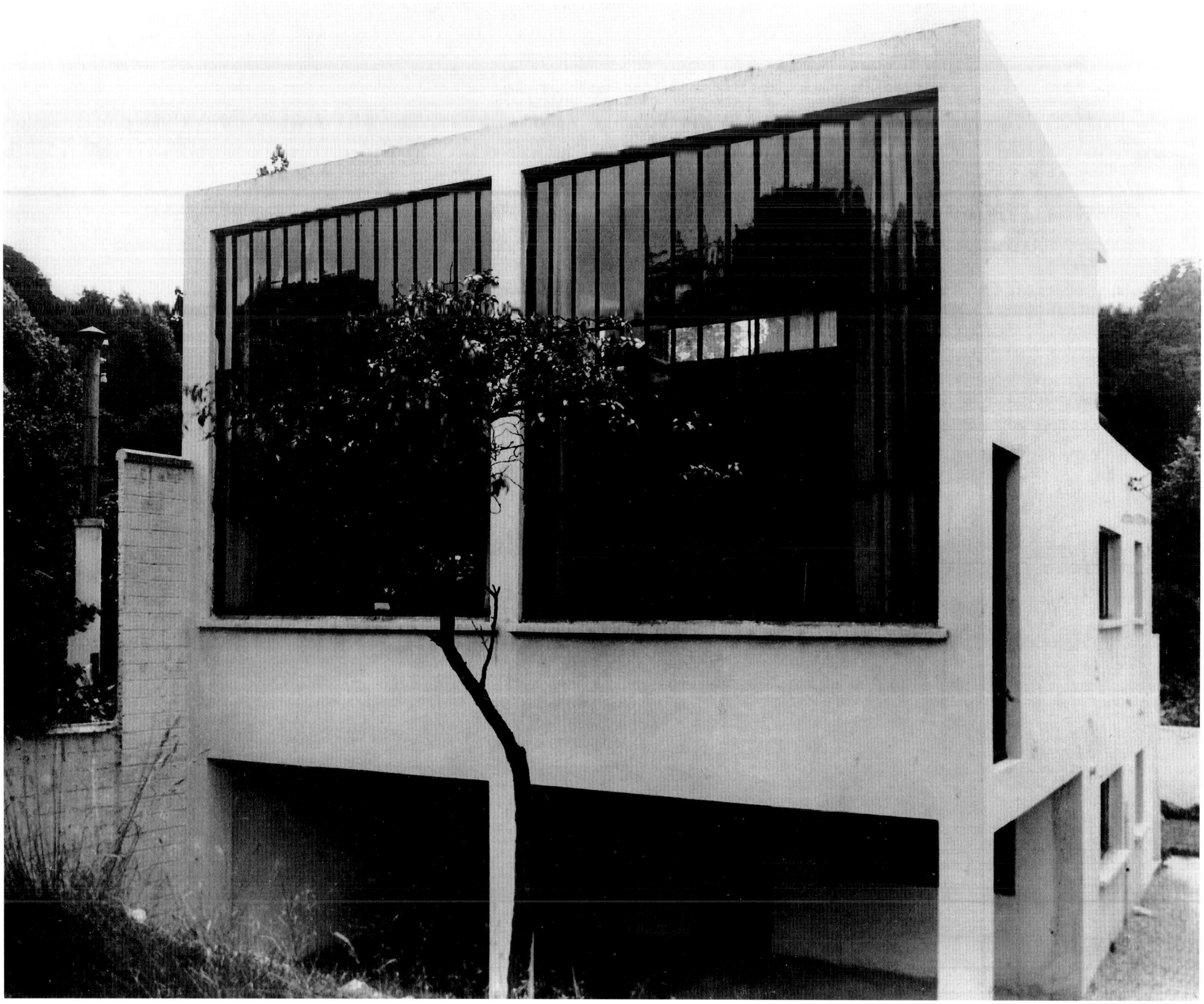

Studio House Theo van Doesburg

This studio house is the culmination of Theo van Doesburg's attempts to translate the tenets of Neo-Plasticism — a Modernist preoccupation with shifting volumes and sliding planes — into a built form. The artist/architect was best known as the incessant polemicist of the De Stijl movement, whose early endeavours at architecture were compelling, unbuilt constructions of intersecting planes of primary colours, similar to the paintings of his colleague Piet Mondrian. However, in this, his last built project, he moved away from spiritual constructions of De Stijl's earlier works towards a more objective, technical solution. Traces of the kinetic spirit of van Doesburg's early compositions can still be seen in the composition of his studio house — the two cubic volumes seemingly pulling apart, the studio in the upper cube and the living quarters in the lower one. Also, his usual palette of primary colours is retained in the doors and openings.

Studio House, Meudon, nr Paris, France, 1929–31. **Theo van Doesburg (Christian Emil Marie Küpper)**. **b** Utrecht, The Netherlands, 1883. **d** Meudon, nr Paris, France, 1931.

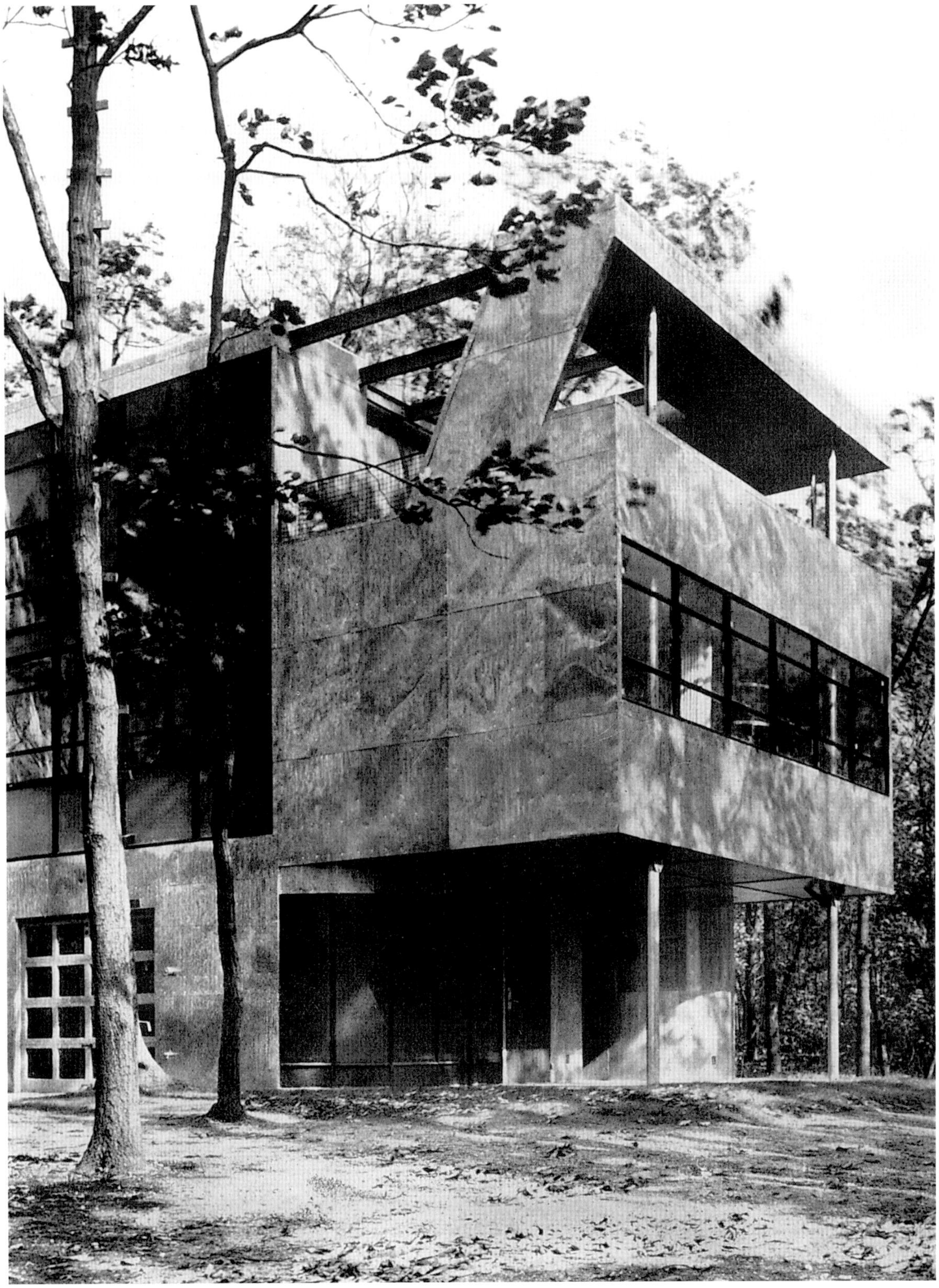

Aluminaire House Lawrence Kocher & Albert Frey

Built for the 'Allied Arts and Building Products' exhibition in New York, the all-metal Aluminaire House was a pioneering structure when erected, in only ten days, in 1931. It was the first steel and aluminium house built in the United States, and one of the earliest examples of the budding International Style. The affordable, lightweight, three-storey house followed the development of the experimental prefabricated houses of Le Corbusier, who proposed the Dom-Ino House in 1914, and Buckminster Fuller's Dymaxion House in 1927. The client, architect Wallace K Harrison, purchased the Aluminaire House as a summer retreat and moved it from its original site to two further locations on Long Island, as if to demonstrate its adaptability. Preservationists fought successfully to save the ageing structure and secure it as a historic landmark. The New York Institute of Technology later purchased it and restored the structure to its original metallic glory.

Aluminaire House, Syosset, NY, USA, 1931. **Lawrence Kocher**. **b** San Jose, CA, USA, 1885. **d** Williamsburg, VA, USA, 1969.
Albert Frey. **b** Zurich, Switzerland, 1904. **d** Palm Springs, CA, USA, 1998.

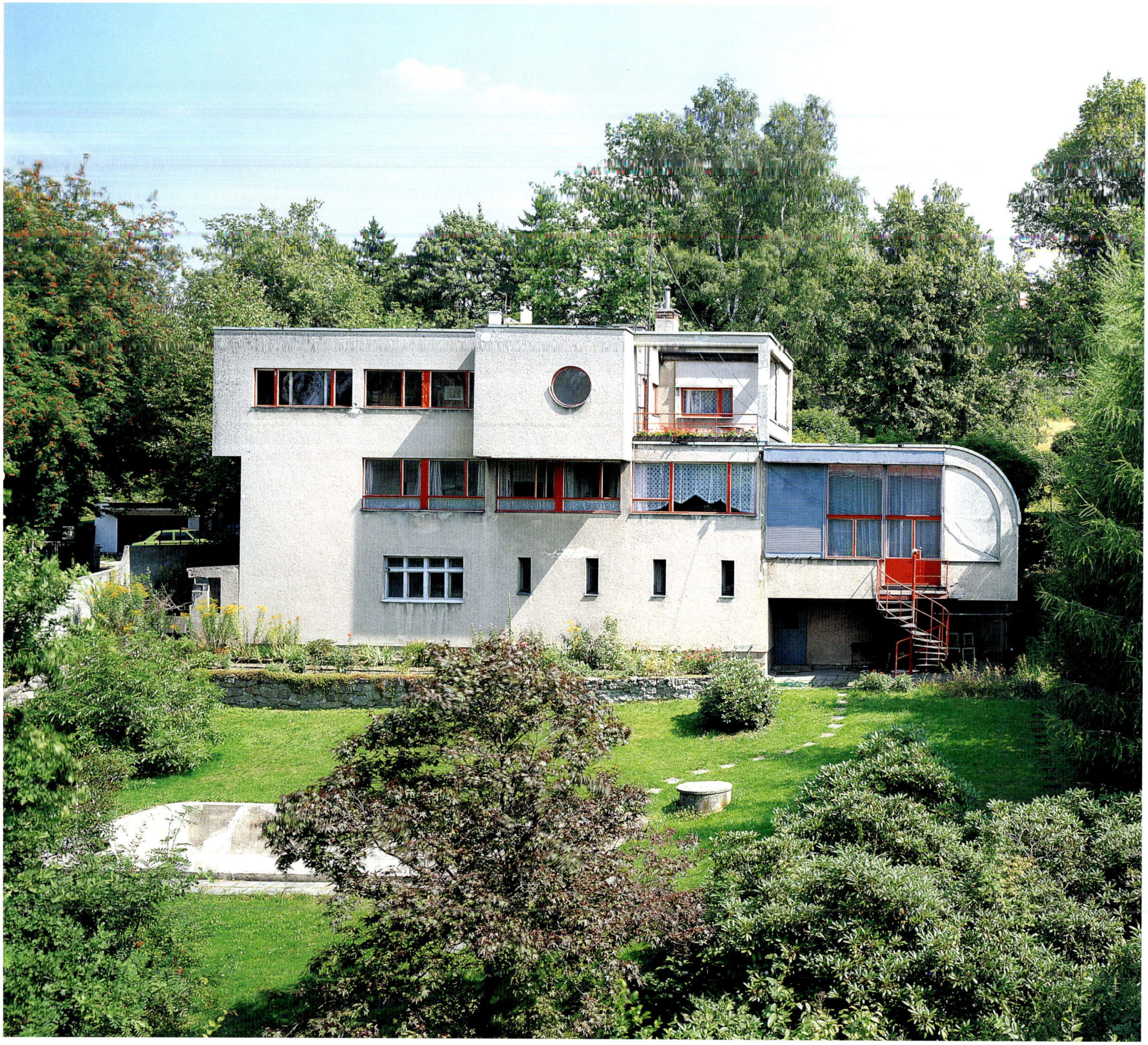

Villa Schmelowsky Heinrich Lauterbach

Combining ocean-liner imagery with clear, cubic forms, this house reflects the Modernist tradition at both a superficial and a profound level. The short cantilevers and open, high-level terrace stake a claim to their space in a consciously Cubist manner, while the porthole lends a nautical air. These two strands come together in the living room, with its balcony resembling a captain's bridge, and its asymmetrical curved roof. Heinrich Lauterbach's composition deals with the same generic problem of a site that slopes steeply away from a road as Mies van der Rohe addressed at his Tugendhat House. Mies may have achieved greater elegance, but Lauterbach was a friend of the organic apostle, Hans Scharoun, and his design has a certain consistency in its awkward compositional devices. Its long, narrow form is essentially self-contained, like a ship, and its connection to its surroundings — a bridge from the road — is the static equivalent of a gangplank.

Villa Schmelowsky, Jablonec nad Nisou, Bohemia (now Czech Republic), 1931. **Heinrich Lauterbach**. **b** Breslau, Germany (now Wroclaw, Poland), 1893. **d** Biberach, Germany, 1973.

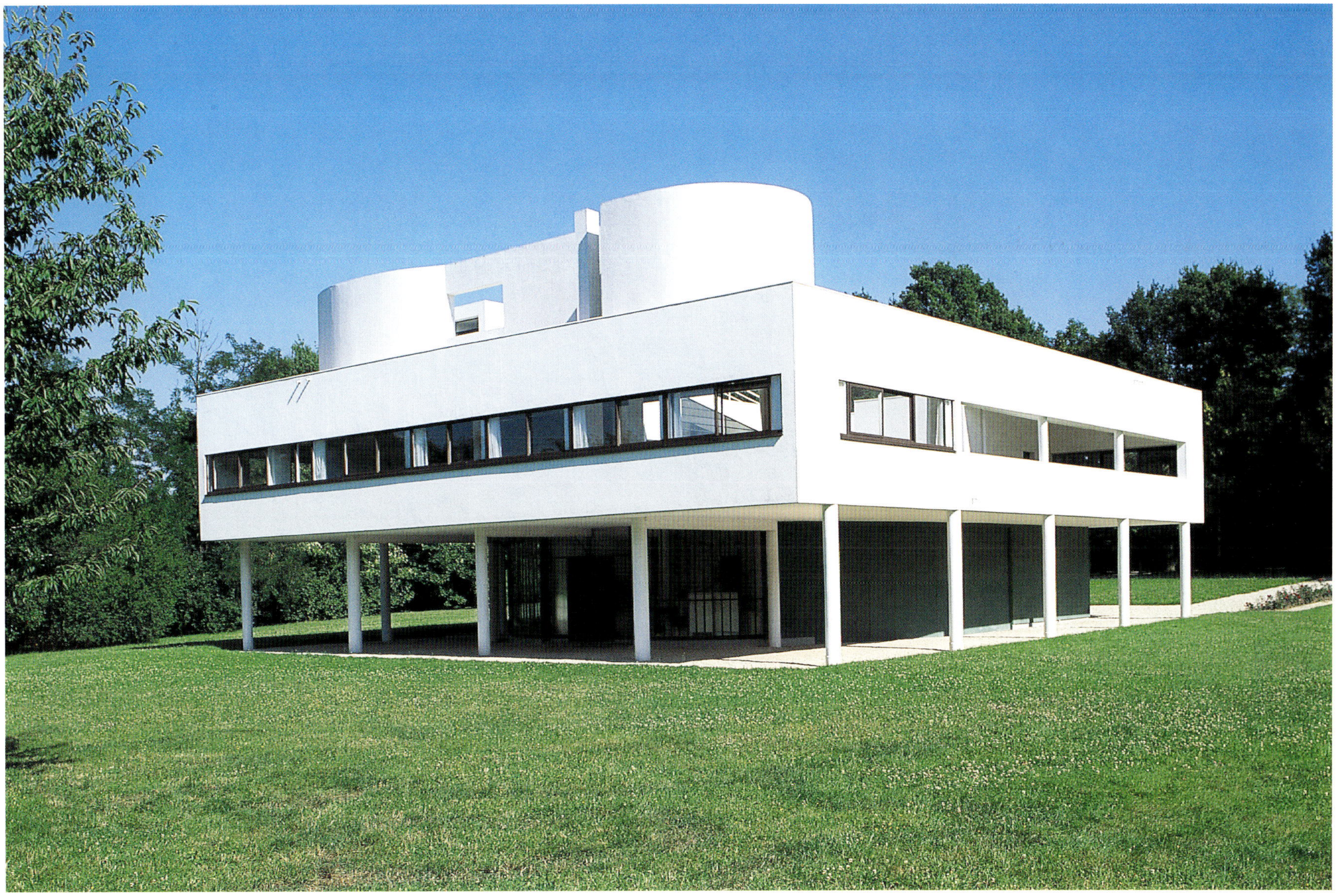

Villa Savoye Le Corbusier

The Villa Savoye is an icon of functionalist, machine-age symbolism, embodying many of Le Corbusier's revolutionary concepts including the 'Five Points of a New Architecture'. The use of the slender columns, *pilotis*, to support the main living accommodation above the ground, gives the house a striking elegance and lightness, while the strip windows on all sides unify the design. Made possible by the development of reinforced concrete technology, the *pilotis* enabled Le Corbusier to separate stationary living space from a ground zone given over to moving objects, or traffic. Inside, a ramp leads from ground level up towards the rooftop solarium, dramatizing a sense of movement through the house, while also distilling associations with the industrial era. This house is an eloquent expression of Le Corbusier's influential vision of a rationalized architecture for the twentieth century, which would lift its inhabitants into a realm of light, air and order.

Villa Savoye, Poissy, France, 1928–31. **Le Corbusier (Charles-Edouard Jeanneret)**. **b** La Chaux-de-Fonds, Switzerland, 1887. **d** Cap Martin, France, 1965.

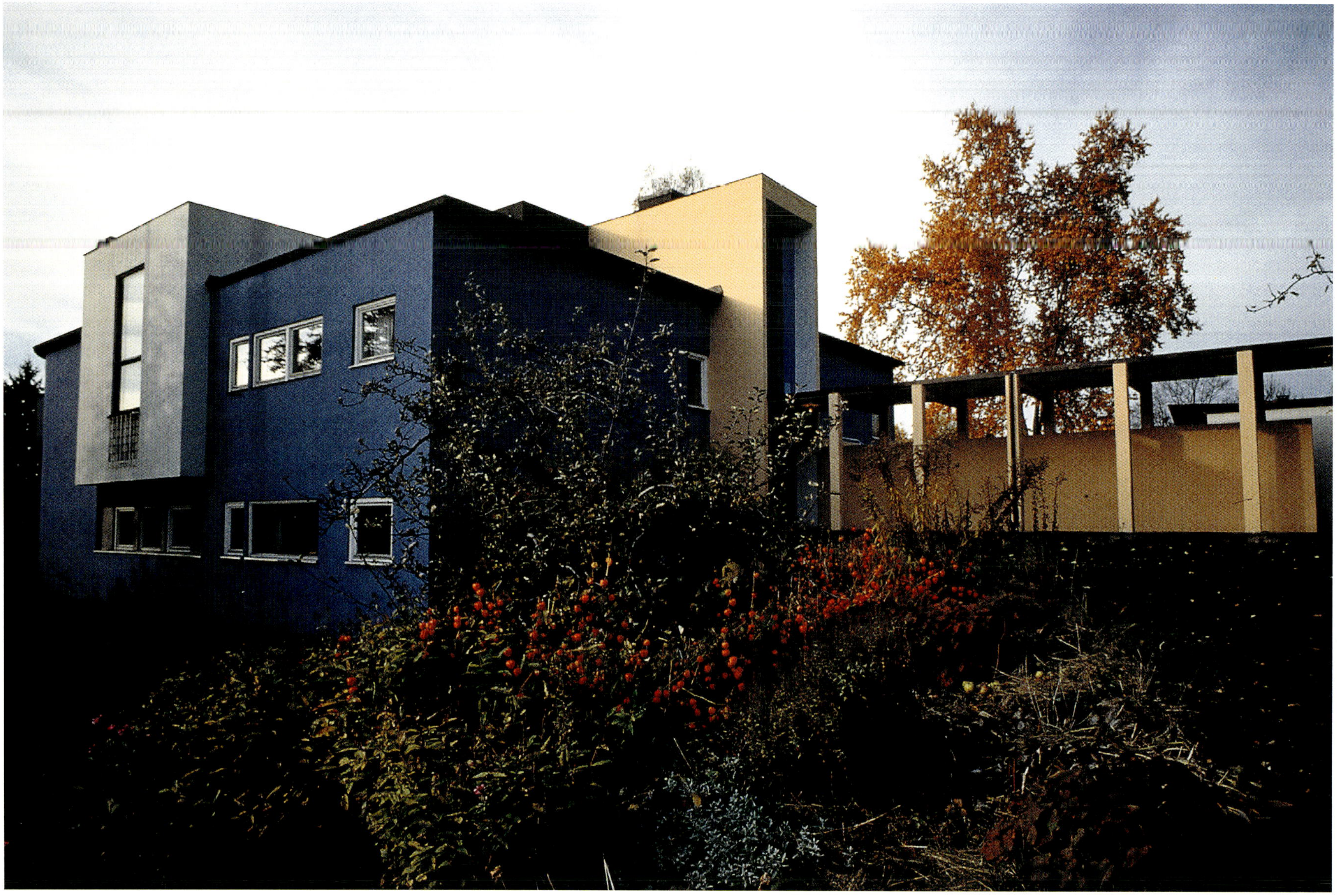

Villa Damman Arne Korsmo

In 1930, Axel Damman commissioned Arne Korsmo to design fourteen houses for the Havna neighbourhood in Oslo, including this, the developer's own house. With its strong plan and play of overlapping forms, the Villa Damman remains one of Korsmo's most important works, and an expression of his commitment to Norwegian Modernism. The street front of the house is dominated by a long walkway leading from the garden to the entrance. The rear facade, facing a fjord, accommodates the living room — which doubles as an art gallery, lit by continuous, high-level strip windows — a dining room and semicircular study. Successfully uniting the articulated forms into a harmonious whole, the concept was taken through into the interior, with much of the furniture also specially designed by Korsmo. Like Le Corbusier, he believed in the ability of a fully designed environment to transform the way people lived and to solve the problems of society.

Villa Damman, Oslo, Norway, 1932. **Arne Korsmo**. **b** Oslo, Norway, 1900. **d** Lima, Peru, 1968.

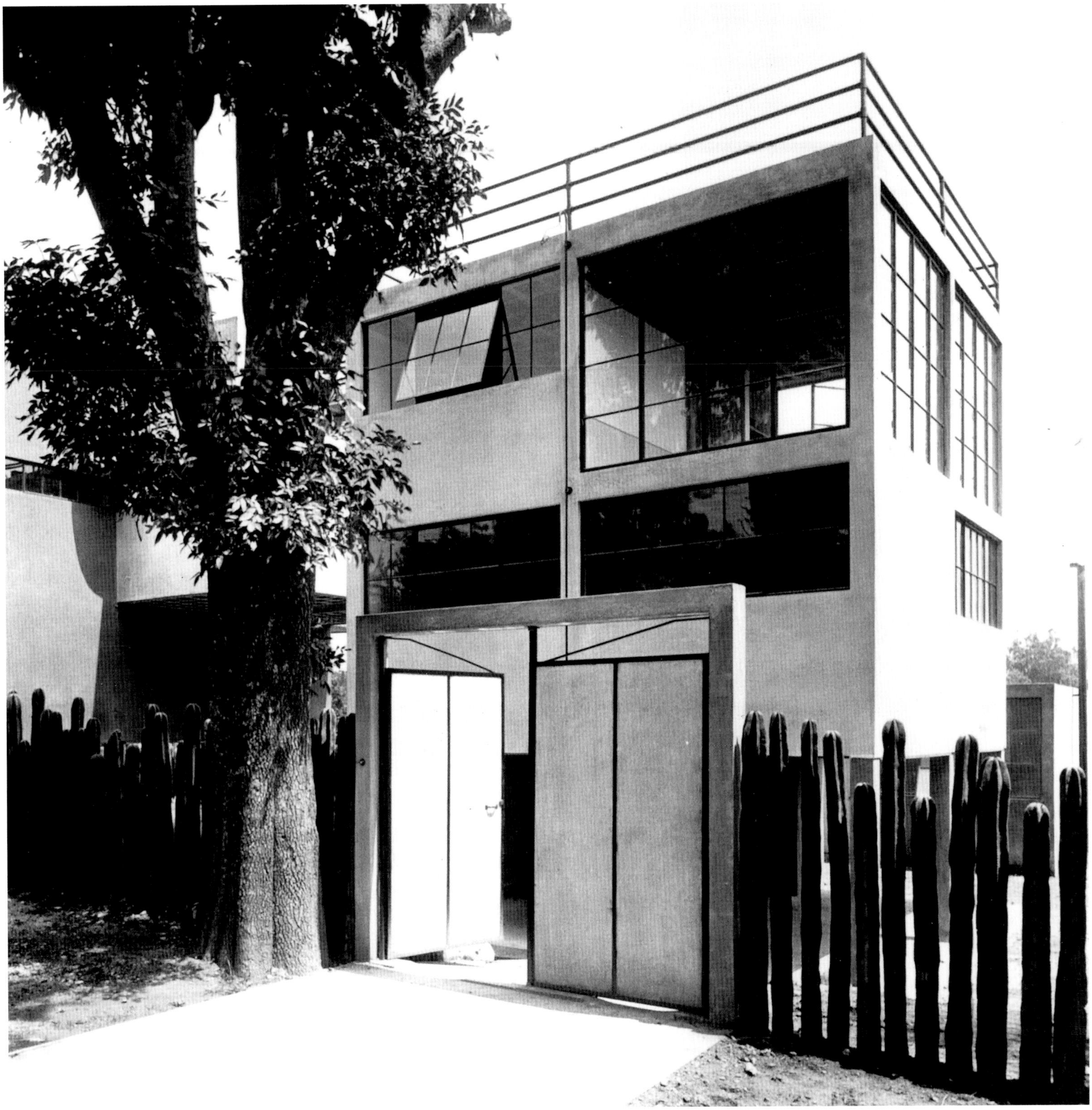

Diego Rivera and Frida Kahlo House Juan O'Gorman

Later in his life, Juan O'Gorman turned away from his early enthusiasm for Le Corbusier's Modernism — his own house, built some twenty-five years after this one, is a sequence of mosaic- and relief-encrusted, cave-like spaces. But here, at the house and studio built for his friends, the artists Diego Rivera and Frida Kahlo, the abstractions of Le Corbusier's early houses are precisely re-expressed. If anything, O'Gorman's expressed functionalism is even more ideological: the concrete frame is more strongly stated (and restated in the entrance gateway with its cactus fence) than in Le Corbusier's otherwise very similar Ozenfant Studio of 1923, for example. Indeed, ideological commitment seems to have led to O'Gorman's withdrawal from architecture for over ten years, and to the very different, architectural concerns of his later practice, where his work as a painter, and that of his artist friends, led to a more local and personal expression.

Diego Rivera and Frida Kahlo House and Studio, Mexico City, Mexico, 1930–2. **Juan O'Gorman**. **b** Mexico City, Mexico, 1905. **d** Mexico City, Mexico, 1982.

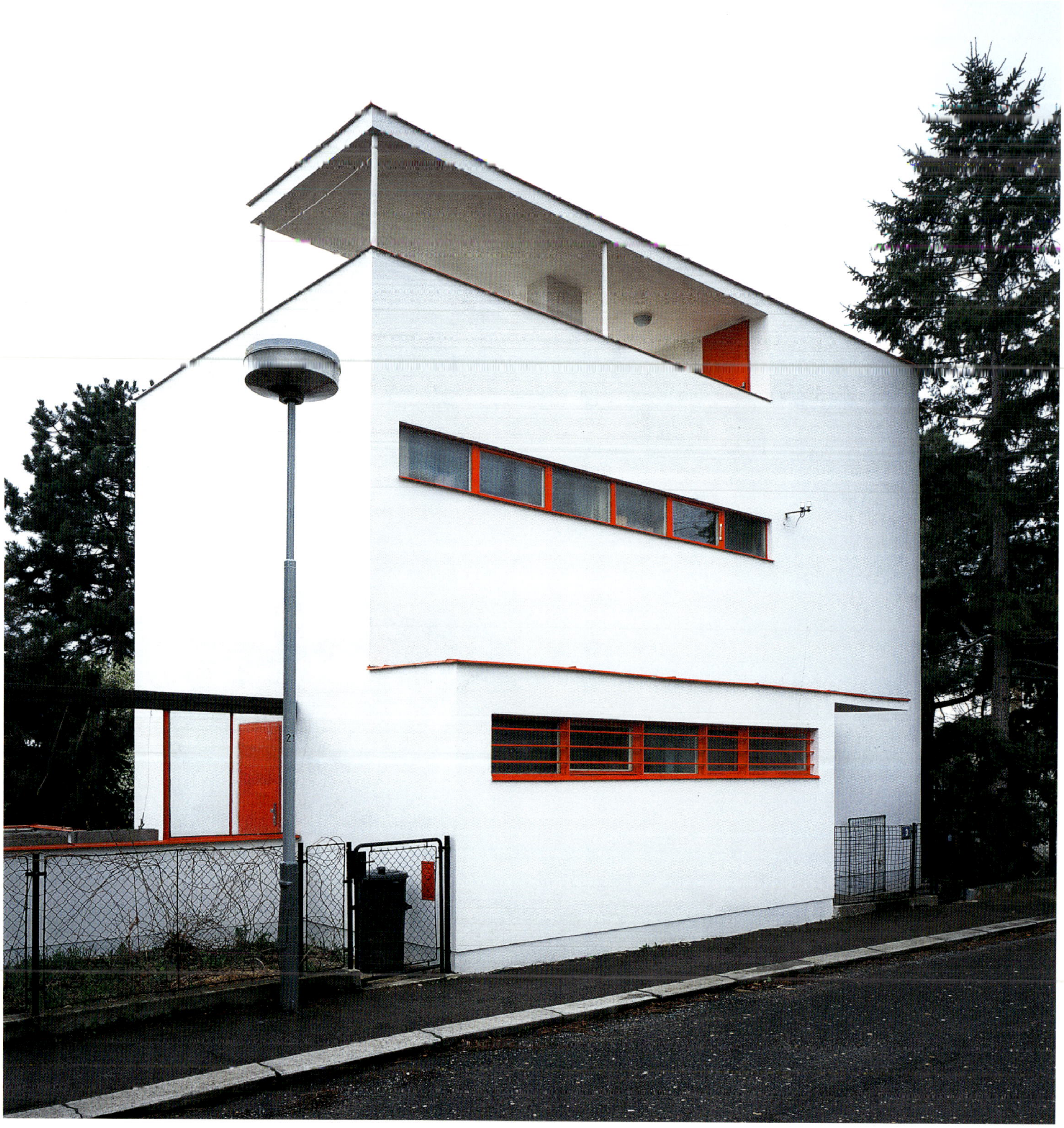

Villa Herain Ladislav Zák

As seen from the street, this modest house has an unassuming presence, with its two long bands of windows set in a plain white, rectilinear facade. By contrast, the garden elevation takes advantage of the scenic hillside site overlooking Prague, with large expanses of glass looking onto the garden and beyond, and a rounded, glazed stair tower. Built as one of twenty original houses at the Baba housing exhibition of 1932, the Villa Herain was one of three designed by the young Ladislav Zák. The estate was built for a series of individual clients — in this case the art historian Karel Herain, who moved in after the exhibition closed to the public. The exhibition was sponsored by the Czechoslovak Werkbund and based on the model of the successful Stuttgart-Weissenhof housing estate in Germany organized by Mies van der Rohe in 1927, which sparked the construction of twelve other housing exhibitions across Europe.

Villa Herain, Prague, Czech Republic, 1932. **Ladislav Zák**. **b** Prague, Czech Republic, 1900. **d** Prague, Czech Republic, 1973.

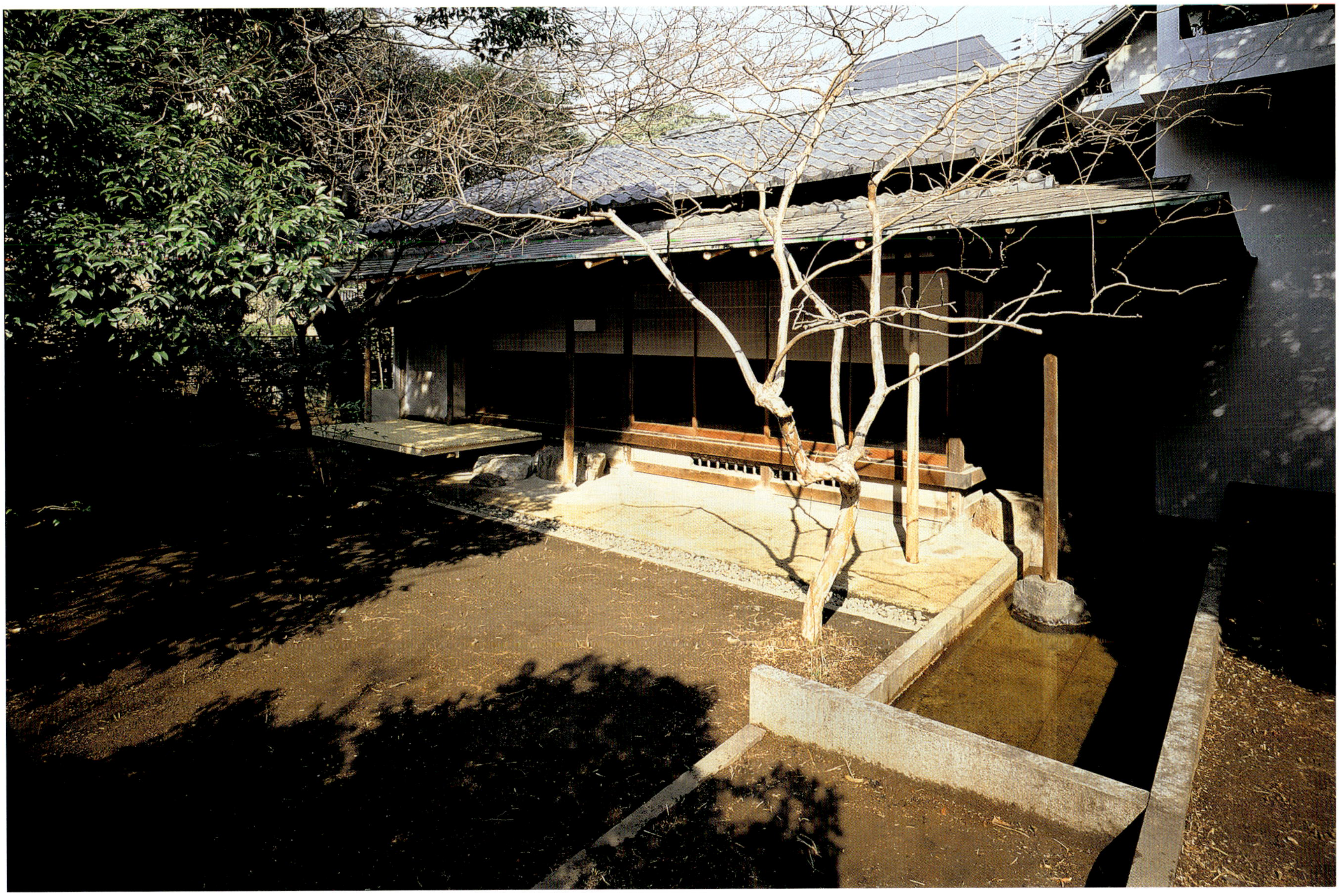

Okada House Sutemi Horiguchi

Okada House, which brings together traditional Japanese architecture and gardens with De Stijl-like compositional principles, has been described as the starting point of Modern architecture in Japan. It consists of a timber-frame Japanese wing, seen here, with a tea room and moon-viewing bamboo veranda recalling the seventeenth-century Katsura Imperial Villa, as well as a reinforced concrete living wing; the two volumes visually intersecting at the long, rectilinear reflecting pool. Horiguchi, a leader of the Japanese Secessionist movement *Bunriha* (1920–7), was one of the first Japanese architects to visit the Bauhaus. In 1924 he wrote an influential book on contemporary Dutch architecture. He also became a noted scholar of Japanese tea room architecture, thereby underscoring an inherent link between the modern and traditional *sukiya* style. The house was demolished in 1995 — only photographs that were published around the world remain.

Okada House, Tokyo, Japan, 1933, demolished 1995. **Sutemi Horiguchi**. **b** Gifu Prefecture, Japan, 1895. **d** Tokyo, Japan, 1984.

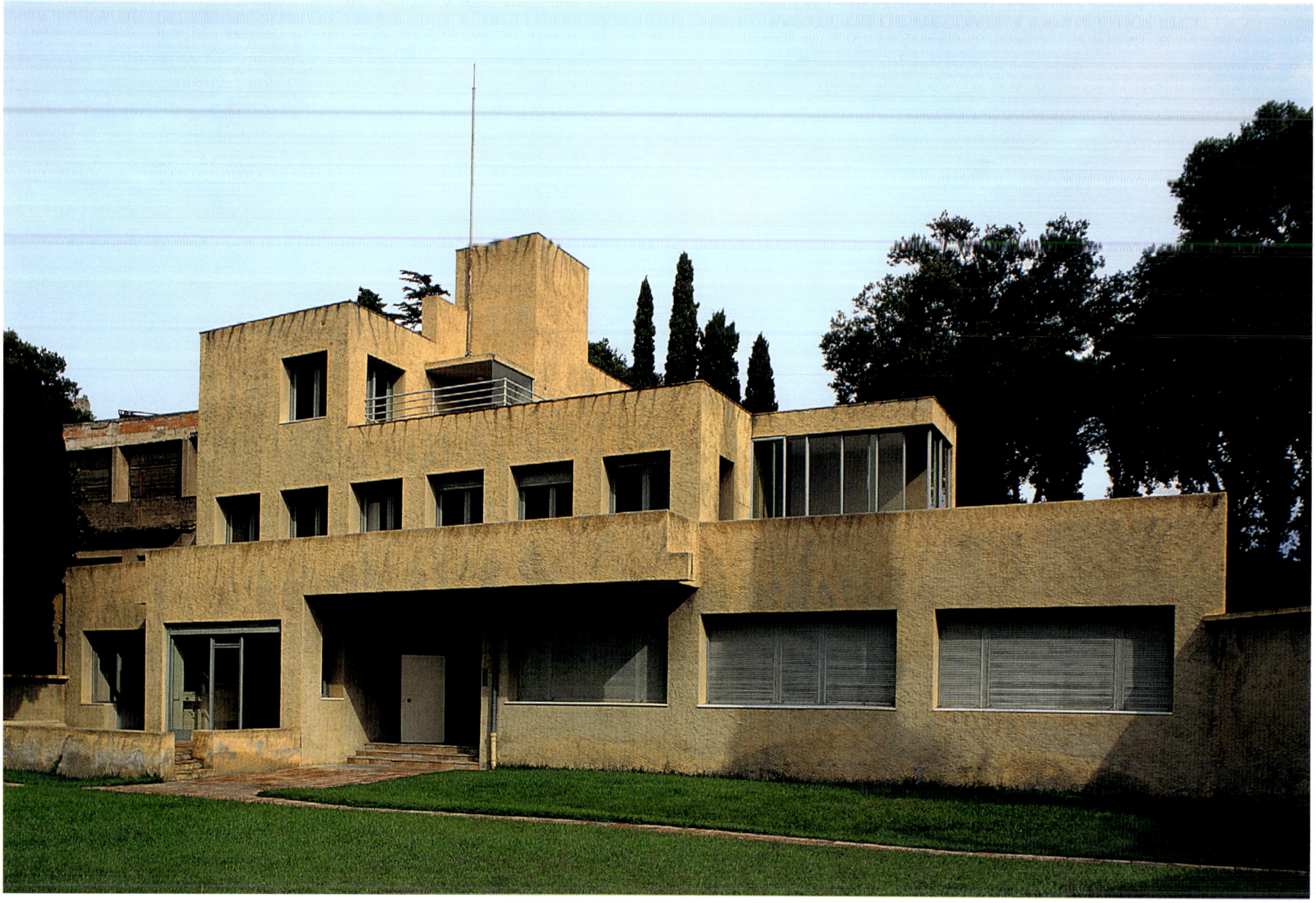

Villa Noailles Robert Mallet-Stevens

Rendered in flat, unadorned stucco, the street facade of this sprawling villa expresses a monumentality that is not compromised by the playful composition of its geometrical volumes and bold windows. Situated on a hillside, the massive facade hides a luxurious retreat with extensively landscaped terrace gardens, a covered swimming pool, gymnasium and squash courts. The original project, a five-bedroom weekend home for film enthusiast and modern art collector Viscount Charles de Noailles, was expanded to include eventually over sixty rooms; some of which were specially designed by other architects, including an open-air room by Pierre Chareau and a flower room by Dutch architect/artist Theo van Doesburg. The client originally intended to commission Mies van der Rohe or Le Corbusier for this project, but settled on the untested Robert Mallet-Stevens whose architectural reputation at the time, aged thirty-seven, was based only on inventive movie set designs.

Villa Noailles, Hyères, France, 1924–33. **Robert Mallet-Stevens**. **b** Paris, France, 1886. **d** Paris, France, 1945.

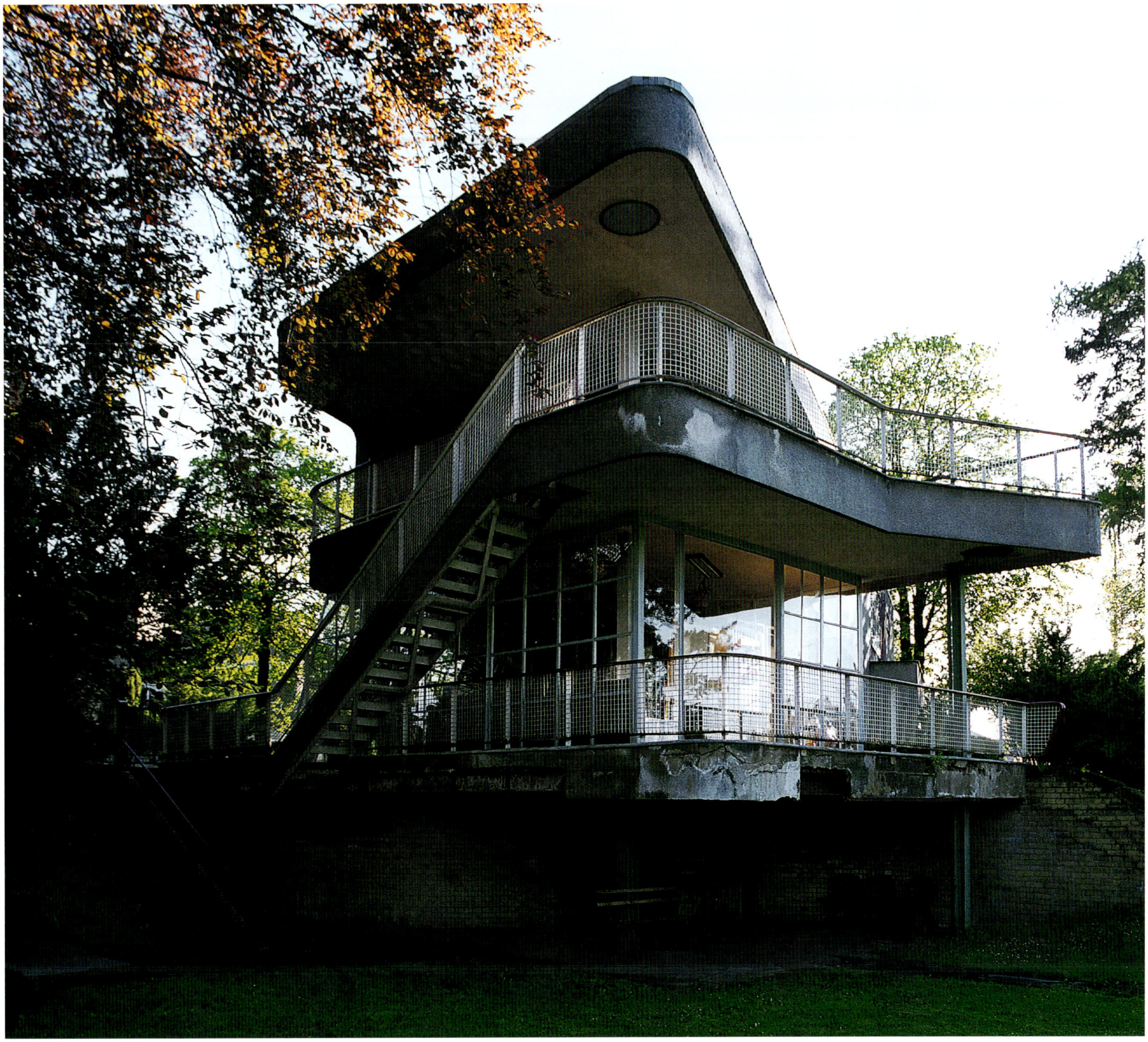

Schminke House Hans Scharoun

The canted relationship between the north–south orientation of the central block of this house and its two side wings, which follow the site boundaries at a 26-degree angle, gives an inherent dynamism to this design. Hans Scharoun exploits this characteristic with transparent walls and double-height spaces. His architecture depended on interpretation of site (note the cantilever off the garden wall), and of the functions that a building would accommodate, in opposition to preconceived Corbusian forms. The imminent Nazi regime — during which Scharoun remained in Germany — repressed the consummation of the refined relationship between form and function he achieved here. After World War II, Scharoun became Director of the Building and Housing Department for Greater Berlin, setting the stage for his greatest works and public buildings, and giving him free rein to influence the next generation of German architects.

Schminke House, Löbau, Germany, 1933. **Hans Scharoun**. **b** Bremen, Germany, 1893. **d** Berlin, Germany, 1972.

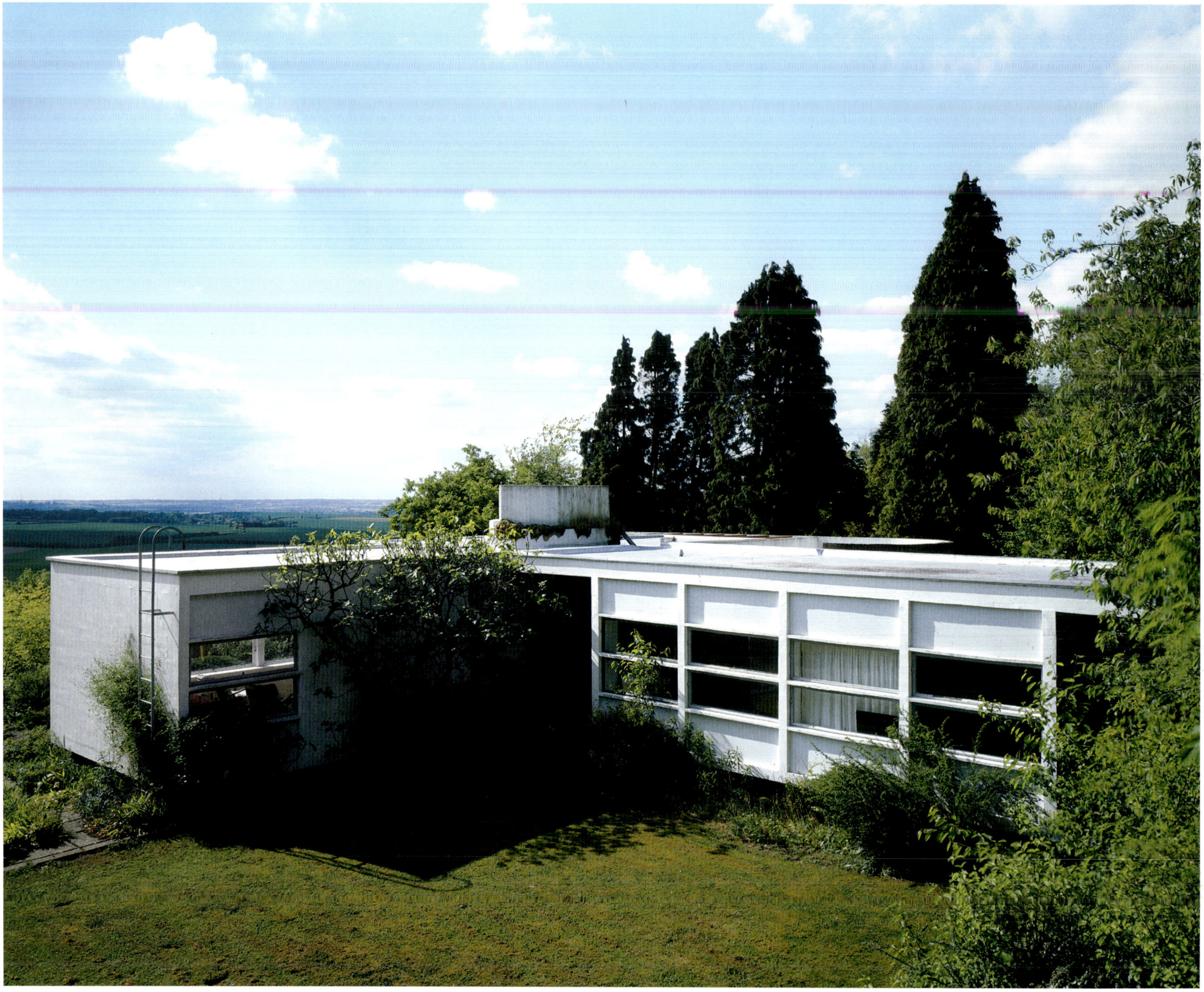

House A at Whipsnade Berthold Lubetkin

As this house was for himself, Berthold Lubetkin took the opportunity to experiment. It was designed for maximum outdoor living, and built on a platform cut into the hill to make the most of the views. The bedrooms are provided with outdoor sleeping porches, and there is also an outdoor fireplace. Lubetkin was not a strict functionalist and he worked in an intuitive way, as demonstrated in the two highly expressive curved elements of the building. First, on the roof is an extended parabolic screen which, below, makes a room-within-a-room for dining, and focuses this space on the view across the valley; second, the entrance is screened by a semicircular 'sun-catch'. Lubetkin came to England in 1931 and set up Tecton (1932–48) with young admirers of his work who had studied at the Architectural Association in London. Although best known for the Penguin Pool (1934) at London Zoo, his deeply-held socialist views led him to concentrate most of his career on public housing.

House A at Whipsnade, Bedfordshire, UK, 1933–6. **Berthold Lubetkin**. **b** Tiflis, Russia (now Tbilisi, Republic of Georgia), 1901. **d** Bristol, UK, 1990.

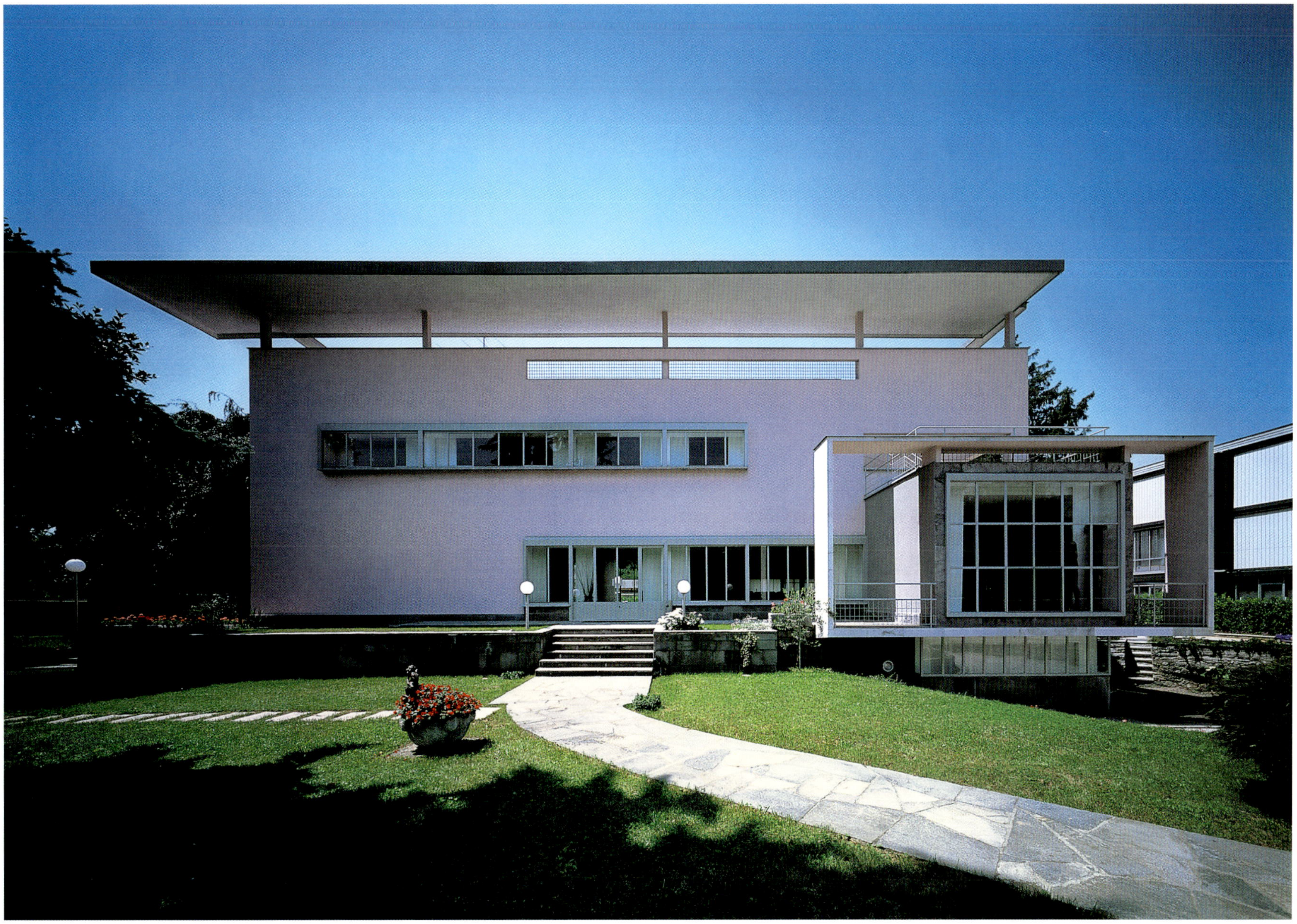

Villa Bianca Giuseppe Terragni

While an indebtedness to Le Corbusier is evident in the cubic volumetric form and horizontal stripped fenestration of the Villa Bianca, Giuseppe Terragni's own brand of Rationalism is also apparent. Architect of the infamous, rather static office building Casa del Fascio, and the unbuilt Danteum museum project of the same period, Terragni, in contrast, here exhibits an obsession with sliding planes, protruding volumes and floating canopies. The conflicting dynamics of the villa's structure constrain and, at the same time, extend the building beyond its proper enclosure, producing an active and fluid series of spaces, both inside and outside its shell. This concern for the displacement of mass is characteristic of Terragni and his Rationalist comrades, who sought to synthesize the values of Italian Classicism and the dynamism of the machine age. Contrary to its name, the villa is painted not white, but a pale pink, named instead after a beloved lost child of the original owner.

Villa Bianca, Seveso, Italy, 1937. **Giuseppe Terragni**. **b** Meda, Italy, 1904. **d** Como, Italy, 1943.

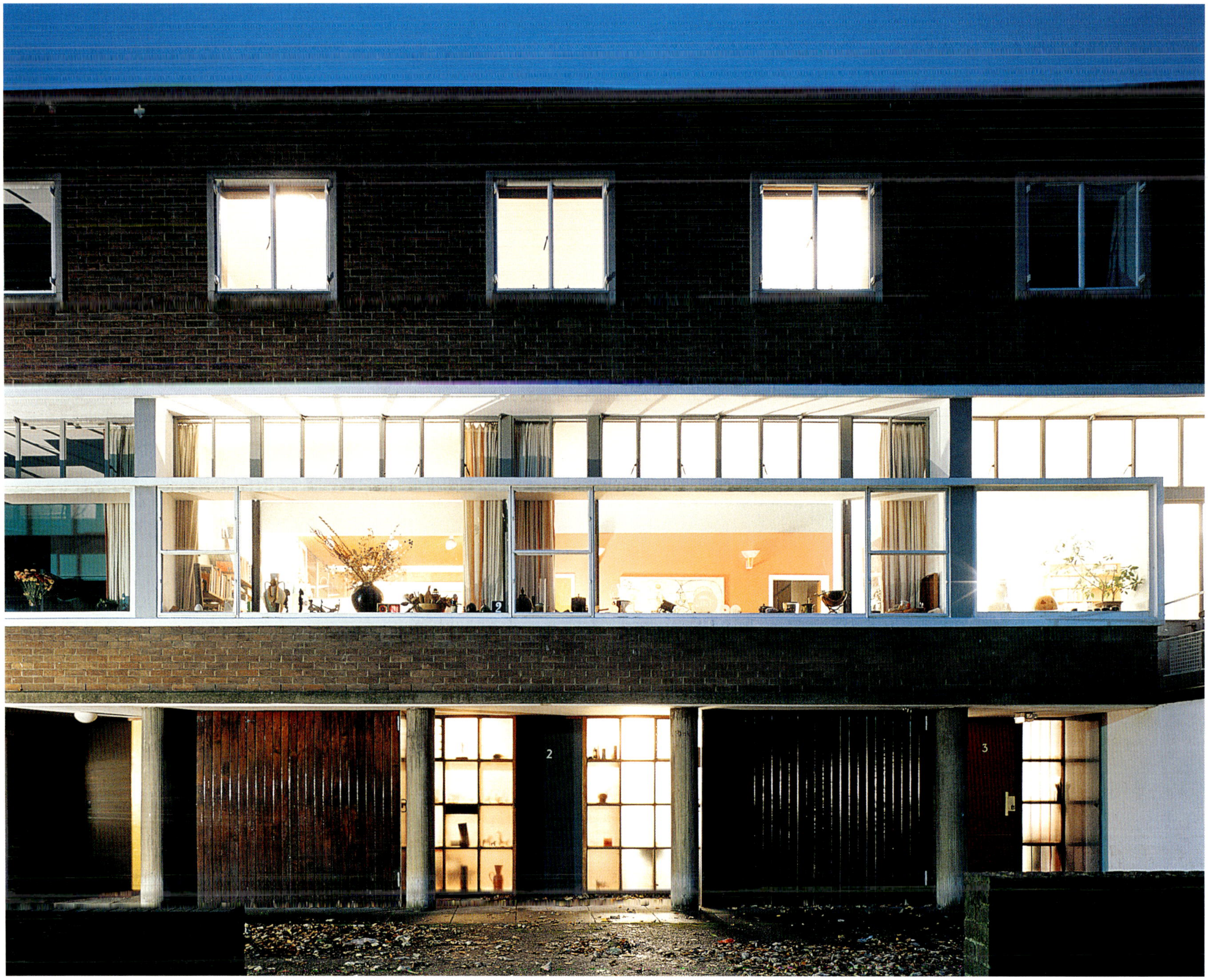

Willow Road Ernö Goldfinger

Ironically, the protest that greeted plans for Ernö Goldfinger's houses at Willow Road was based on the mistaken belief that they were to be white concrete, like other Modern houses of the time. In fact, they were the most successful integration of pre-war Modernism into the powerful and much-loved British tradition of the Georgian terrace. Three houses are grouped into a single, elegantly proportioned terrace, the piano nobile visible through large first-floor windows. The proportions are Georgian, the brickwork contextual, but the language is clearly Modernist. The horizontal windows feature Goldfinger's first use of the 'photobolic screen', the horizontal plane at the top of the window that bounces light deep into the room. Inside, many of the walls fold away; on the top floor, the three children's bedrooms open to form a single playroom. Goldfinger's own house was the slightly larger, middle of the three, and is now a museum owned by the National Trust.

Willow Road, London, UK, 1937. **Ernö Goldfinger**. **b** Budapest, Hungary, 1902. **d** London, UK, 1987.

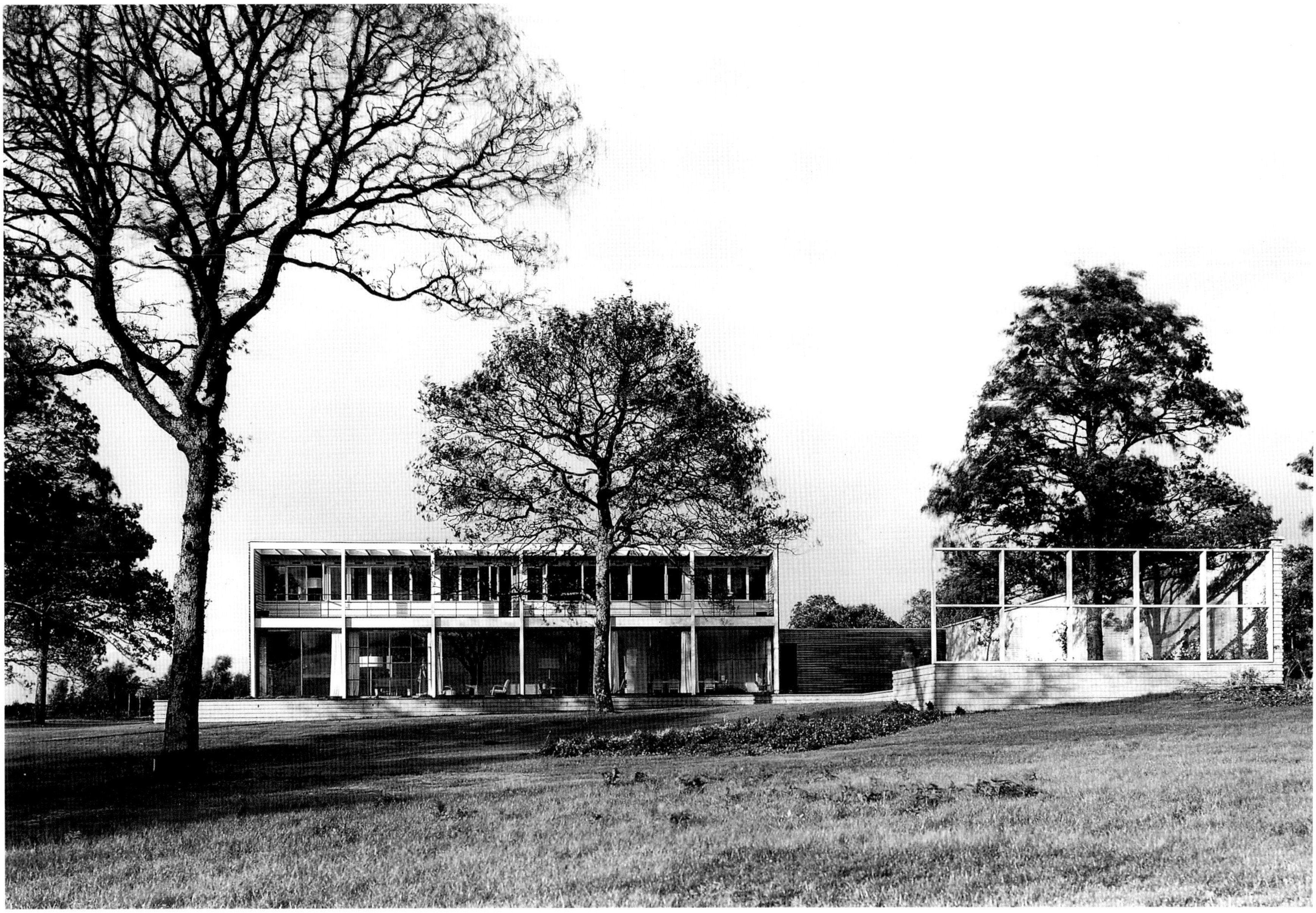

Bentley Wood Serge Chermayeff

This two-storey, long-fronted house stands in a broad landscape, stretching out an arm to one side where, as if held in the hand, a majestic stone carving by Henry Moore surveys the distant scene. Completed shortly before World War II, Bentley Wood was recognized as the most mature of English Modern houses of the 1930s. Serge Chermayeff integrated its white-painted, timber-frame structure and cladding with its grid-like visual form, using timber unsentimentally, as if it were steel. The plan, a model for relaxed weekend living, was designed for the architect and his family, with furnishings chosen to complement the abstract paintings by John Piper and Ben Nicholson. Frank Lloyd Wright visited in the summer of 1939, remarking, 'It'll take a little time for God to make it click', but contemporary critics recognized Bentley Wood's aristocratic poise and the effortless convergence of Modern ideas of space with older themes in landscape design.

Bentley Wood, Halland, UK, 1937–8. **Serge Ivan Chermayeff**. **b** Grozny, Chechen Republic, Russia, 1900. **d** Wellfleet, MA, USA, 1996.

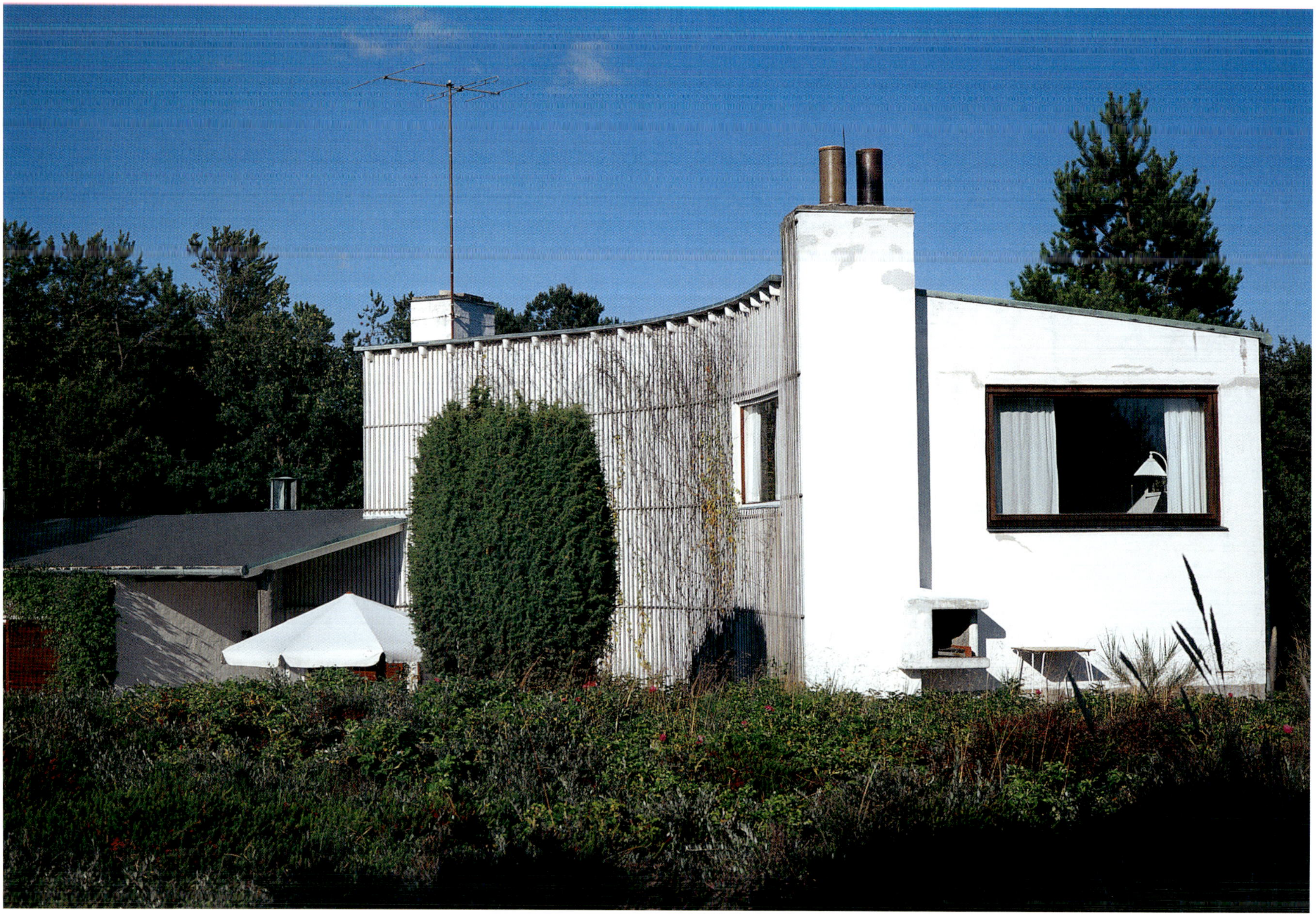

Summer House Arne Jacobsen

The shed roof that gently attaches itself to the wall, the outdoor fireplace that hangs on the chimney, the picture window and the patio, all exemplify the informality and relaxed relationship to the outdoors of much Scandinavian architecture of this period. Even the potentially monumental curved wall, which organizes the more casual components of the architect's own summer house, is broken down through texture and horizontal articulation. But the whiteness and proportion of the house set it apart from nature, and this tension makes it a pivotal design in Arne Jacobsen's career. One of the key figures in the development of Scandinavian Modernism, he was educated to balance new techniques and functions with tradition and culture, and later on, his houses were closely attuned to a northern European climate. He was also a designer of tableware and furniture, and is possibly most well known today for his cult-status Egg chair (1957).

Summer House, Gudmindrup Lyng, Denmark, 1938. **Arne Jacobsen**. **b** Copenhagen, Denmark, 1902. **d** Copenhagen, Denmark, 1971.

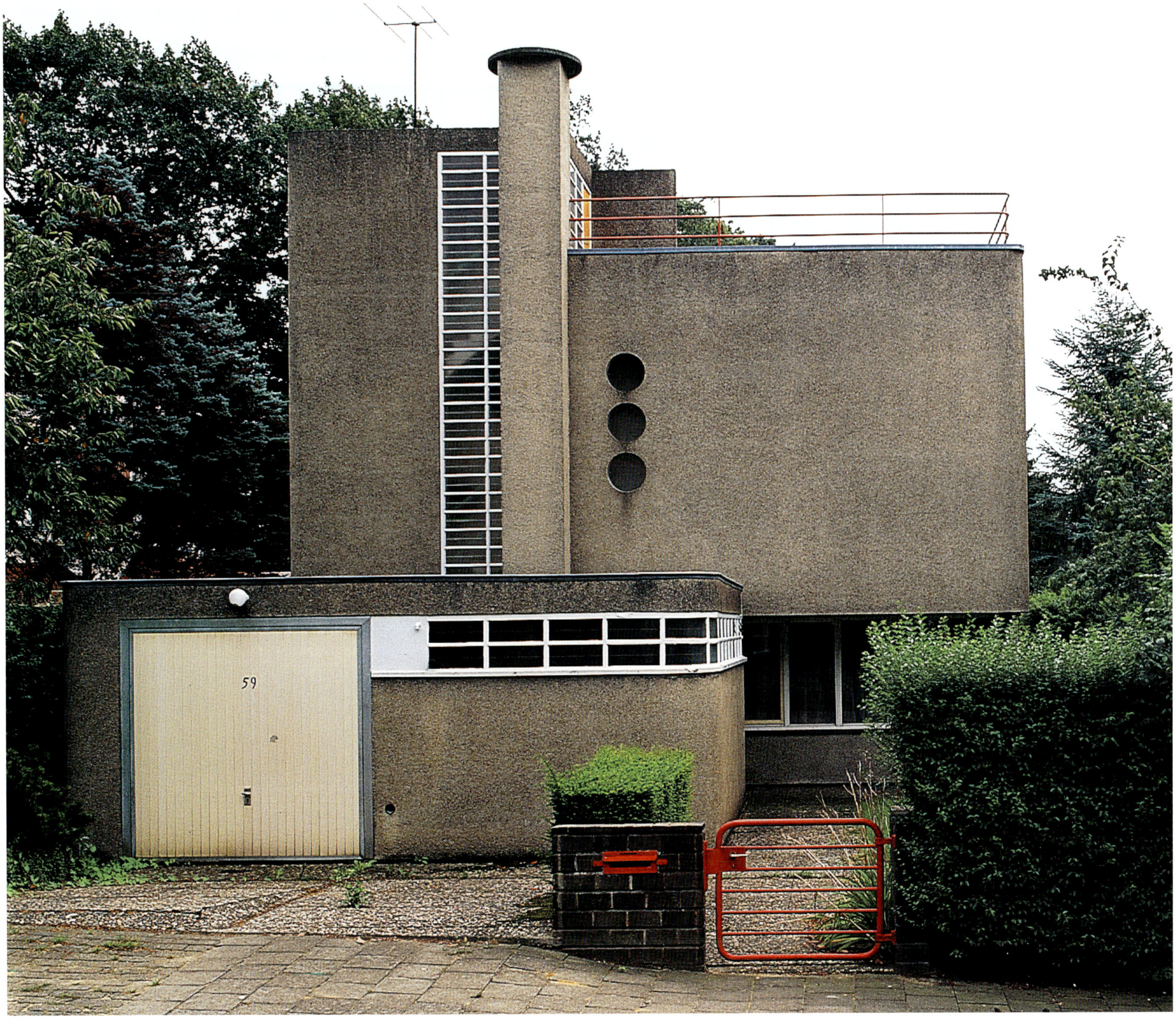

Villa Berteaux Louis Herman de Koninck

Inspired in his early days by the Art Nouveau architecture of fellow Belgian, Victor Horta, Louis Herman de Koninck's interpretation of the Modern style was formally more creative and less rigid than many of his European contemporaries. This is shown at the Villa Berteaux in the interplay between horizontal and vertical windows; this playful composition also borrowed the porthole windows and metal handrails from ship designs, a favourite Modernist source. De Koninck was renowned for his technological innovation; he introduced the exterior reinforced concrete wall to Belgium. This house, built for an engineer, displays his mastery of construction techniques, with smooth, rounded corners and elegantly composed volumes. De Koninck was best known internationally for the CUBEX kitchen, which was designed as a series of modular components that could be assembled in various configurations to fit a client's needs.

Villa Berteaux, Uccle, Belgium, 1936–8. **Louis Herman de Koninck**. **b** Brussels, Belgium, 1896. **d** Brussels, Belgium, 1984.

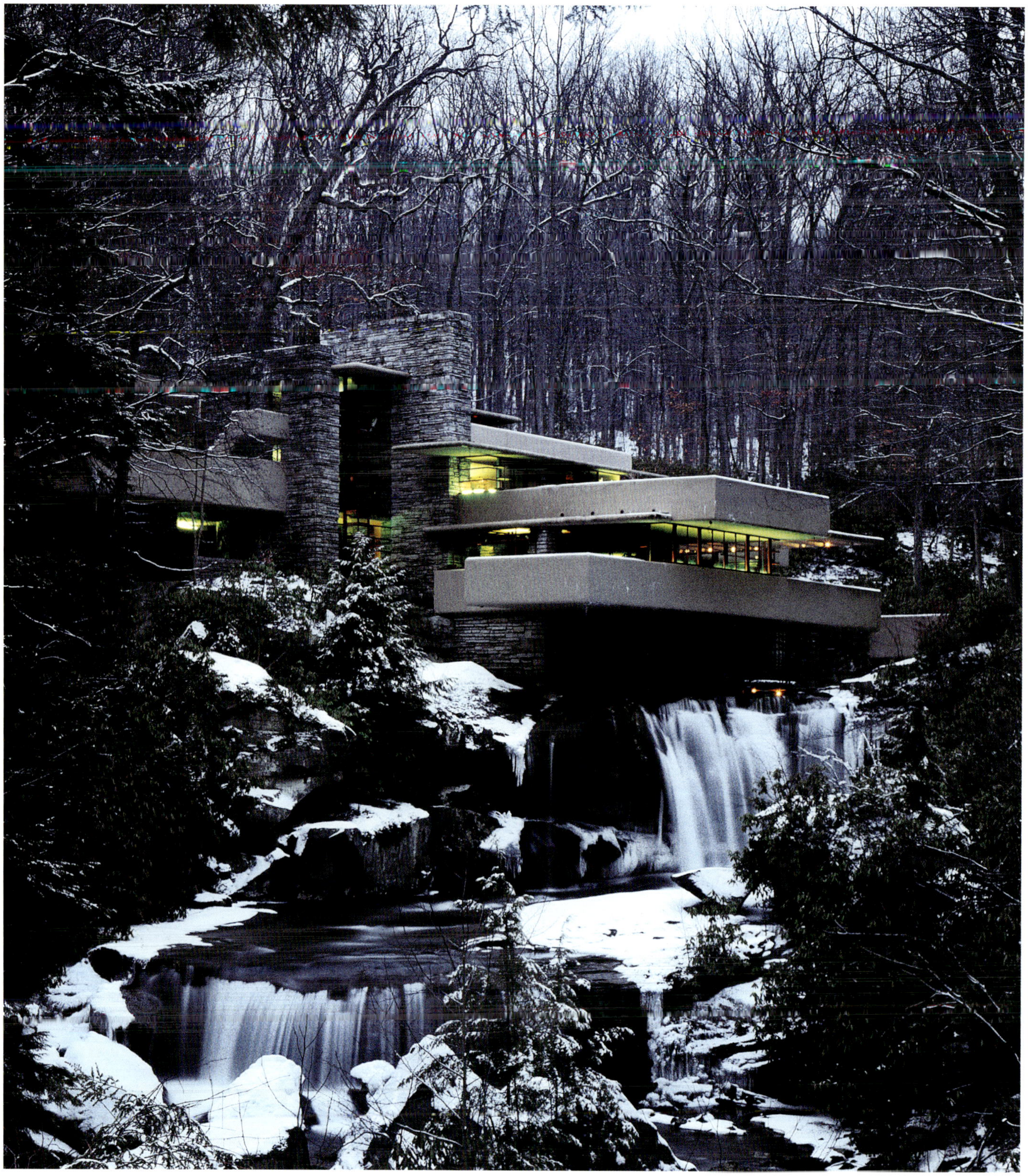

Fallingwater Frank Lloyd Wright

With its dramatic, horizontal concrete slabs cantilevered over the roaring crescendo of a waterfall, Fallingwater symbolizes both the romance of nature and the triumph of man. At first glance, the horizontal emphasis is reminiscent of the prevalent International Modernism of the time; however, the natural materials and handcrafted details — evident in the stacked stone walls — betray its roots in the Arts and Crafts tradition, while the plan is derived from Frank Lloyd Wright's earlier Prairie House-type, with volumes developing from a central core. The contrast between man and nature continues on the inside: the polished flagstone floor appears as though a river had flowed over it for centuries, yet the recessed ceilings float overhead as man-made works of art. Arguably the most important twentieth-century house in the United States, Fallingwater was built towards the latter part of Wright's extraordinarily prolific and influential career.

Fallingwater (Kaufmann House), Bear Run, PA, USA, 1935–9. **Frank Lloyd Wright**. **b** Richland Center, WI, USA, 1867. **d** Phoenix, AZ, USA, 1959.

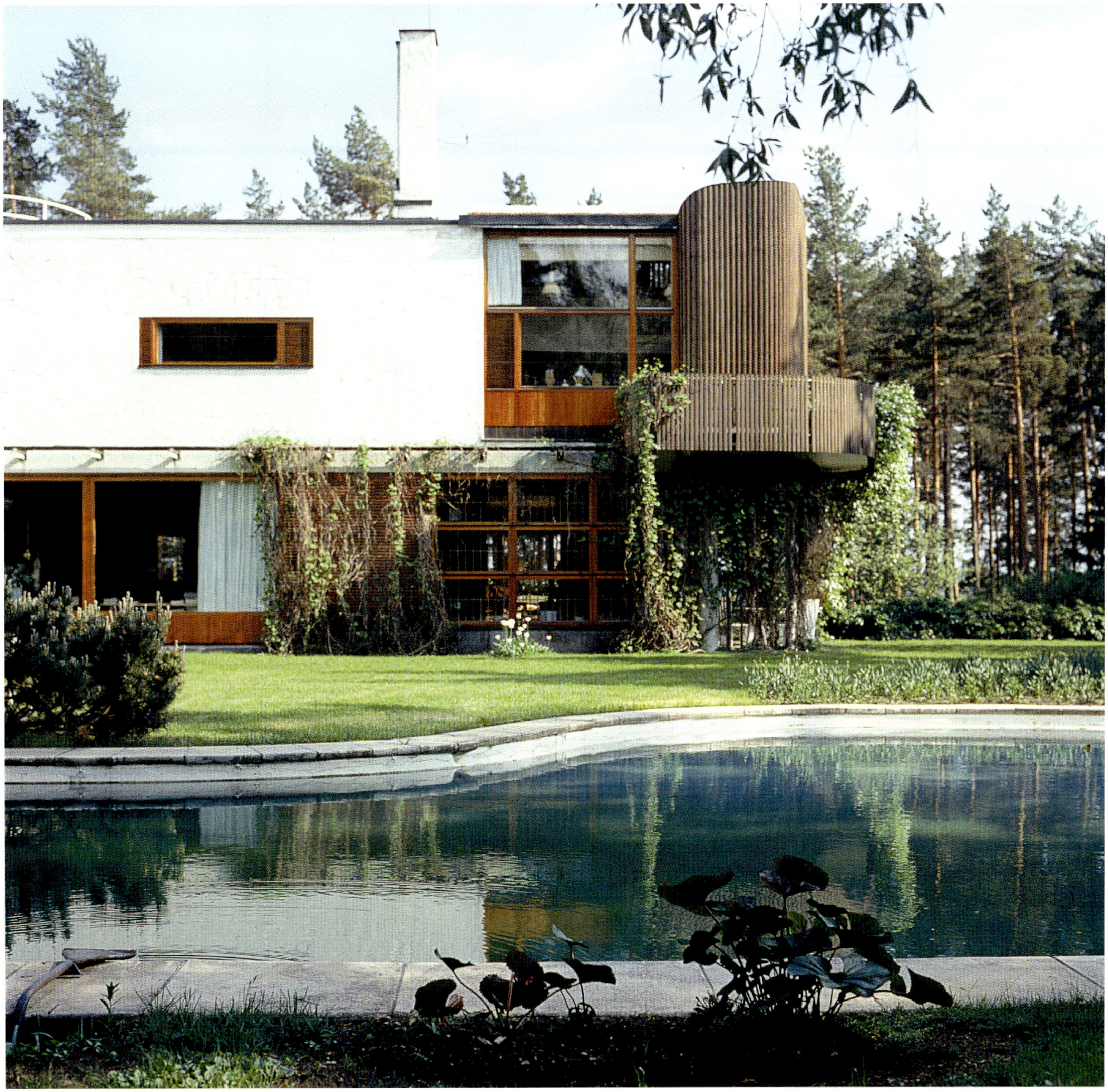

Villa Mairea Alvar Aalto

Instructed by his clients to take an experimental approach when designing this rural retreat, Alvar Aalto took the opportunity to test out ideas that he hoped could be adapted for future use in mass-produced housing programmes. The two-storey flat-roofed structure combines machine-made angularity with a warmth derived from the use of natural materials, sometimes lacking in the work of his contemporaries. The austere functionalism of European Modernism is juxtaposed with traditional Finnish peasant vernacular so that the apparently stark white box is richly decorated with luxurious natural materials. The L-shaped plan presents a formal facade to the public while creating an enclosed private area housing a swimming pool to the rear. The proximity of the surrounding woodland is celebrated and emphasized by the tree-like supporting pillars and a grass roof on concrete beams. Inside, the open-plan layout maximizes light and views while the rectangular spaces are broken up with a curved hall.

Villa Mairea, Noormarkku, Finland, 1937–9. **Hugo Alvar Henrik Aalto**. **b** Kuortane, nr Jyväskylä, Finland, 1898. **d** Helsinki, Finland, 1976.

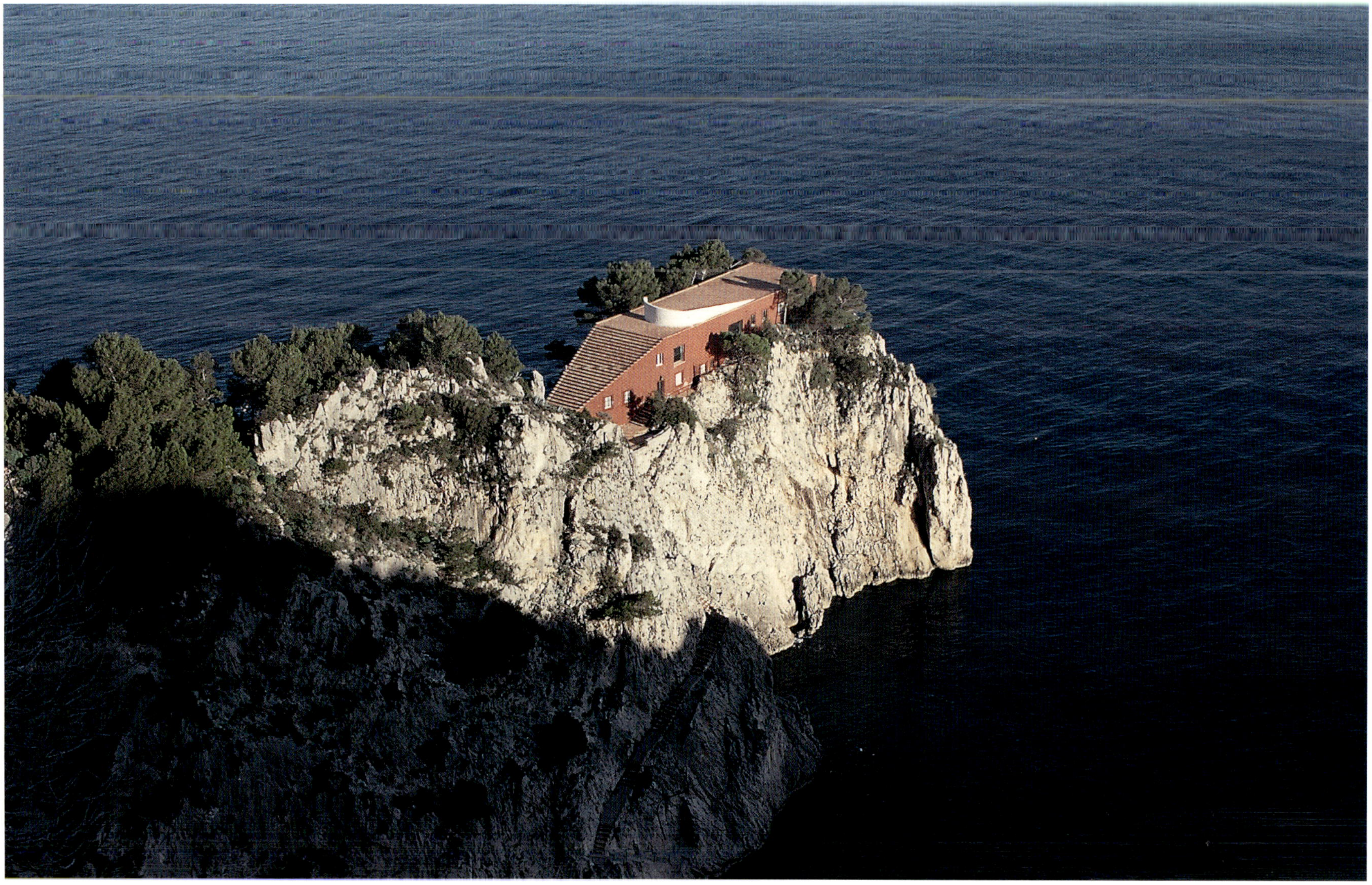

Casa Malaparte Adalberto Libera

In building the inter-war Casa Malaparte, Rationalist architect Adalberto Libera, together with his client, the writer Curzio Malaparte, reinforced something of the myth of the writer in his solitary study on this bare rock of his Capri island exile. Conceived as a simple stone house, the design was soon developed to incorporate a broad, ritualistic flight of tapering steps that lead to the plain roof terrace. This detail ties the house to its rocky setting, demonstrating how a building can be treated as a geographical accent, part of the landscape itself. This relationship with nature is continued inside by a series of small windows framing intense views along the dramatic coastline or glimpses of rocks and waves in the distance. Although more Modern than Classical in its architectural heritage, Casa Malaparte manages to evoke an antique ruin; indeed, it was built almost in sight of Tiberius' Villa Iovis which had, at the time, just been excavated.

Casa Malaparte, Capri, Italy, 1938–41. **Adalberto Libera**. **b** Trento, Italy, 1903. **d** Rome, Italy, 1963.

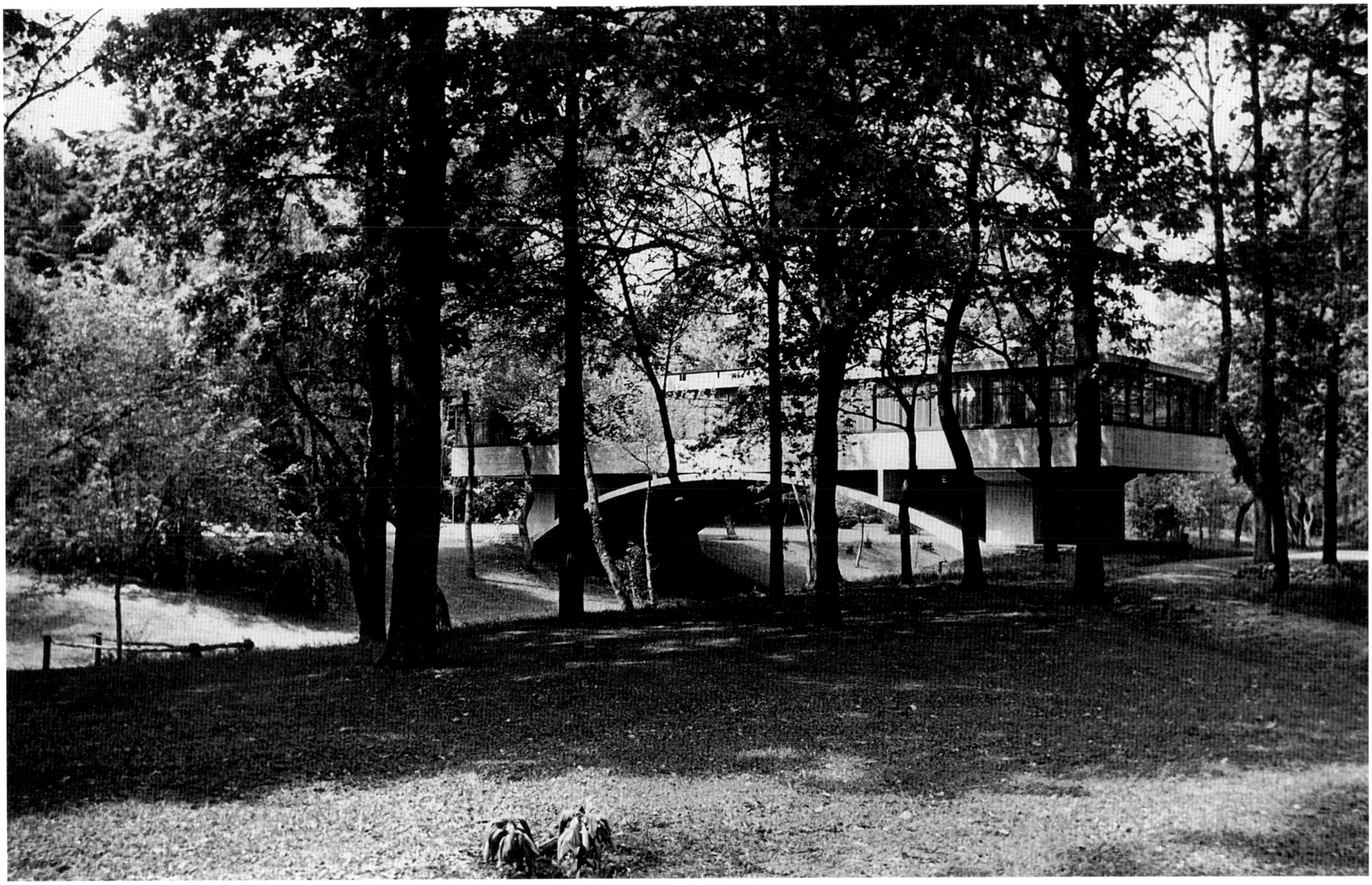

House over the Brook Amancio Williams

This house represents a dynamic synthesis of Le Corbusier's principles with Latin American imagination and daring. Amancio Williams, who worked as an aviator for a number of years before studying architecture, designed and built the house for his father, a well-known musician. Located in Mar del Plata, some 500 km (310 miles) from Buenos Aires, the house takes advantage of the bucolic setting by spanning a small brook that runs through the property. The bridge-like house is entirely constructed of formed, exposed concrete, with the flat floor slab and curved supporting slab below forming an integral whole, so that, according to Williams, 'form, structure and quality are thus here the same thing'. With the uninterrupted glazing and rooftop terrace, every advantage is taken of the views of this idyllic setting. The most complete of only a handful of built designs by Williams, the house embodies his innovative and meticulous approach to architecture.

House over the Brook, Mar del Plata, Argentina, 1943–5. **Amancio Williams**. **b** Buenos Aires, Argentina, 1913. **d** Buenos Aires, Argentina, 1989.

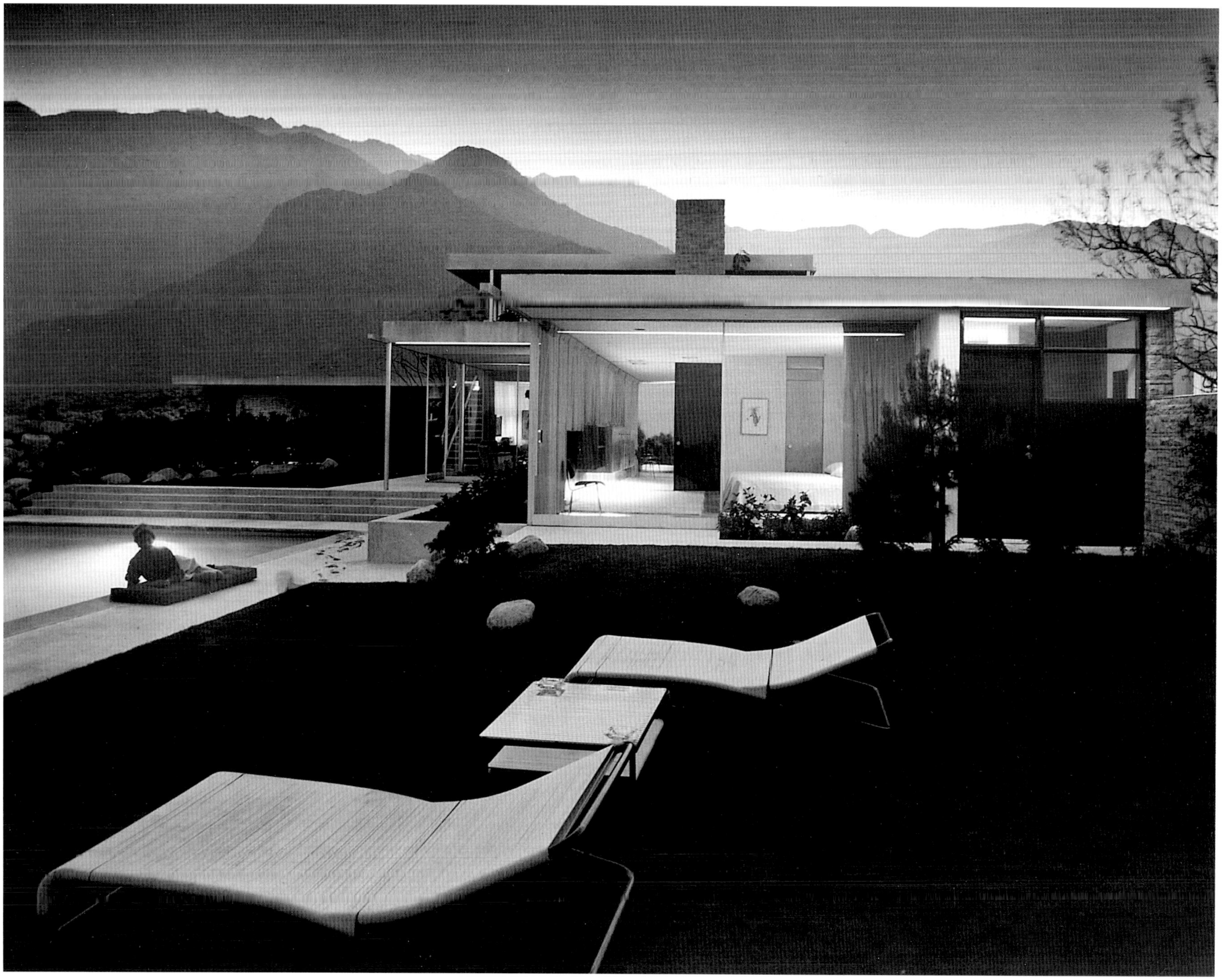

Kaufmann Desert House Richard Neutra

Designed as a pavilion for inhabiting and encountering the arid desert of Palm Springs, the Kaufmann Desert House radiates out from its centre like a pinwheel, with each wing only one room wide in order to maximize the views of the surrounding mountains and landscape. The house sensitively adapts the International Style to this hot, harsh climate, using strong horizontal lines to contrast with the mountainous landscape. Working in the California regionalist tradition of Rudolph Schindler, Neutra combines a Modernist vocabulary with a distinctive American accent, evocative of Frank Lloyd Wright's Taliesin West. Here, however, the steel-frame house retains an intrusive presence, unlike Wright's organicism. The house fulfils Neutra's aspiration that his architecture combine 'the goal of building environmental harmony, functional efficiency, and human enhancement into the experience of everyday living'.

Kaufmann Desert House, Palm Springs, CA, USA, 1946–7. **Richard Josef Neutra**. **b** Vienna, Austria, 1892. **d** Wuppertal, Germany, 1970.

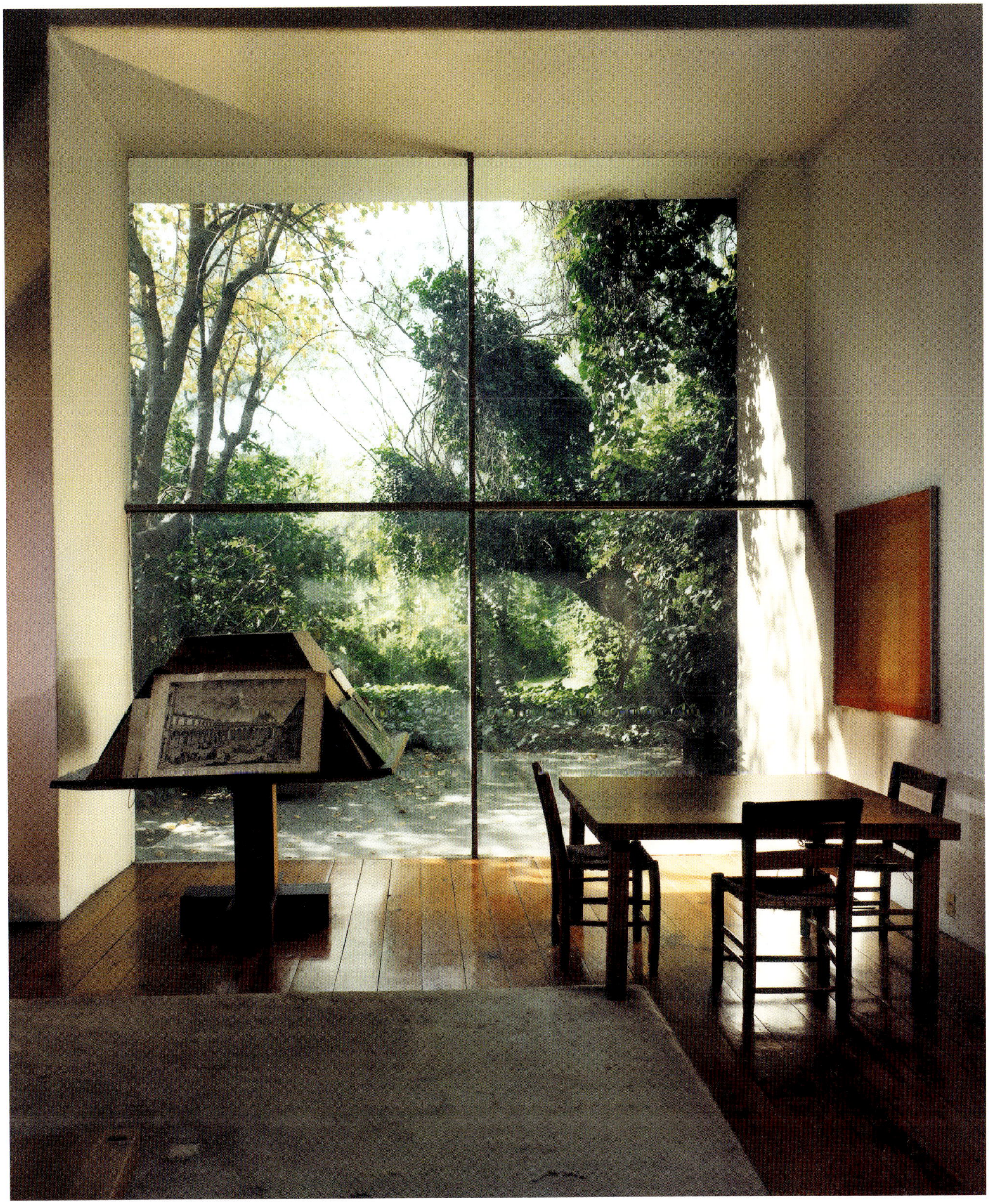

Barragán House Luis Barragán

The house and studio of Luis Barragán is an outstanding example of his innovative use of colour, texture and form. Externally, the building has a stark, unmemorable facade in keeping with the existing aspect of the street. Inside, the house reveals a vibrant juxtaposition of traditional Modernist philosophies with a warm Mexican flavour defined by simple geometric spaces and brightly coloured painted surfaces. Low walls subdivide the interior and sunlight is diffused throughout the house via skylights and large rear windows. These offer visual access to the walled garden which serves as an extension of the interior space. Barragán was an advocate of emotional architecture rather than cool functionalism, and he personalizes the house by intergrating found objects symbolizing horses, death and religion into his design. This house represents a masterpiece of Modernism, combining old and new concepts to form a fresh architectural synthesis that has been highly influential in contemporary landscape design.

Barragán House, Tacubaya, Mexico City, Mexico, 1947–8. **Luis Barragán**. **b** Guadalajara, Mexico, 1902. **d** Mexico City, Mexico, 1988.

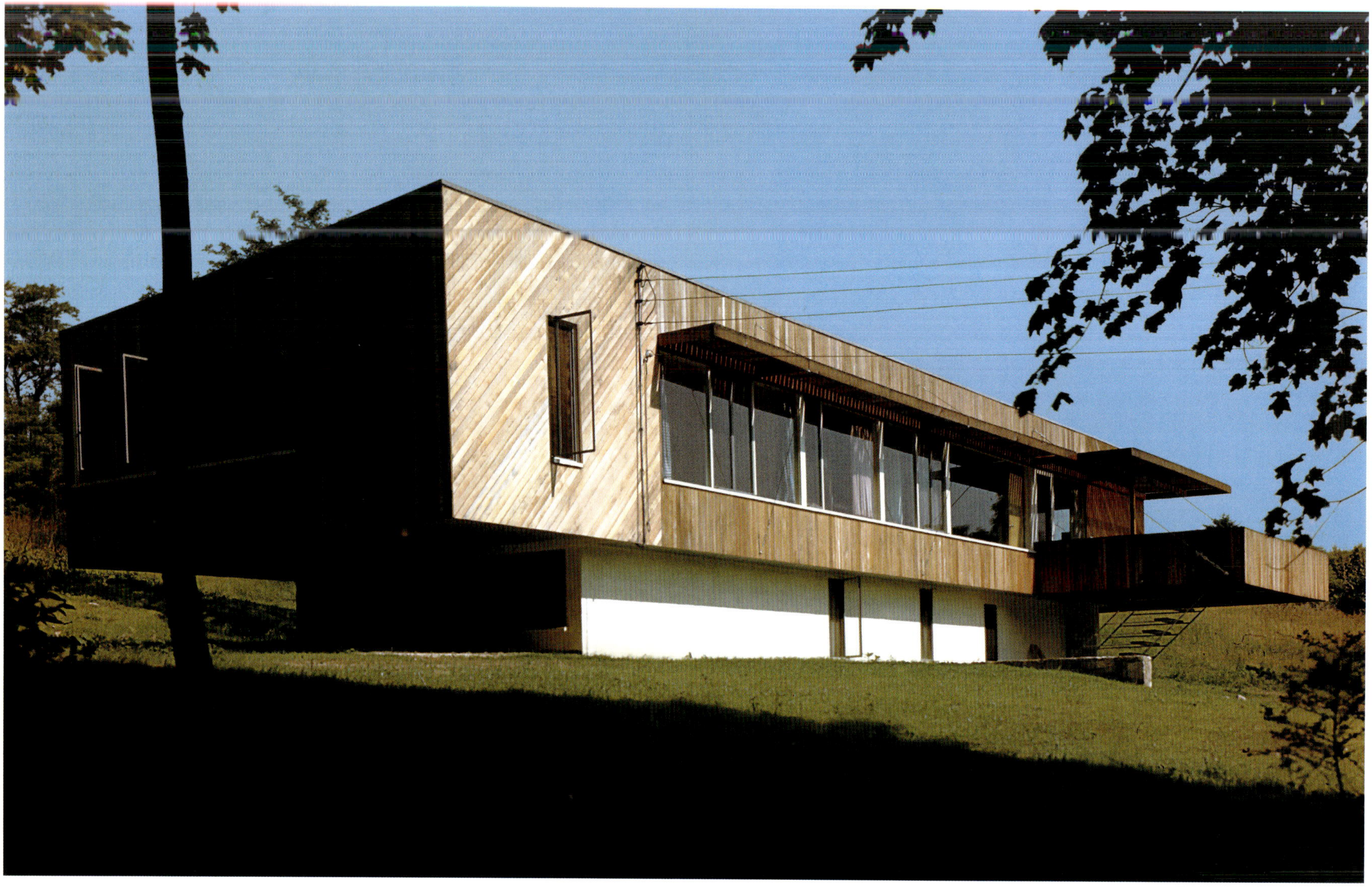

Breuer House II Marcel Breuer

The controlled simplicity of this Breuer house — essentially two rectangular forms, one of natural timber cantilevered over another of white-washed concrete — demonstrates his direct and rational design method. Such a disarmingly simple organization, stemming from a very straightforward idea, is characteristic of both Breuer's architecture and his furniture designs, such as his famous tubular chrome and black leather Wassily armchair (1925) from his time at the Bauhaus school. Built into a hillside, this house is relatively small but very open, with large banks of windows and an overhanging balcony suspended by thin, steel cables; a workshop is contained within the concrete base. His attention to detail, as in the diagonal boarding of the cantilevered portions of the house, helps to define the importance of each element. Breuer's iconic housing designs have often been used as prototypes for practical solutions to domestic design.

Breuer House II, New Canaan, CT, USA, 1947–8. **Marcel Breuer**. **b** Pécs, Hungary, 1902. **d** New York, NY, USA, 1981.

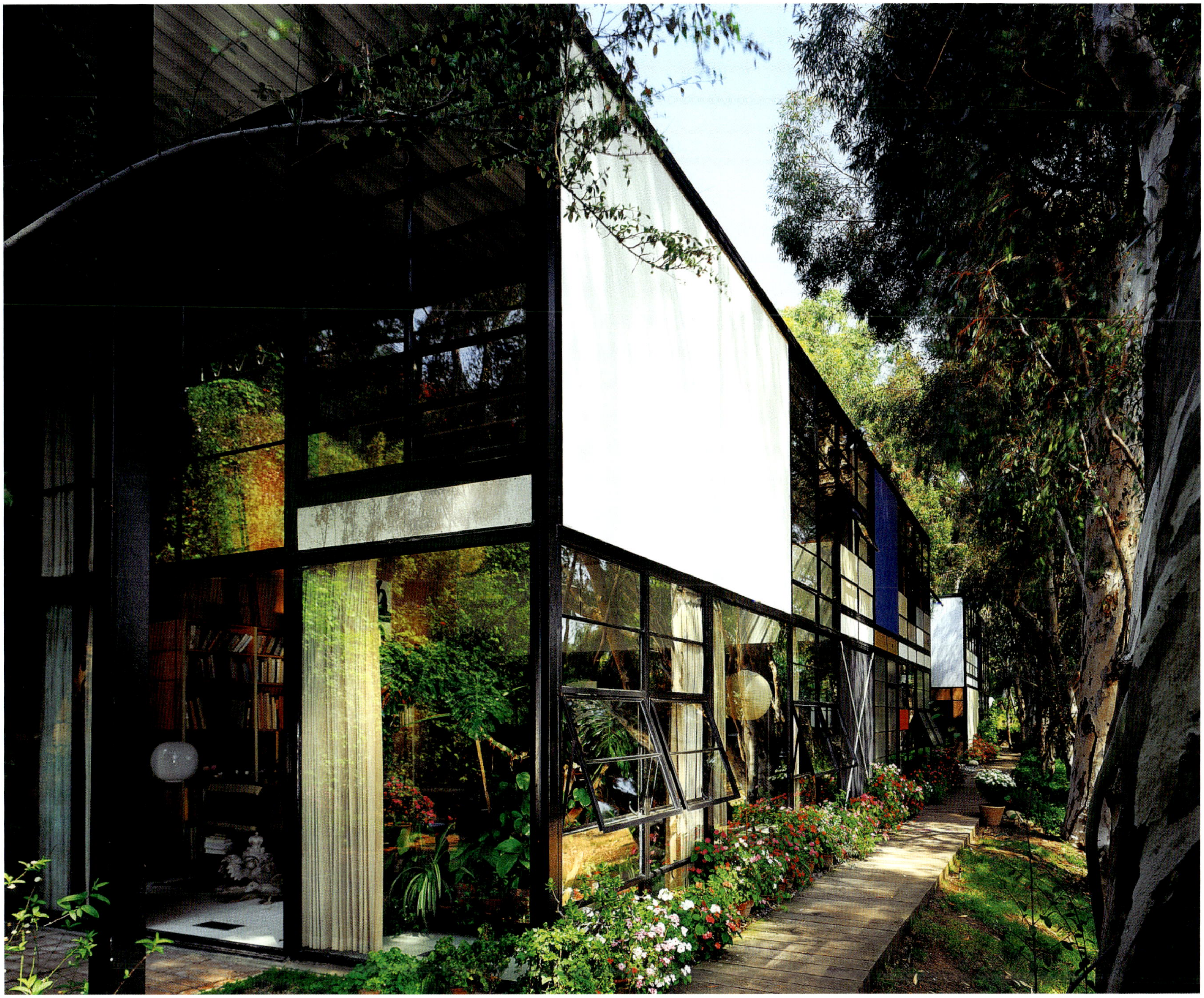

Eames House Charles & Ray Eames

Lightweight, steel and glass, and in the perpetual sunshine of southern California, the Eames House presented an enticing image to other architects, but especially to British architects: Norman Foster, Richard Rogers, John Winter and Michael Hopkins have all paid tribute to it. If one building launched British 'High Tech', this is it. The husband and wife team responded to the Case Study House Program, initiated by the magazine *Arts & Architecture*, to demonstrate the applicability of Modern design to domestic buildings. The house and its associated studio (visible beyond the house) create as much space as possible with minimal materials. Developing an identifiable aesthetic out of such practical construction gave it an enduring place in the canon of great architectural works. Elevating the ordinary, the everyday and 'found objects' became the Eames's hallmark, particularly in the eclectic mix of artfully ordered objects inside the house.

Eames House (Case Study House No.8), Pacific Palisades, CA, USA, 1949. **Charles Eames**. **b** St Louis, MO, USA, 1907. **d** St Louis, MO, USA, 1978. **Ray Eames**. **b** Sacramento, CA, USA, 1912. **d** Los Angeles, CA, USA, 1988.

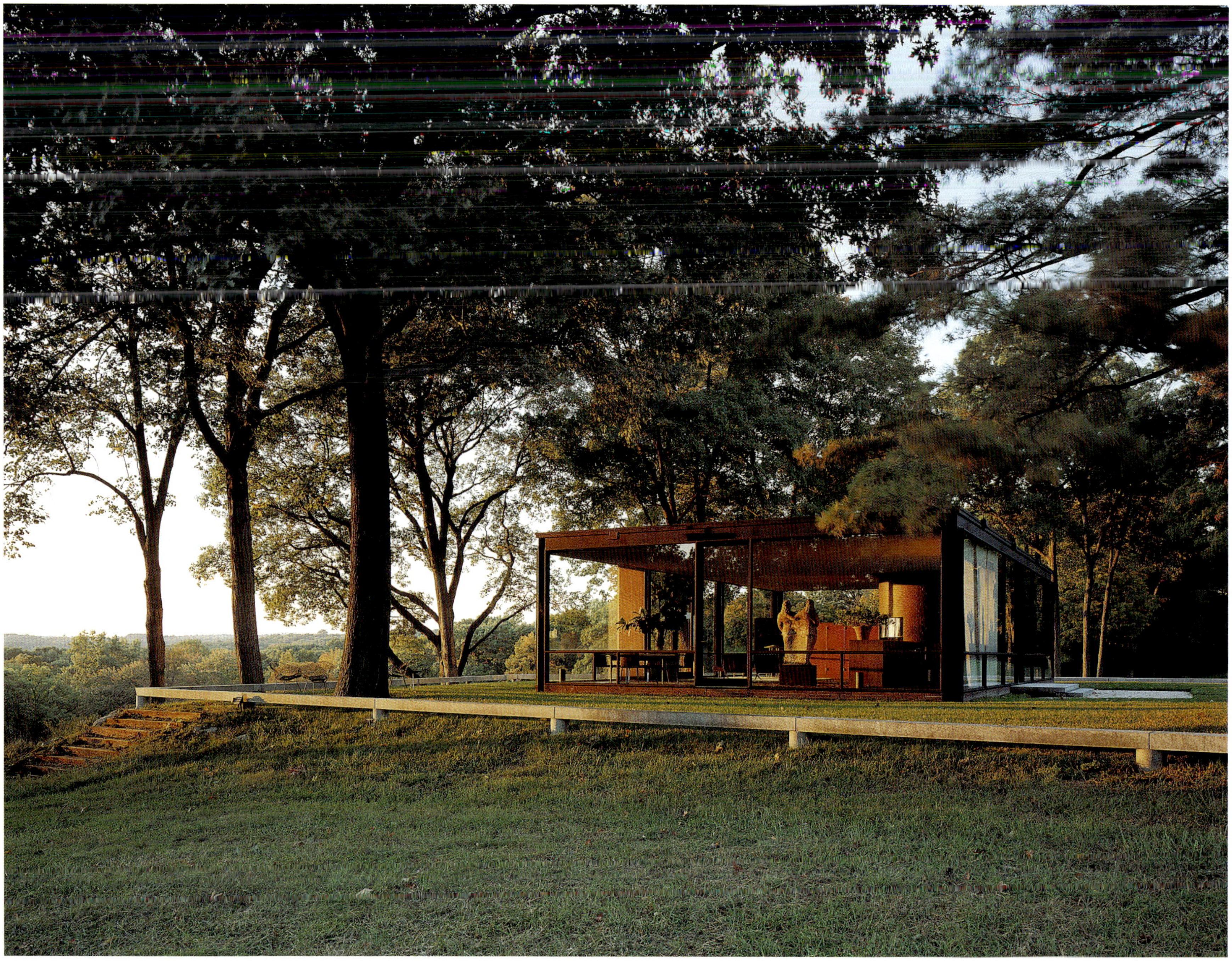

Glass House Philip Johnson

This structure, small in scale yet prodigious in terms of its influence, shows Philip Johnson's indebtedness to the work of Mies van der Rohe — in the use of standard steel sections for a strong yet decorative finish of the facade, in the corner treatment and the relation of the column to the 1945 sketches for the as yet unbuilt Farnsworth House — and is an iconic work in the International Style. But Johnson is working here almost as a landscape designer, treating the house as a frame for its natural environment; he uses the lawn, extended onto the raised platform, as a well-groomed carpet on which to place the architectural object. The house is externally symmetrical, and organized around an interior brick cylinder, which stands in contrast to the incorporeality of the glass envelope. The French architect, Auguste Perret, on visiting the house reportedly remarked, 'Trop de verre' (Too much glass).

Glass House, New Canaan, CT, USA, 1949. **Philip Cortelyon Johnson**. **b** Cleveland, OH, USA, 1906. **d** New Canaan, CT, USA, 2005.

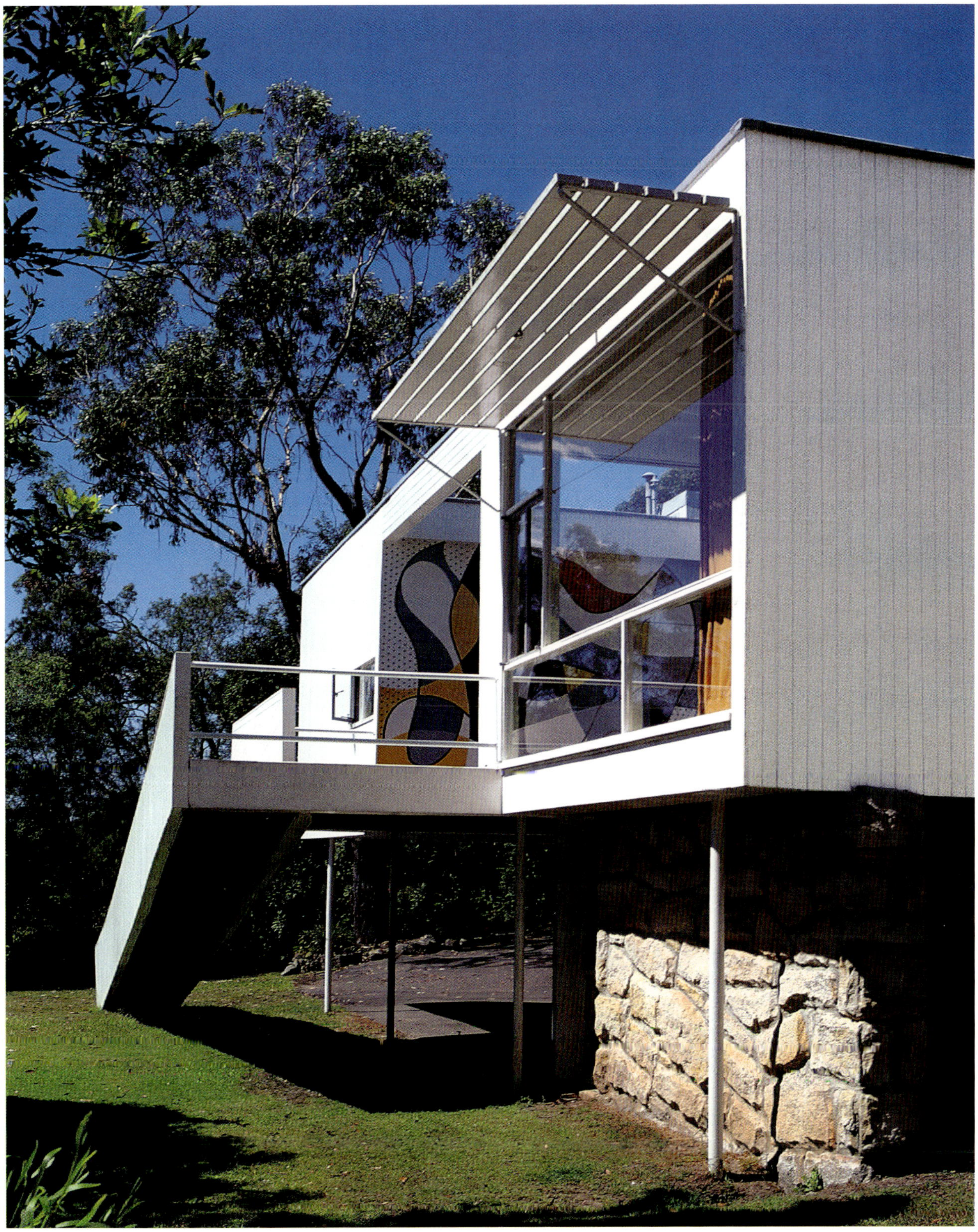

Rose Seidler House Harry Seidler

Graduating from Harvard University in 1946, where he was taught by ex-Bauhaus members, Walter Gropius and Marcel Breuer, Harry Seidler left for Australia to design a house in Sydney for his parents. The Rose Seidler House, one of a small group of dwellings that Seidler designed for his family and friends, was the first building of a prolific career, now spanning over fifty years and ranging from small domestic projects to high-rise apartments and office towers. A hollowed-out, floating white box, the house is anchored to the ground by a series of elements that extend from the main volume, such as the garden retaining walls and the visually dominant ramp. The open terrace, with its Seidler mural links the living and bedroom spaces. In 1988 the Historic Houses Trust opened the house to the public, reinforcing its status as an important work of Modernism and one of the most influential houses in Australia.

Rose Seidler House, Wahroonga, Sydney, NSW, Australia, 1948–50. **Harry Seidler**. **b** Vienna, Austria, 1923. **d** Killara, NSW, Australia, 2006.

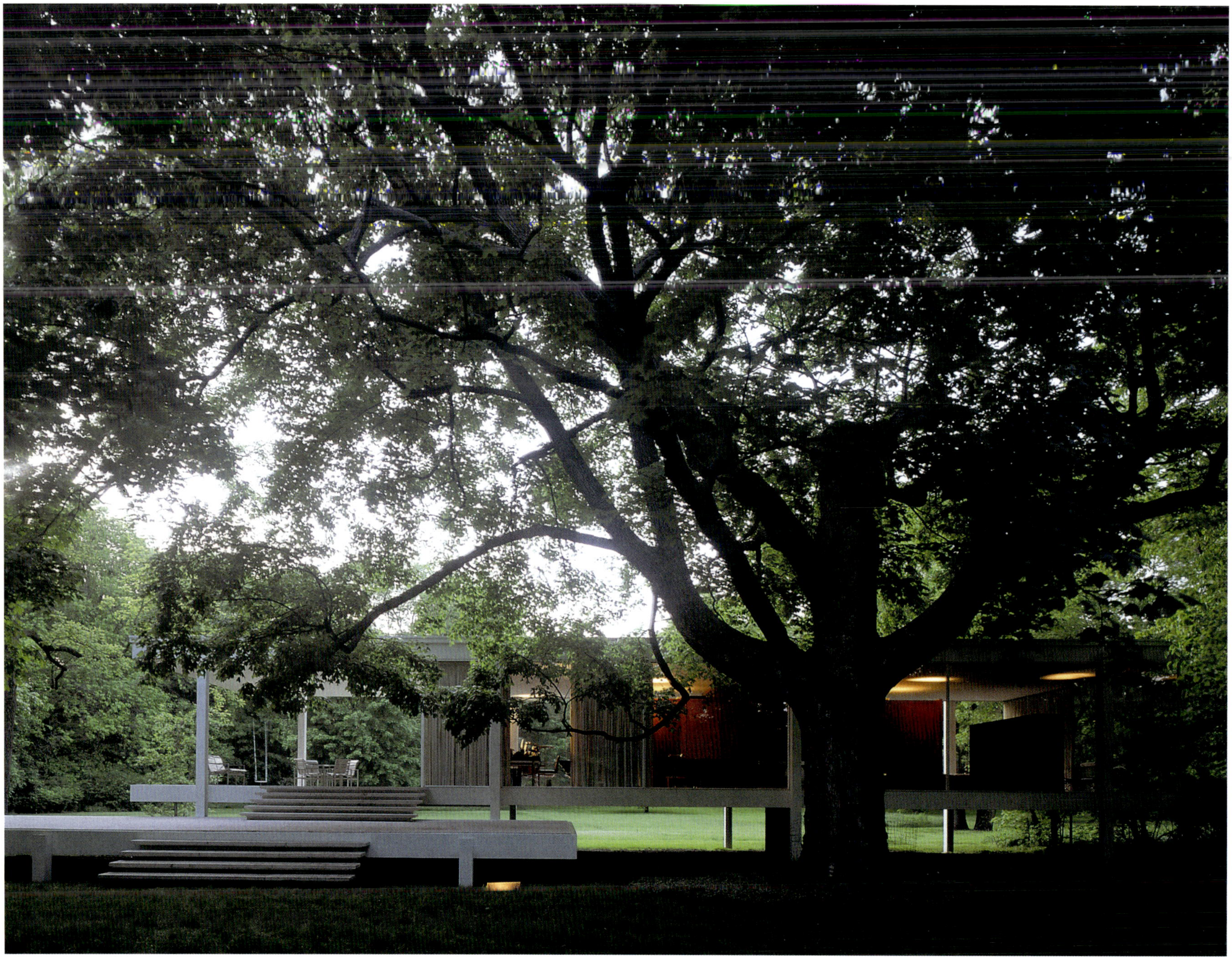

Farnsworth House Ludwig Mies van der Rohe

The view of the Farnsworth House through the trees is one of the supreme delights of Modern architecture. The most exquisite of the glass-box houses, it hangs from a steel frame, its travertine floor suspended well above ground level, which is liable to heavy (sometimes devastating) flooding from the nearby Fox River. Designed as the perfect weekend retreat, it is a single volume completely open to view, with an elegant, timber-veneered service core enclosing a fireplace on one side, kitchen and services on the other, and a bathroom at each end. Its open entrance porch occupies one-third of the entire floor space. As the ultimate example of International Style minimalism applied to domestic living, it has been much debated — not least by the client, whose relationship with Mies deteriorated into legal action as the estimated price rocketed. The house has been widely quoted and inspired Philip Johnson's Glass House.

Farnsworth House, Plano, IL, USA, 1946–50. **Ludwig Mies van der Rohe (Ludwig Mies)**. **b** Aachen, Germany, 1886. **d** Chicago, IL, USA, 1969.

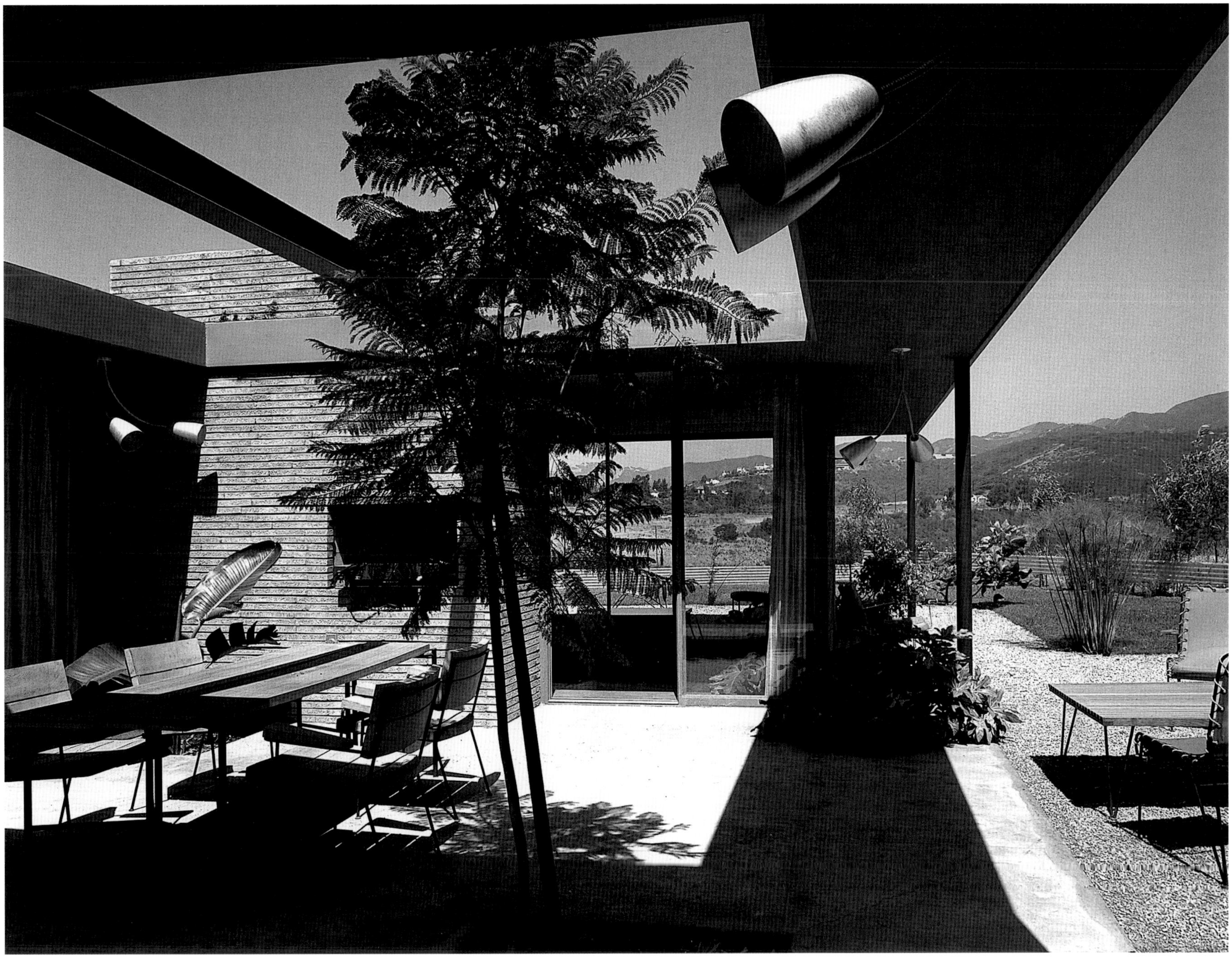

Case Study House Raphael Soriano

Blurring the boundaries between interior and exterior, this austere California home was an experiment in residential, light steel-frame construction, and marked Raphael Soriano's shift from Bauhaus white cubes to more informal structures. Designed for the Case Study House Program — sponsored by *Arts & Architecture* magazine to showcase the work of young architects — all of the structural building components were prefabricated and assembled on site in three days. Soriano delighted in working with off-the-shelf materials, such as plywood partitions and window panels that fitted into a standardized grid system, the fundamental ordering principle behind all his work. By leaving portions of the roof grid open, he created interior patios and allowed light to penetrate unexpectedly into the living spaces. Soriano began his career in the office of Richard Neutra, whose Lovell House (1927–9) was an early example of domestic steel construction.

1950 Case Study House, Pacific Palisades, CA, USA, 1950. **Raphael Soriano**. **b** Rhodes, Greece, 1907. **d** Los Angeles, CA, USA, 1988.

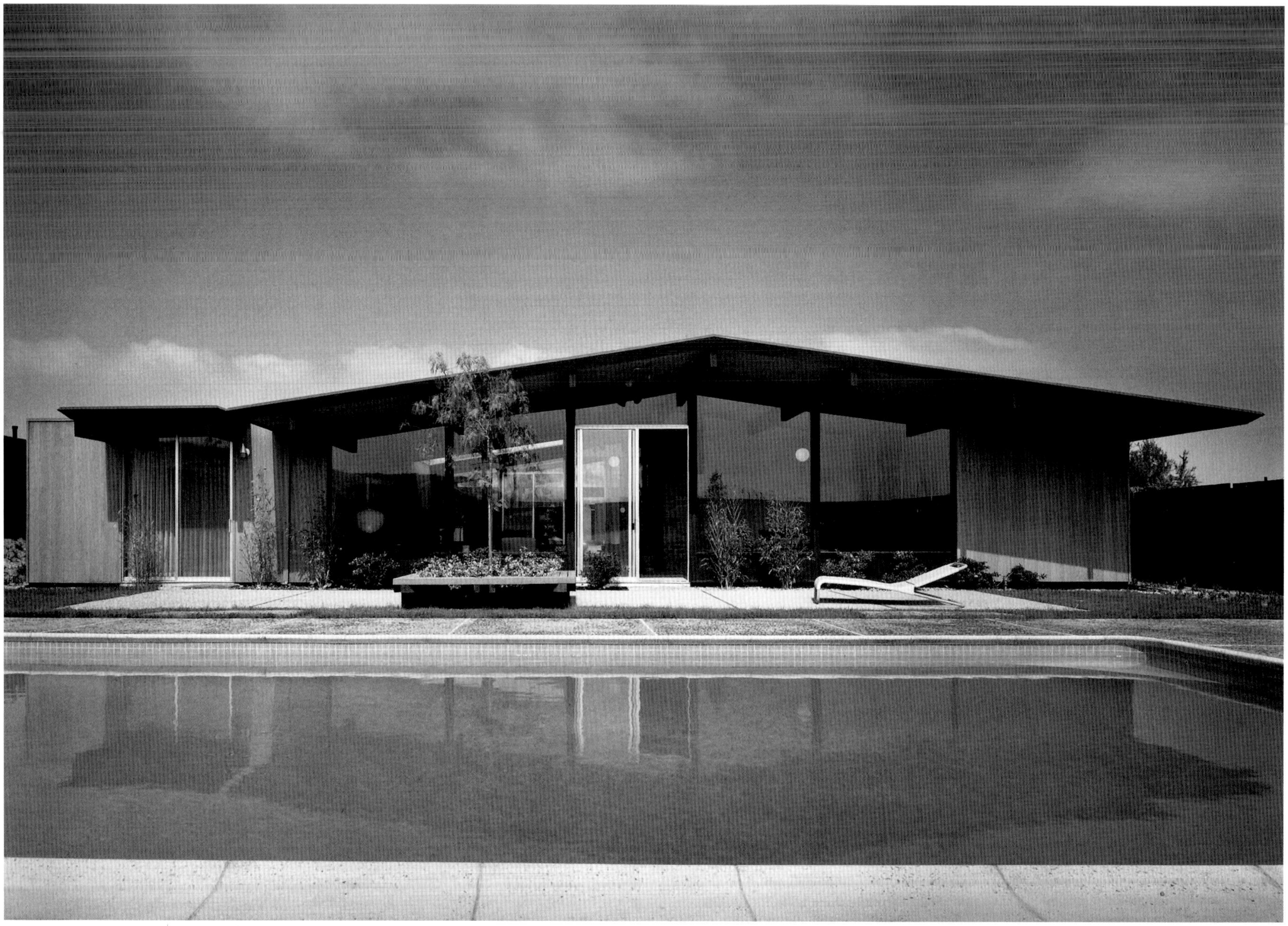

Eichler Home Joseph Eichler

This typical Eichler Home turns its back on the street and focuses all of its attention on the ample leisure area in the private back yard. Well-designed, inexpensive modern homes were hard to find in the San Francisco Bay area before businessman-turned-building-contractor Joseph Eichler built his first housing development in 1950. While living in a rented Frank Lloyd Wright house, Eichler conceived of a new breed of affordable housing that would not sacrifice quality for cost. Although modest in scale, Eichler Homes have impressive features, such as open floor plans, high ceilings, exposed redwood beams and underfloor heating. Bedrooms and bathrooms are often on the street side to reinforce the private nature of the main living space. The characteristic rear glass facades create continuous views overlooking the yard and remain one of the most popular features of the homes. Today, 11,000 Eichler Homes still survive in the San Francisco Bay area.

Eichler Home, various locations, San Francisco Bay area, CA, USA, as built 1950s and 1960s. **Joseph Eichler**. **b** New York, NY, USA, 1900. **d** San Francisco, CA, USA, 1974.

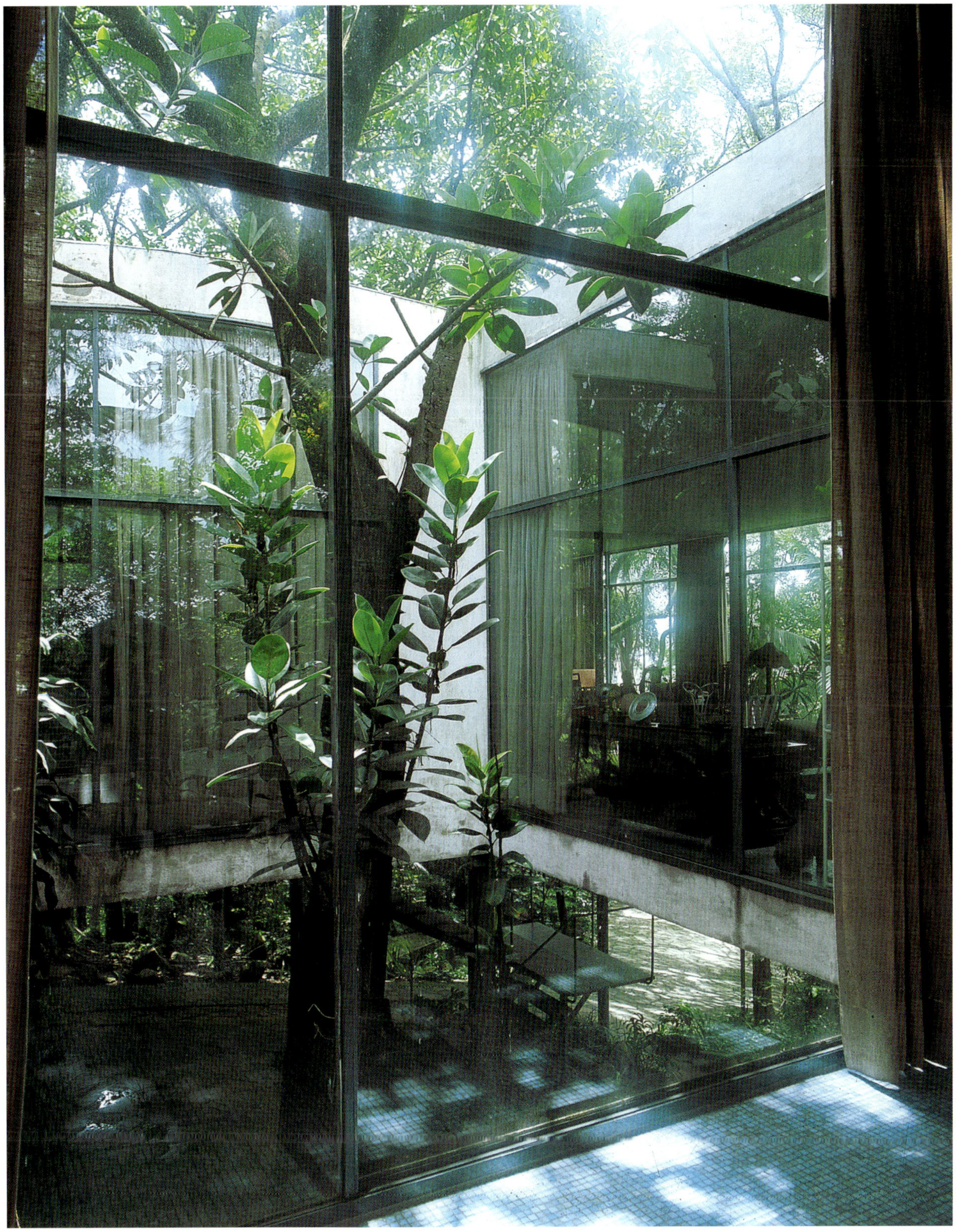

Glass House Lina Bo Bardi

Designed by Lina Bo Bardi early in her career for herself and her husband, the Glass House has been described as elegant and poetic by its many visitors; however, it would not meet today's building regulations. The remarkably slender columns that support the building, and elevate it above the sloping ground, are complemented by thin horizontal sections of reinforced concrete and fully glazed facades, resulting in a high degree of transparency and lightness. The main living space is arranged on the first-floor level around a central atrium full of lush tropical plants, underscoring the close relationship of the house with the surrounding Brazilian forest, which was once visible on all sides, but has since given way to development. In her subsequent commissioned work, Bo Bardi avoided working on private houses, stating, 'I have a horror of designing homes for madams', and mainly concentrated on public buildings in which she could achieve an expression of collective identity.

Glass House, São Paulo, Brazil, 1951. **Lina Bo Bardi**. **b** Rome, Italy, 1914. **d** São Paulo, Brazil, 1992.

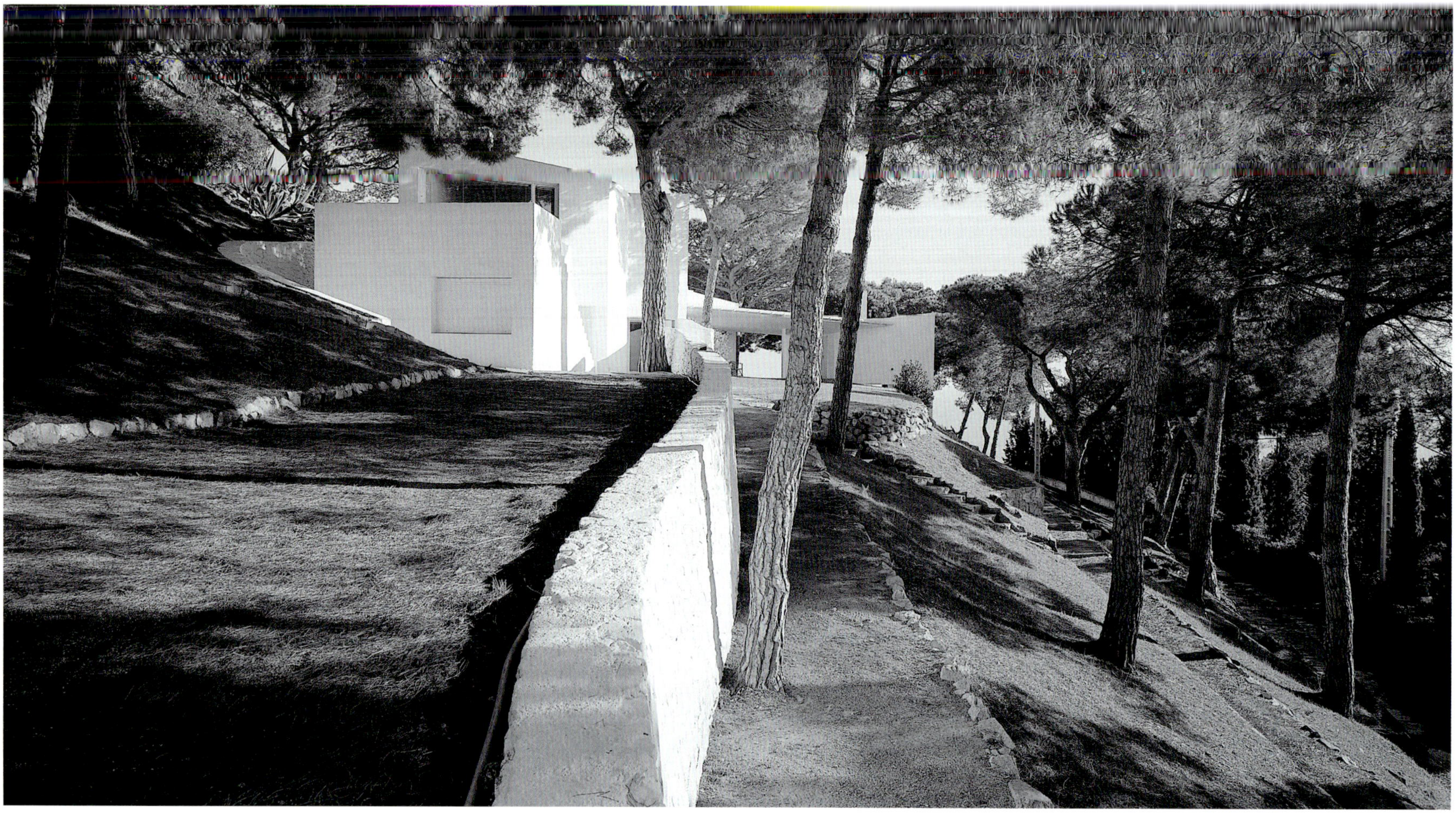

Casa Ugalde José Antonio Coderch

José Antonio Coderch was a founding member of the Grupo R, a group of Modernist architects active in Barcelona in the 1950s, whose aim was the renewal of Catalan architecture. His Casa Ugalde is perhaps the single, most important piece of architecture in Catalonia since Mies van der Rohe's German Pavilion of 1929. But whereas Mies employed a universal grid to delineate the Modernist concept of interiority/exteriority, the Casa Ugalde, built on the coast as a weekend home, takes its cue from the undulating terrain and lush landscape to define the internal and external spaces. No plans can explain these interweaving spaces, and indeed Coderch made extensive revisions to the layout of the building as the construction progressed. The result is a sequence of interior spaces that are tailored to specific vistas, gradually opening up the house through a series of angled and undulating planes to the spectacular ocean-scape beyond.

Casa Ugalde, Caldes d'Estrac, Barcelona, Spain, 1951. **José Antonio Coderch**. **b** Barcelona, Spain, 1913. **d** Barcelona, Spain, 1984.

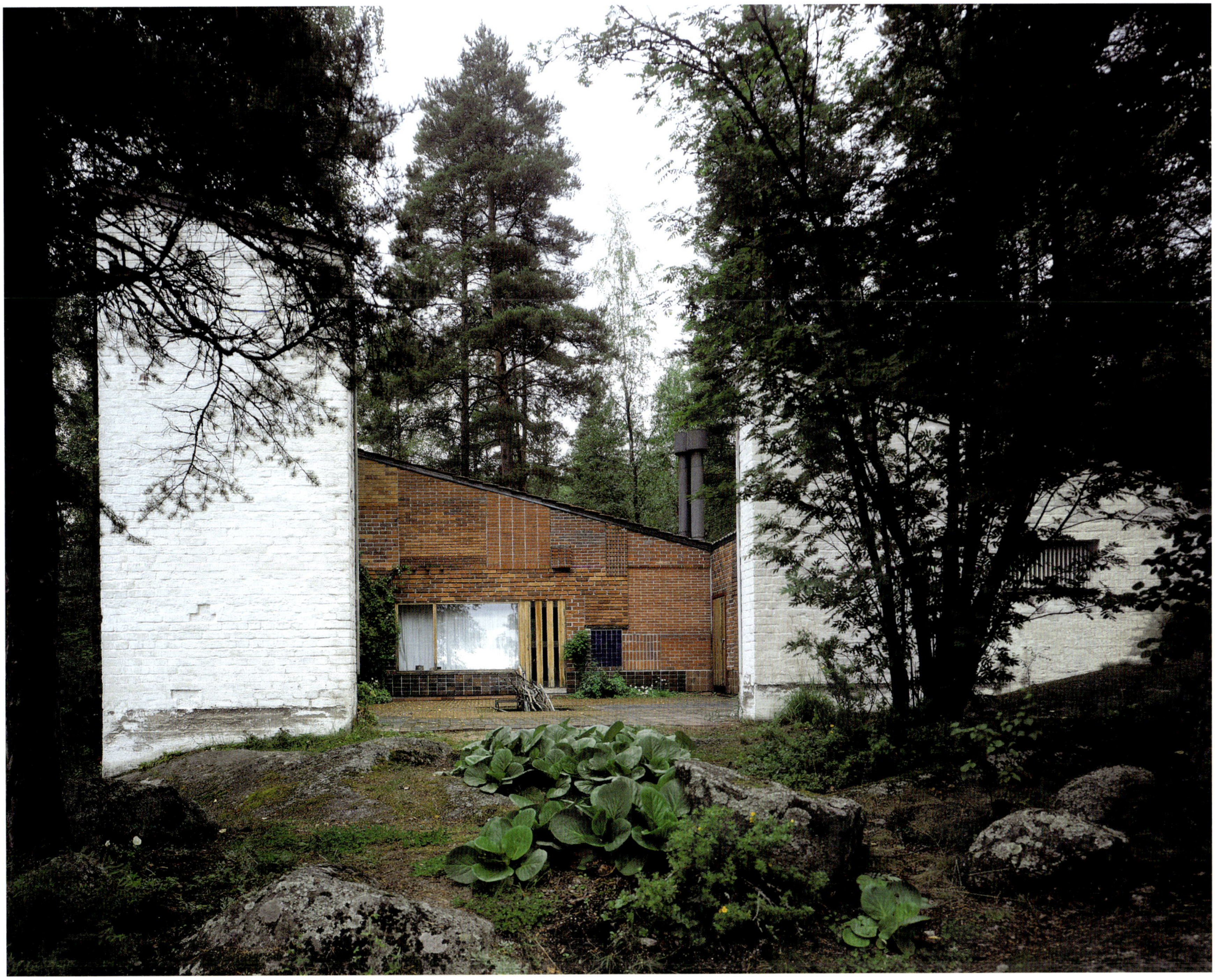

Summer House Alvar Aalto

One hour by boat from the nearest railway station, in a forest overlooking a lake in north-central Finland, this summer house was both a retreat and a test-bed where one of the most important twentieth-century architects developed his own particular contribution to Modernism. Under the influence of this sylvan, Scandinavian setting, the house marks a decisive shift away from the more familiar Modernist planar, abstract surfaces towards consciously varied tactile and aesthetic effects, a principal feature of the Finnish tradition in which Alvar Aalto was pre-eminent. The composition of the house is simple: two equal wings at right angles enclose the courtyard, with a separate guest annex. Fifty different types of brick and ceramic tile line the courtyard, while the walls frame stunning yet contrived views through a large, white-painted timber grid. Sensibility to site and manipulation of surface are hallmarks extending to Aalto's large public commissions.

Summer House, Muuratsalo, Jyväskylä, Finland, 1953. **Hugo Alvar Henrik Aalto**. **b** Kuortane, nr Jyväskylä, Finland, 1898. **d** Helsinki, Finland, 1976.

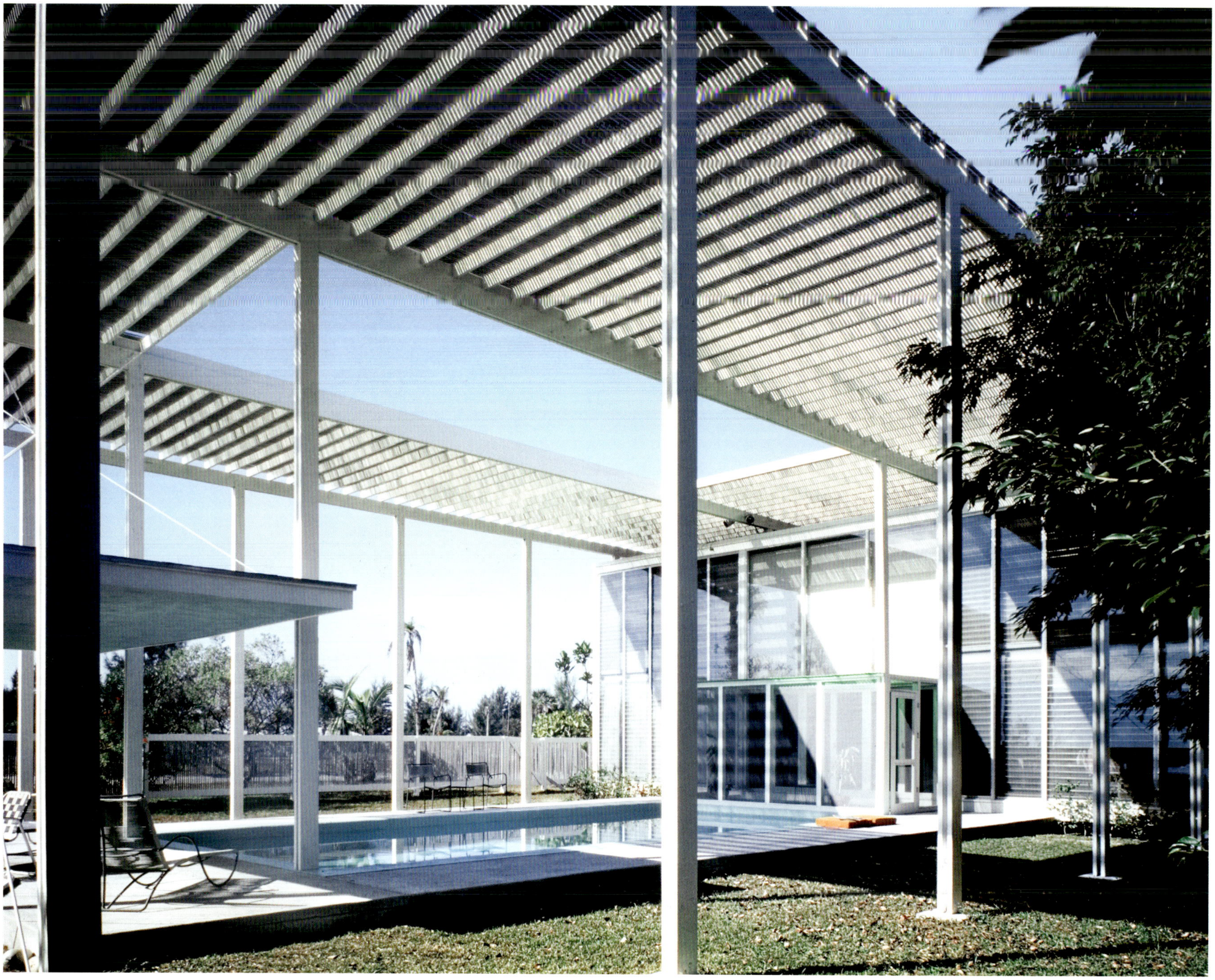

Umbrella House Paul Rudolph

Paul Rudolph believed that an aesthetically unified form could be created only by the successful realization of its function, as seen in his Umbrella House, its distinctive characteristics due to his response to the Lido Shores site. Sheltering from the subtropical sun under a timber canopy, this home is a structurally independent glass and steel box, yet the 'umbrella', house, pool and terrace form one unit. Glass walls, open floor plan and double-height living space accentuate the interdependence of internal and external volumes. Jalousies set into the north and south walls provide ventilation and shade. Inspired by Gropius's design philosophy while at Harvard, Rudolph endeavoured to 'build meaningfully', focusing on qualities such as simplicity, use of light and shadow, and continuity of space. A major figure of the Sarasota School of Architecture (a post-war Florida style), he developed a new expression for American Modernism that was influenced by the Brutalist aesthetic, which is most evident in his civic architecture.

Umbrella House, Lido Shores, Sarasota, FL, USA, 1953. **Paul Rudolph**. **b** Elkton, KY, USA, 1918. **d** New York, NY, USA, 1997.

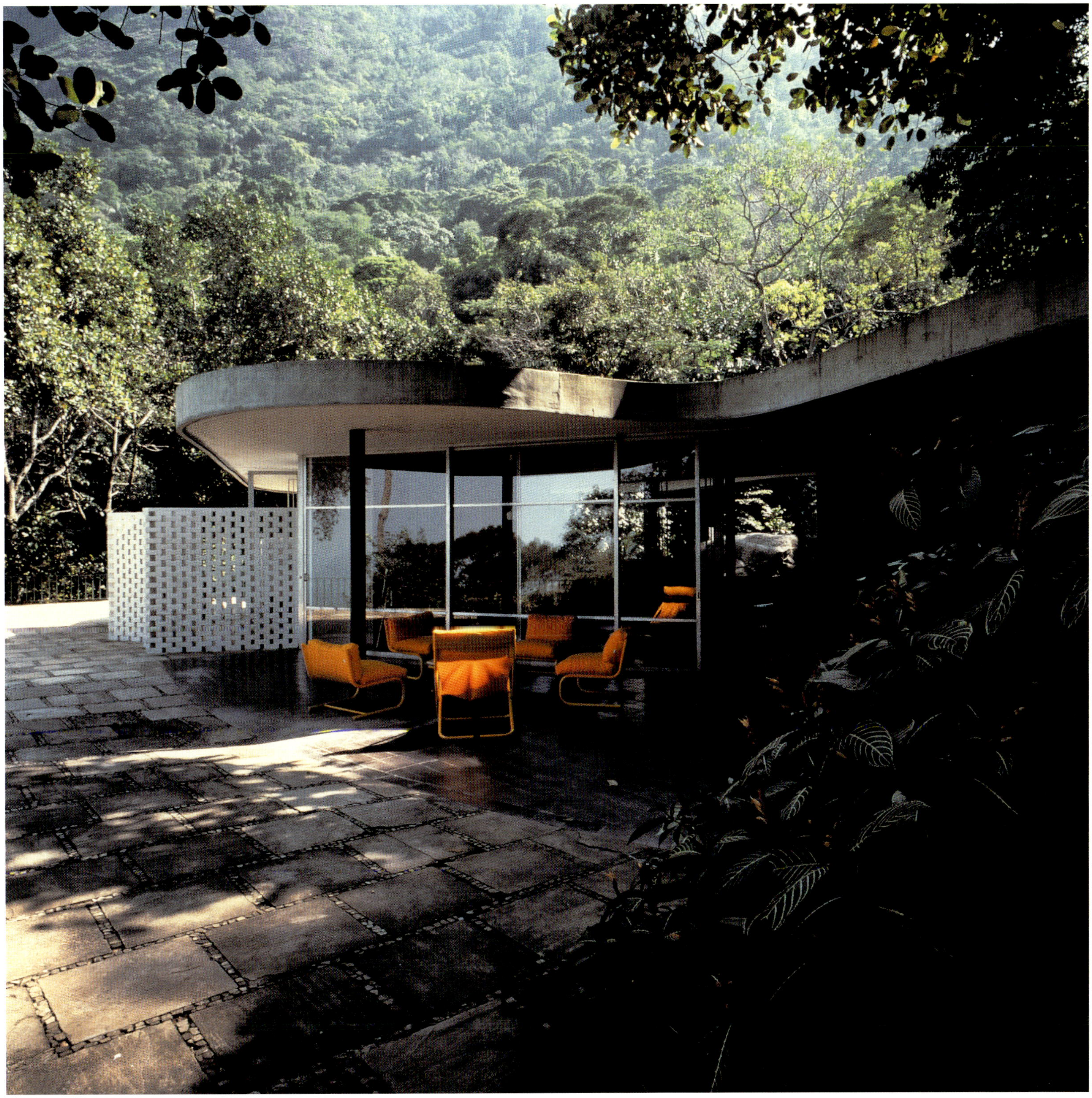

Canoas House Oscar Niemeyer

The free, curving roofline is the intuitive gesture that sets the organic organization for Oscar Niemeyer's own house, whose fluid spaces revolve freely around a natural boulder. The house's unassuming nature and embracing patio confirm Niemeyer as one who is recognized for a humility born of his love for the customs and people of his native country. While influenced by Le Corbusier, with whom he worked early in his career, in 1936, Niemeyer nonetheless continues to draw his primary inspiration from the spirit and imagery of Brazil. 'The straight line, hard, inflexible, created by man, does not attract me,' he wrote. 'What does draw me is the free and sensual curve … The curve I find in the mountains of my country, in the clouds of the sky, and the waves of the sea.' This plasticity inspires Niemeyer even in his famous, large-scale projects, such as the many public buildings of the new city of Brasilia, 1957–60.

Canoas House, São Conrado, Rio de Janeiro, Brazil, 1954. **Oscar Niemeyer**. **b** Rio de Janeiro, Brazil, 1907.

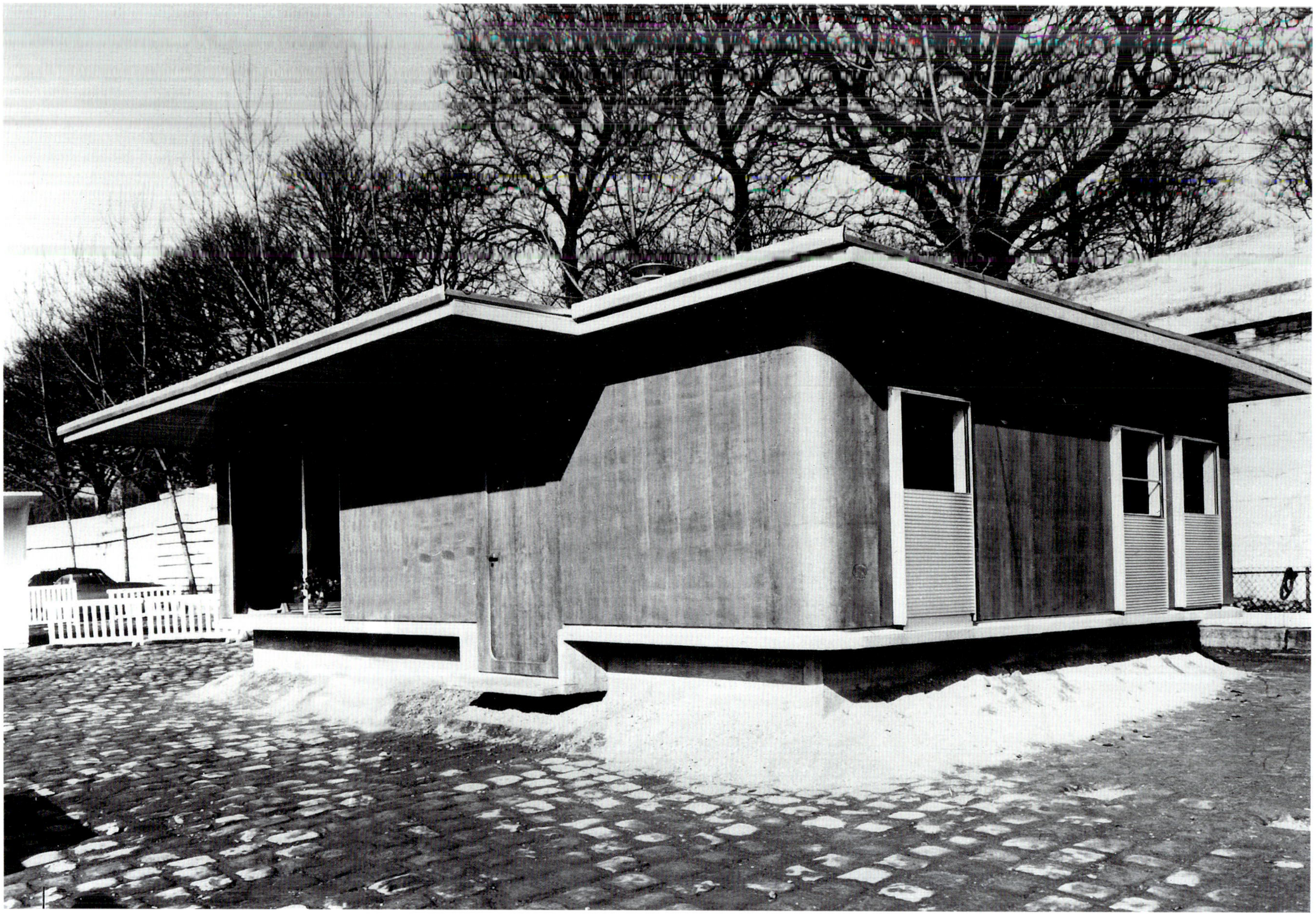

Prototype House Jean Prouvé

In so far as prefabricated houses can achieve apocryphal status, this one has. The house was designed by the hugely influential and innovative manufacturing designer, Jean Prouvé, of whom Le Corbusier said, 'Everything he touches and conceives immediately assumes an elegant plastic form while offering brilliant solutions with regard to strength and manufacture.' Prouvé's prolific work, which includes furniture as well as buildings, is often overlooked or has vanished. Designed and produced in six weeks in 1955 in response to Abbé Pierre's controversial condemnation of the French housing crisis, the prefab houses were funded by the public sending in tokens from packets of washing powder. A demonstration model was shipped to Paris and erected in seven hours, the kitchen and bathroom pod craned into place with saucepans already in the cupboards. Prouvé trained as a blacksmith and produced his own furniture and building components in his workshop.

Prototype House, demonstration model erected in Paris, France, 1955. **Jean Prouvé**. **b** Paris, France, 1901. **d** Nancy, France, 1984.

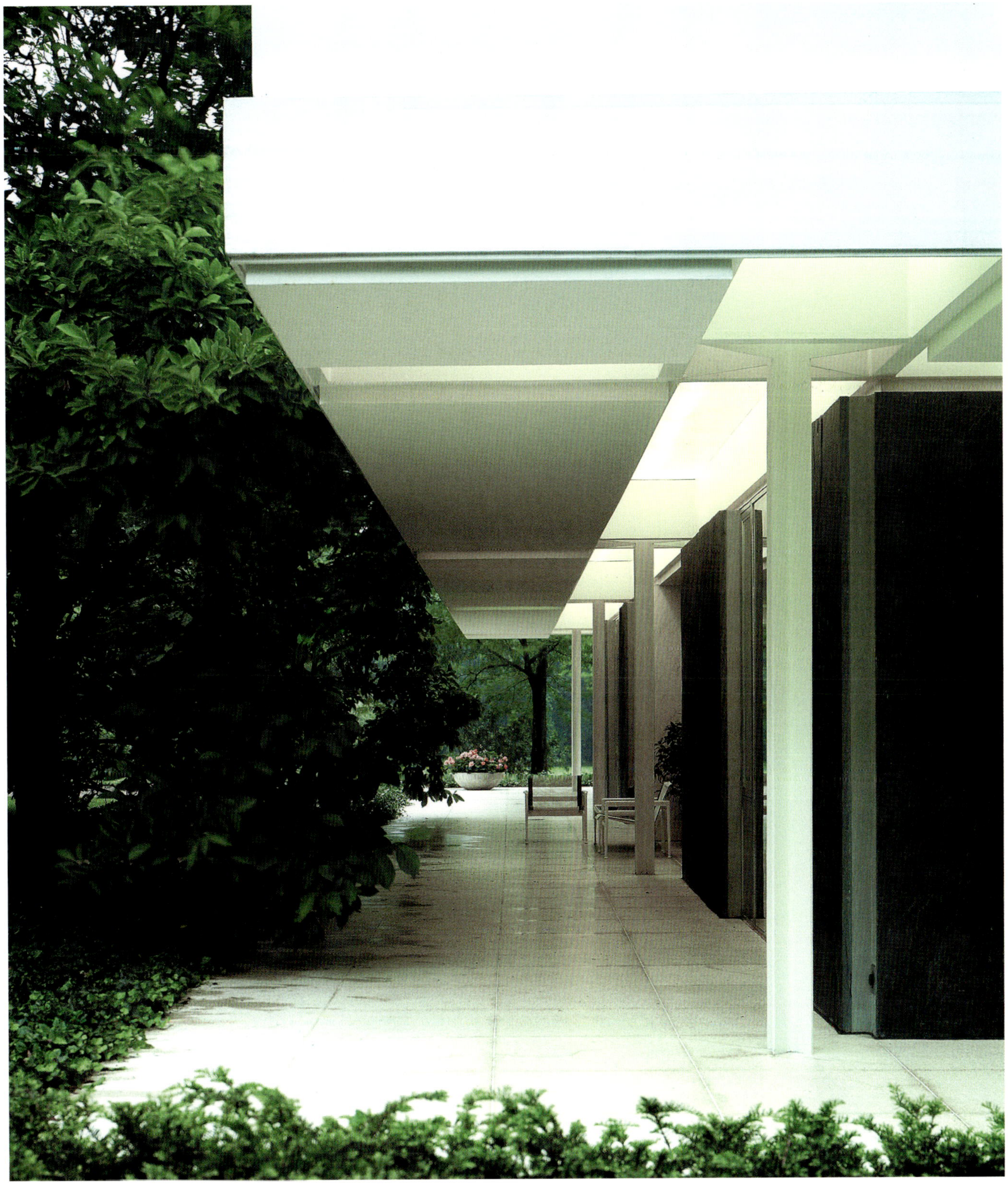

J Irwin & Xenia Miller House Eero Saarinen

Eero Saarinen, the son of Finnish architect Eliel Saarinen, already had a long-time familial connection with J Irwin Miller when he was asked to design this house on the Flatrock River in Columbus. This classically Modern house is actually four separate structures arranged into one unit under a skylighted metal roof and has been likened to a modern version of Palladio's Villa Rotunda. On the interior, Saarinen used marble for walls and travertine for the floor, which extends out onto an all-round veranda; the furnishings included rugs and chairs that Saarinen designed himself. The Millers commissioned two of only four built single-family residences by Saarinen, who is better known for his more famous public buildings, such as the TWA terminal at Kennedy Airport (1956–62) with its wing-like vaulting roofs. In this building, he used form in an abstract and highly symbolic manner quite different to the contained and geometric form of the Miller House.

J Irwin & Xenia Miller House, Columbus, IN, USA, 1953–7. **Eero Saarinen**. **b** Kirkkonummi, Finland, 1910. **d** Ann Arbor, MI, USA, 1961.

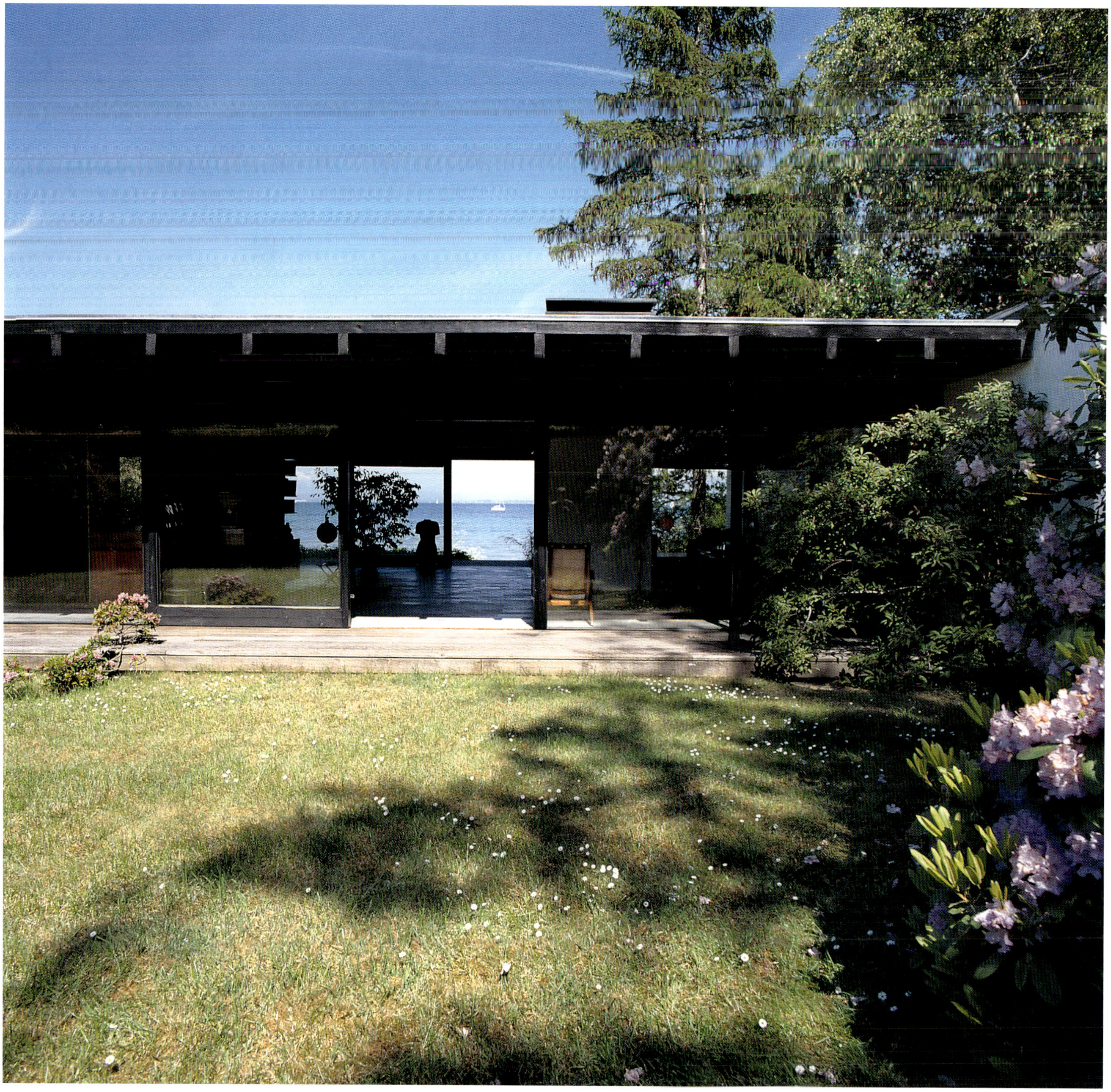

Gunnløgsson House Halldor Gunnløgsson

One of the protagonists of the 'new tradition' in post-war Danish architecture, Halldor Gunnløgsson imbued this simple house with his interpretation of a traditional Danish lifestyle. The house acknowledges the impact on Danish architecture of such influential figures as Mies van der Rohe and Frank Lloyd Wright. This can be seen in the rigorous modular plan laid out on a 2 m (6.5 ft) grid and the simple load-bearing timber structure with brick infill. In contrast to these influences, Gunnløgsson incorporated more traditional elements, such as the central fireplace and fir-board ceilings. Furniture and fittings designed by some of his well-known contemporaries and countrymen, such as Poul Kjaerholm, Kåre Klint and Arne Jacobsen, were selected to complement the open spatial quality of the house. With its simple, open plan and finely detailed traditional timber, stone and brick, the house constitutes one of the finest Modern houses built in Denmark.

Gunnløgsson House, Rungsted, Denmark, 1958. **Halldor Gunnløgsson**. **b** Copenhagen, Denmark, 1918. **d** Rungsted, Denmark, 1985.

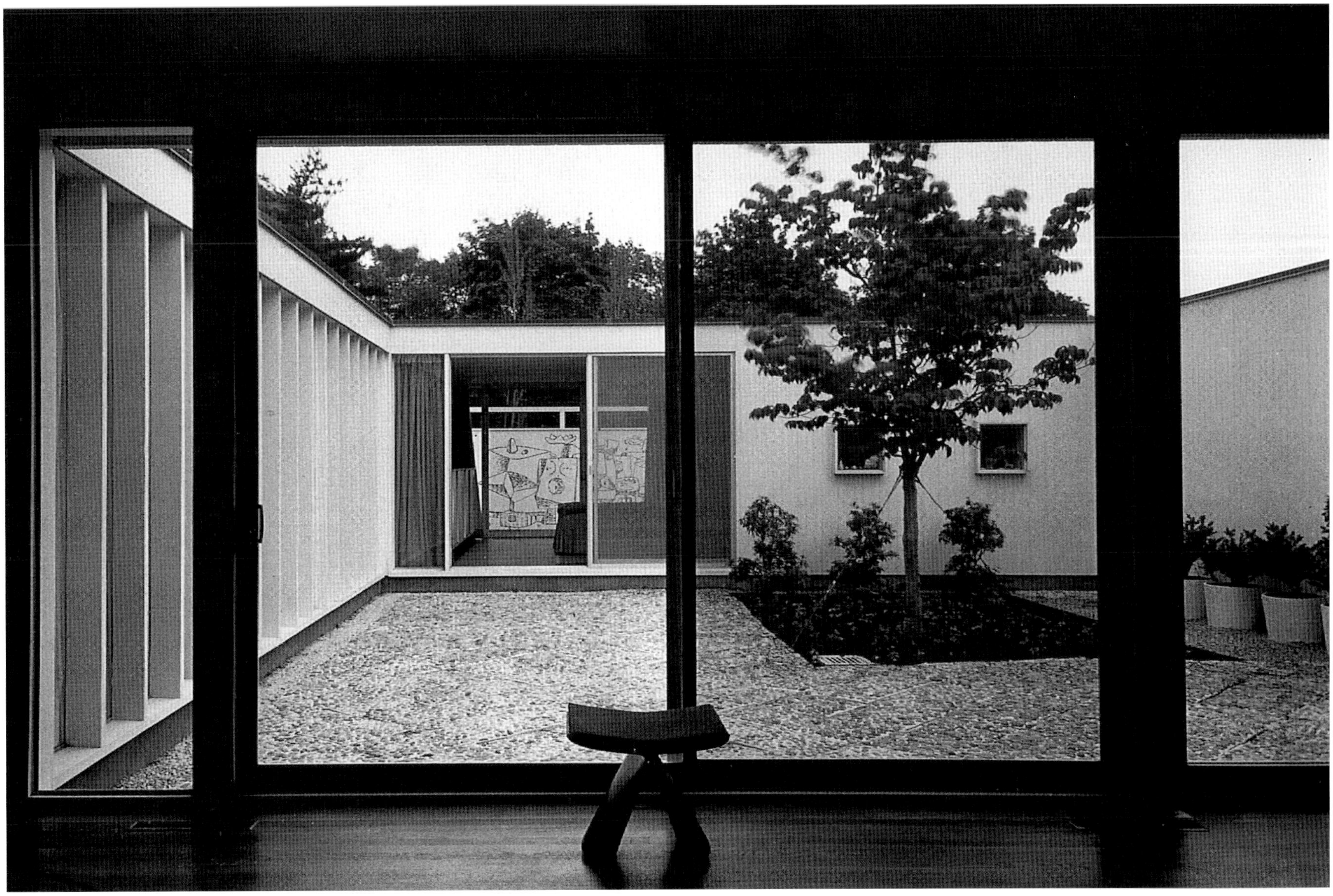

Sert House Josep Lluís Sert

This tightly organized courtyard is the heart of the house that Catalan-born architect Josep Lluís Sert built for himself near Boston in 1958, during his tenure at Harvard. Although the open atrium plan was used in ancient Roman houses, it takes on a thoroughly Modern image when carried out in Sert's rigid, highly rational language. Instead of symmetry and axial sequences, the architect created off-centred alignments of sliding doors and square windows. The furnishings are deliberately minimal; a simple Japanese 'butterfly' stool by Sori Yanagi takes on great visual and symbolic stature when seen against such an austere backdrop. Sert was an alumnus of Le Corbusier, one of Modernism's founding figures. He emigrated to the United States during the Spanish Civil War, and succeeded Bauhaus master, Walter Gropius, at the helm of Harvard's Graduate School of Design from 1953 to 1969.

Sert House, Cambridge, MA, USA, 1958. **Josep Lluís Sert**. **b** Barcelona, Spain, 1902. **d** Barcelona, Spain, 1983.

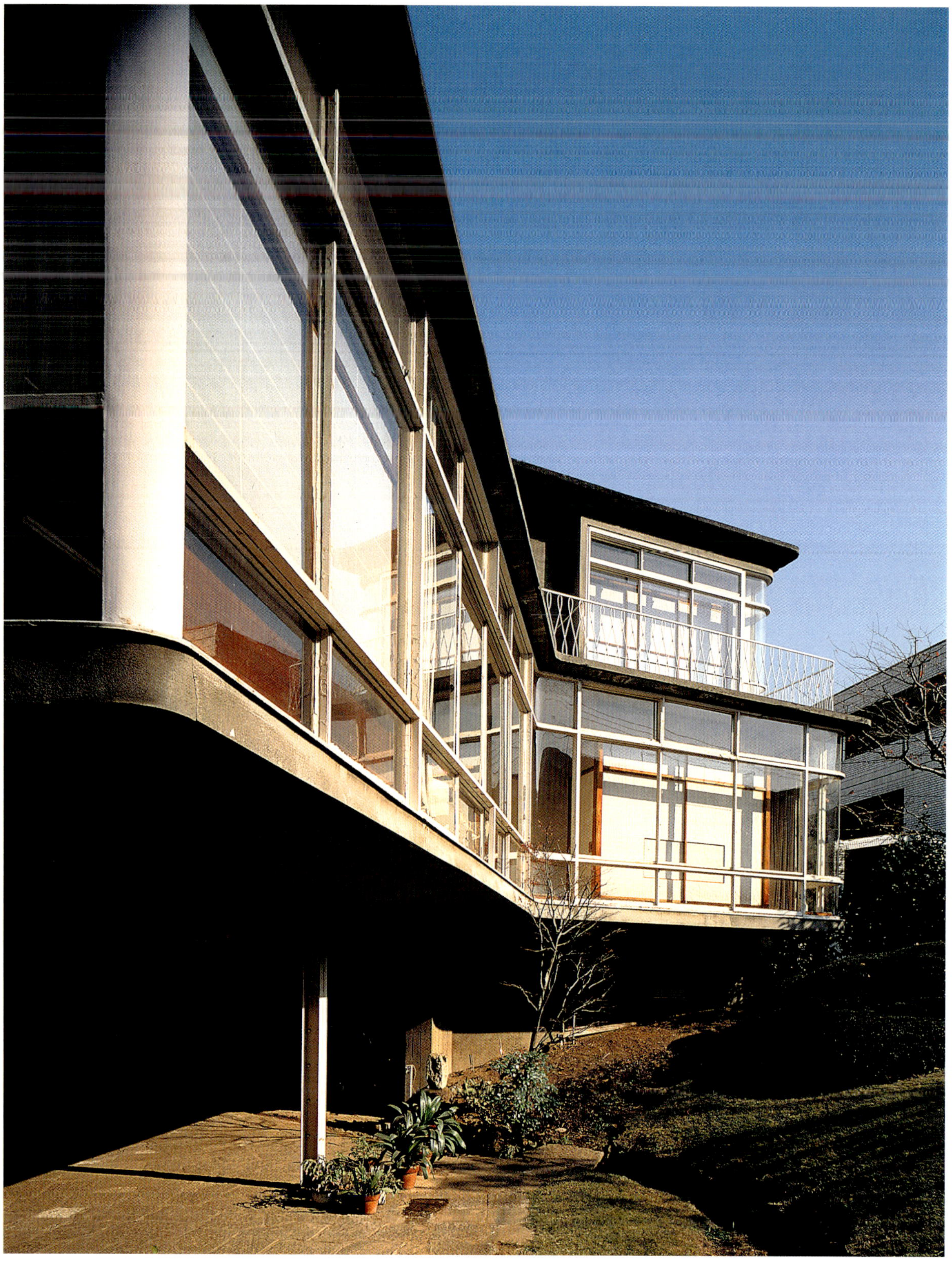

Mamoru Yamada House Mamoru Yamada

As a unique Expressionist transformation of the traditional Japanese house, Mamoru Yamada's own house and studio brings together a curvilinear freedom — similar to that of Hans Scharoun or Oscar Niemeyer — within the context of Japan. Yamada sought to create a new urban dwelling in this three-level, reinforced concrete house that was built in a section of Tokyo formerly dominated by single-level dwellings. The main living space, which is lifted off the ground by *pilotis* and accessed via a spiral stair, retains *tatami* mats and *shoji* screens, but has subtly different proportions and lacks the customary *tokobashira* symbolic wooden columns in the traditional decorative alcove. Yamada was the only Asian architect featured in the 1932 *International Style* book, and like Sutemi Horiguchi, his co-founder of the Bunriha Japanese Secessionist movement of 1920–7, sought to create a new, Modern architecture.

Mamoru Yamada House, Tokyo, Japan, 1959. **Mamoru Yamada**. **b** Gifu Prefecture, Japan, 1894. **d** Tokyo, Japan, 1966.

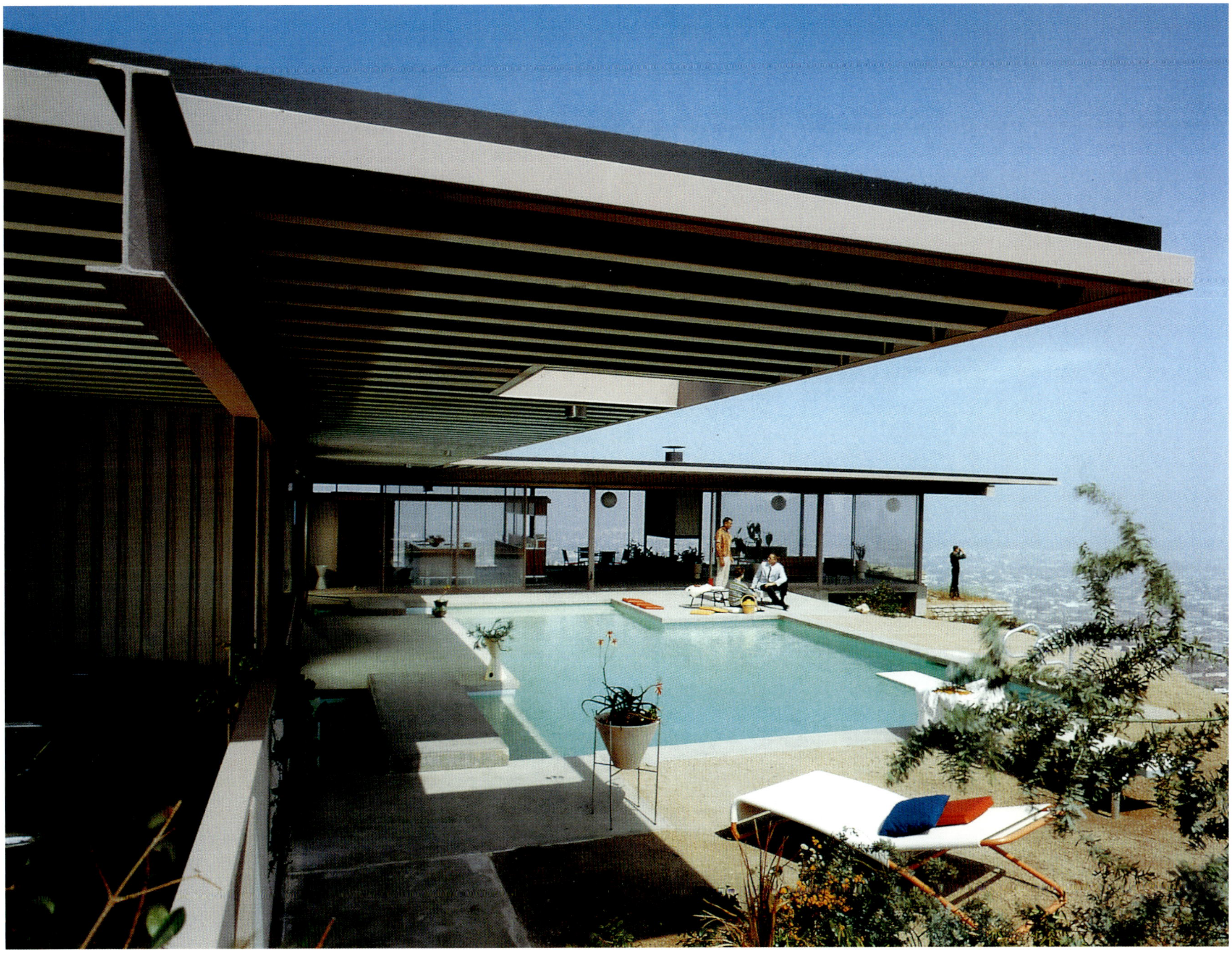

Stahl House Pierre Koenig

'Los Angeles is their back yard' was the way the *Los Angeles Examiner* described the new house of the Stahls in 1960. Pierre Koenig's second house for John Entenza's Case Study House Program is the epitome of the reductivist architecture of the 'Contemporary' style of 1950s California. With its welded steel frame and roof deck, overhanging eaves and open-air swimming pool, it still features regularly in many fashion and film shoots. Built on a relatively cheap site, due to its poor soil and steeply sloping aspect, the owners wanted to take full advantage of the impressive view. Koenig cantilevered the main living space of the steel-frame house out over the slope on massive reinforced concrete beams supported by huge caissons bored into the ground. In 1989, a Case Study exhibition, 'Blueprints for Modern Living', produced a full-scale mock-up of the house, using television screens to represent the lights of the city below.

Stahl House (Case Study House No.22), Los Angeles, CA, USA, 1960. **Pierre Koenig**. **b** San Francisco, CA, USA, 1925. **d** Los Angeles, CA, USA, 2004.

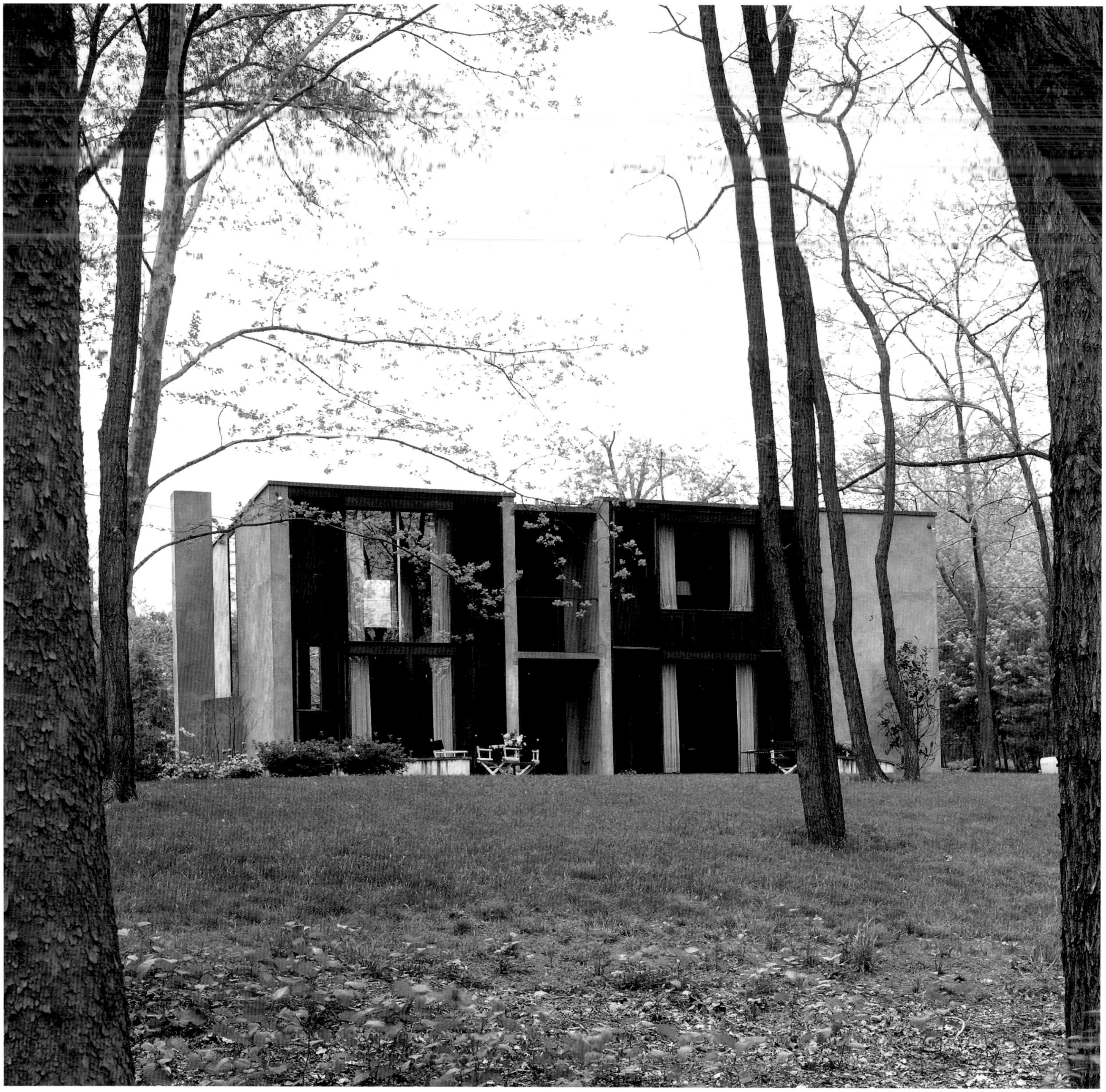

Esherick House Louis I Kahn

In this building, Louis Kahn endowed what is, in effect, a small suburban house — constructed in the stuccoed, timber-frame vernacular of countless such houses — with something of the monumentality of ancient architecture. He achieved this using two means. First, a plan of almost Palladian simplicity: two long, deep rooms either side of a staircase hall, one side a double-height living room, the other a dining room with a bedroom above it, and a service block to the side. Second, the facades onto the street and garden have deep alcoves — solid with bookshelves on the street side, and largely open on the garden side. Solid timber doors to the garden, set back the whole depth of the reveal, alternate with wider bays of glazing set flush to the outer face of the wall, forming full-height bay windows. In his later public buildings Kahn would achieve a greater monumentality using more solid materials, but even in this modest house the grandeur of his aim remains impressive.

Esherick House, Chestnut Hill, PA, USA, 1959–61. **Louis Isidore Kahn**. **b** Saaremaa, Estonia, 1901. **d** New York, NY, USA, 1974.

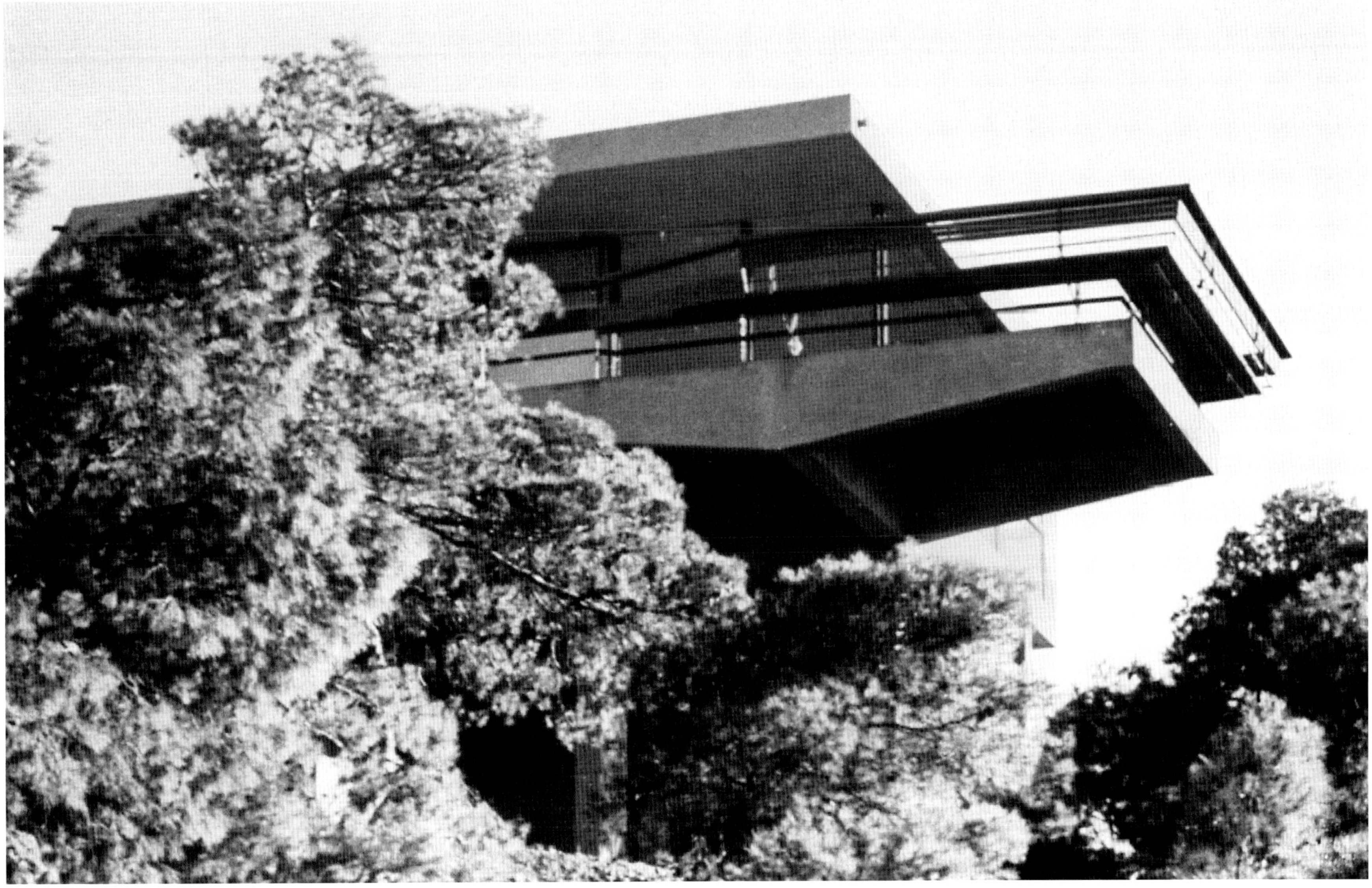

Single-Family House Takis Zenetos

Central to the dramatic, cantilevered design of this house is the architect's philosophy of approaching every project from a new angle in order to achieve a unique solution. In this particular case, the relationship between the building and the site was, naturally, of great importance. The living area is raised above the ground by means of concrete columns, and is part of a daring cantilever that projects both the interior living space and the adjacent terrace into the surrounding pine trees. The balustrade of the terrace is articulated as a bench and establishes an experiential threshold between the built and the natural environment, while providing dramatic views towards the sea. Takis Zenetos was distinguished as the most radical, Modernist post-war architect in Greece during the 1960s and 1970s and was dedicated to the idea of progress through technology in architecture.

Single-Family House, Kavouri, Attica, Greece, 1959–61. **Takis Zenetos**. **b** Athens, Greece, 1926. **d** Athens, Greece, 1977.

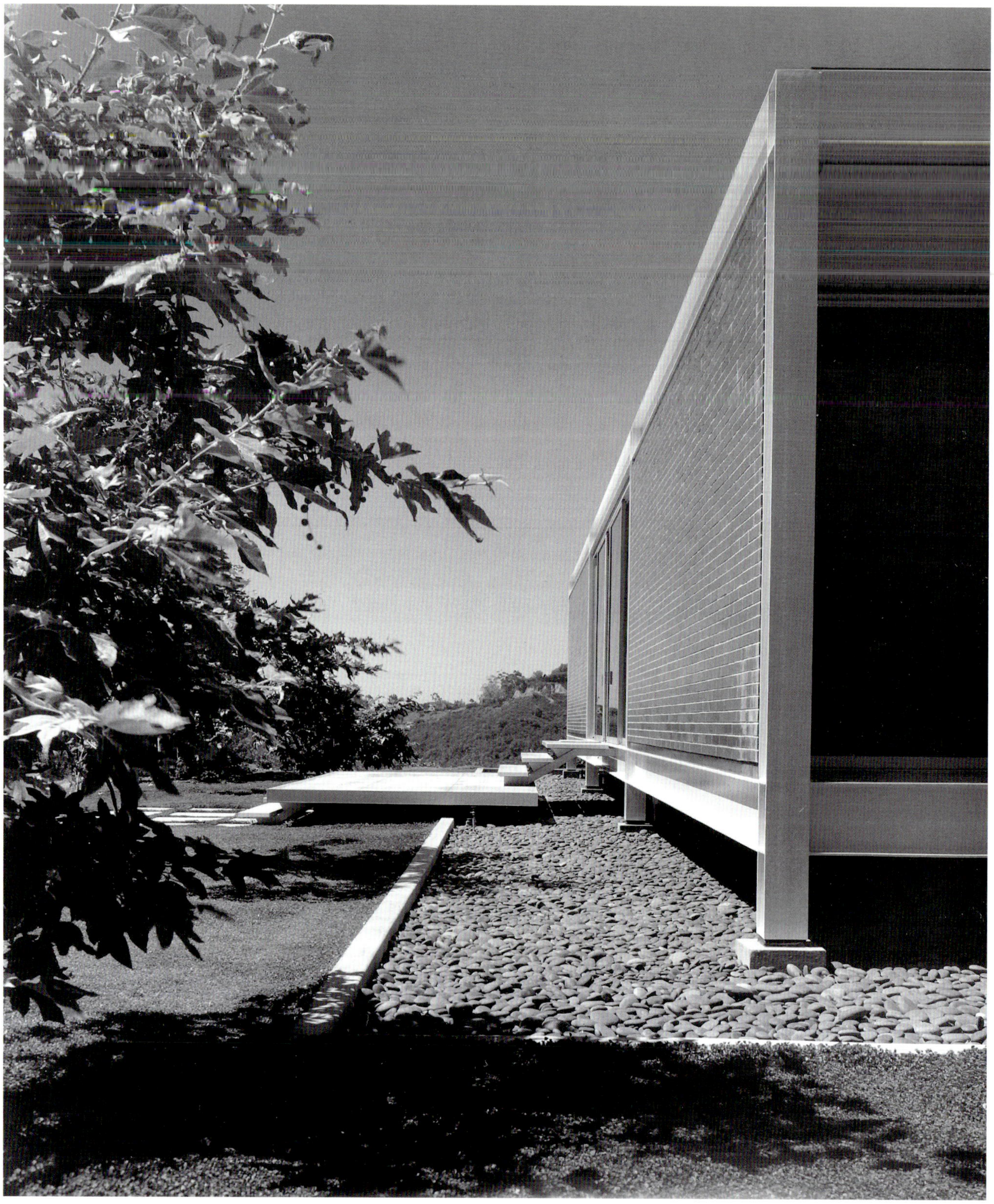

Rosen House Craig Ellwood

Craig Ellwood, who came to prominence during the post-World War II expansion of Los Angeles in the 1940s, designed this elegant house for a banker. The pristine spareness of the steel frame, with its iconic, welded box details, the grey plate glass and brick infill panels, clearly dominates its economical expression. The plan, influenced by a Mies van der Rohe-educated associate in Ellwood's office, is made up of a nine-square-grid, the central square being an open courtyard. However, unlike Mies's Farnsworth House or Philip Johnson's Glass House — both of which were designed for one person — the Rosen House manages to accommodate comfortably the complexities of a five-bedroom, six-bathroom family home. The house has a sense of spaciousness achieved through the use of large expanses of glass, which opens up the house both to the courtyard and the grounds, while providing a reflection of the landscape on the surface of the house itself.

Rosen House, Brentwood, CA, USA, 1962. **Craig Ellwood**. **b** Clarendon, TX, USA, 1922. **d** Pergine Valdarno, Italy, 1992.

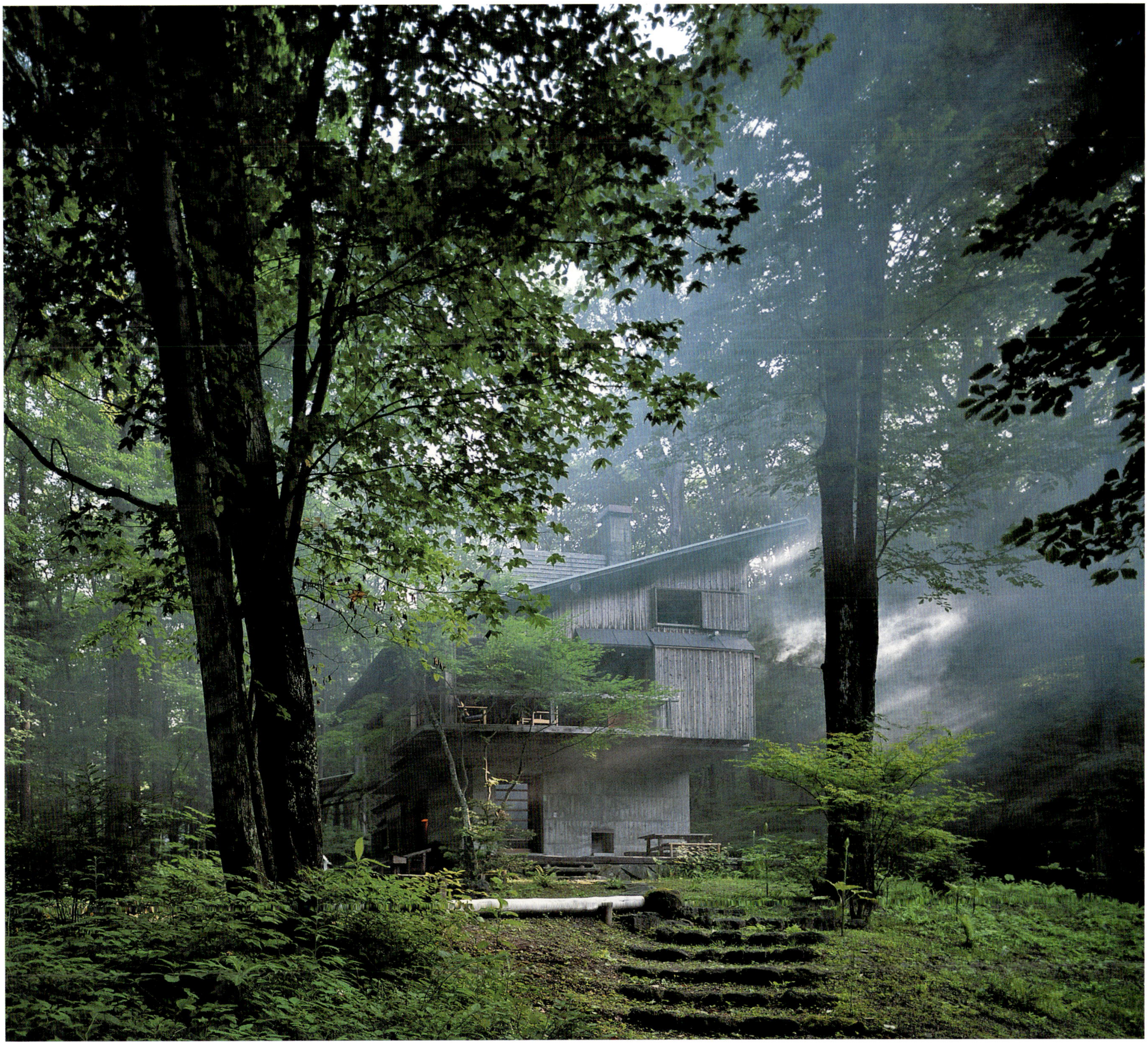

Summer House Junzo Yoshimura

Junzo Yoshimura, the designer of many celebrated post-World War II houses, is known for his superb handling of what is termed the 'Japanese Modern House'. Apprenticed to the Czech-born architect, Antonin Raymond, in the United States, Yoshimura's architecture combined western Modernism with traditional Japanese materials and construction methods. Located in a mountain forest, this villa was designed to be used all year round by the architect and his family. A light, timber-framed living space, topped with an attic containing a study and *tatami* room, sits on a contrasting solid concrete base. The living and sleeping quarters are highly adaptable, despite their small size. As in traditional Japanese houses, screens and panels divide and open up the spaces as function, mood and weather dictate. The central fireplace provides the architectural and spiritual focus at the heart of this simple house, designed as a place in which to experience nature.

Summer House, Karuizawa, Japan, 1962. **Junzo Yoshimura**. **b** Tokyo, Japan, 1908. **d** Japan, 1997.

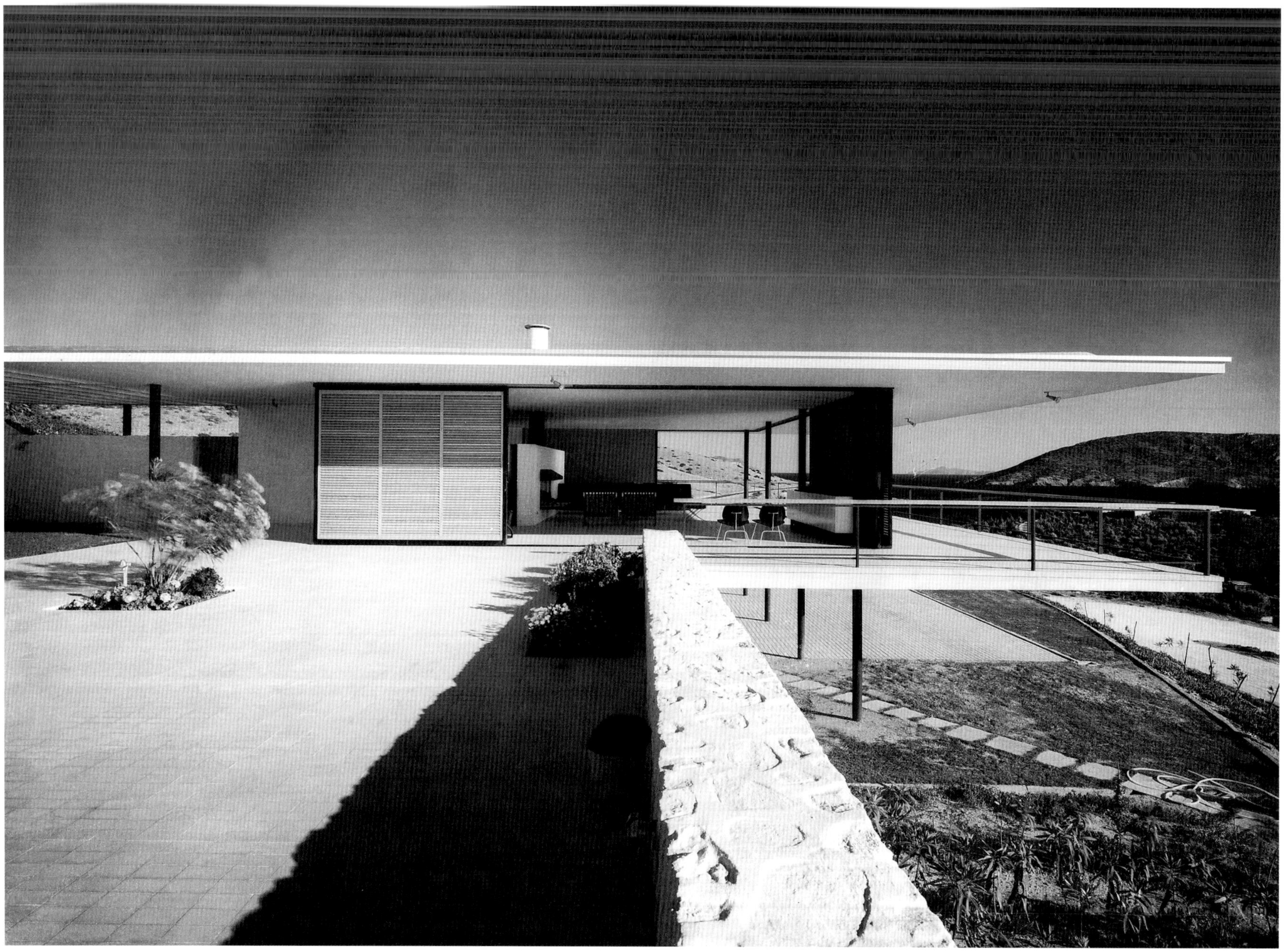

Lanaras Residence Nicos Valsamakis

The Lanaras Residence was designed as a vacation house for a family of four. The generative principle for its design was that of obtaining unobstructed views from the main living area towards the Saronic Gulf, above which the house is located. The living and dining rooms are situated in the glazed volume contained between the two concrete slabs cantilevered out over the sloping site. The slabs, supported by slender steel columns, extend to create a large covered terrace that provides shelter from the sun. The design of the house makes a sensitive and playful response to its context by establishing a dialogue between the internal spaces and the setting, and is, in many ways, reminiscent of the 1950s Case Study Program houses of California. Functionalism, compositional clarity and, at the same time, clear references to context are typical qualities of the architecture of Nicos Valsamakis, as is his attempt to adapt Modernism to Greek regional culture.

Lanaras Residence, Anavyssos, Attica, Greece, 1961–3. **Nicos Valsamakis**. **b** Athens, Greece, 1924.

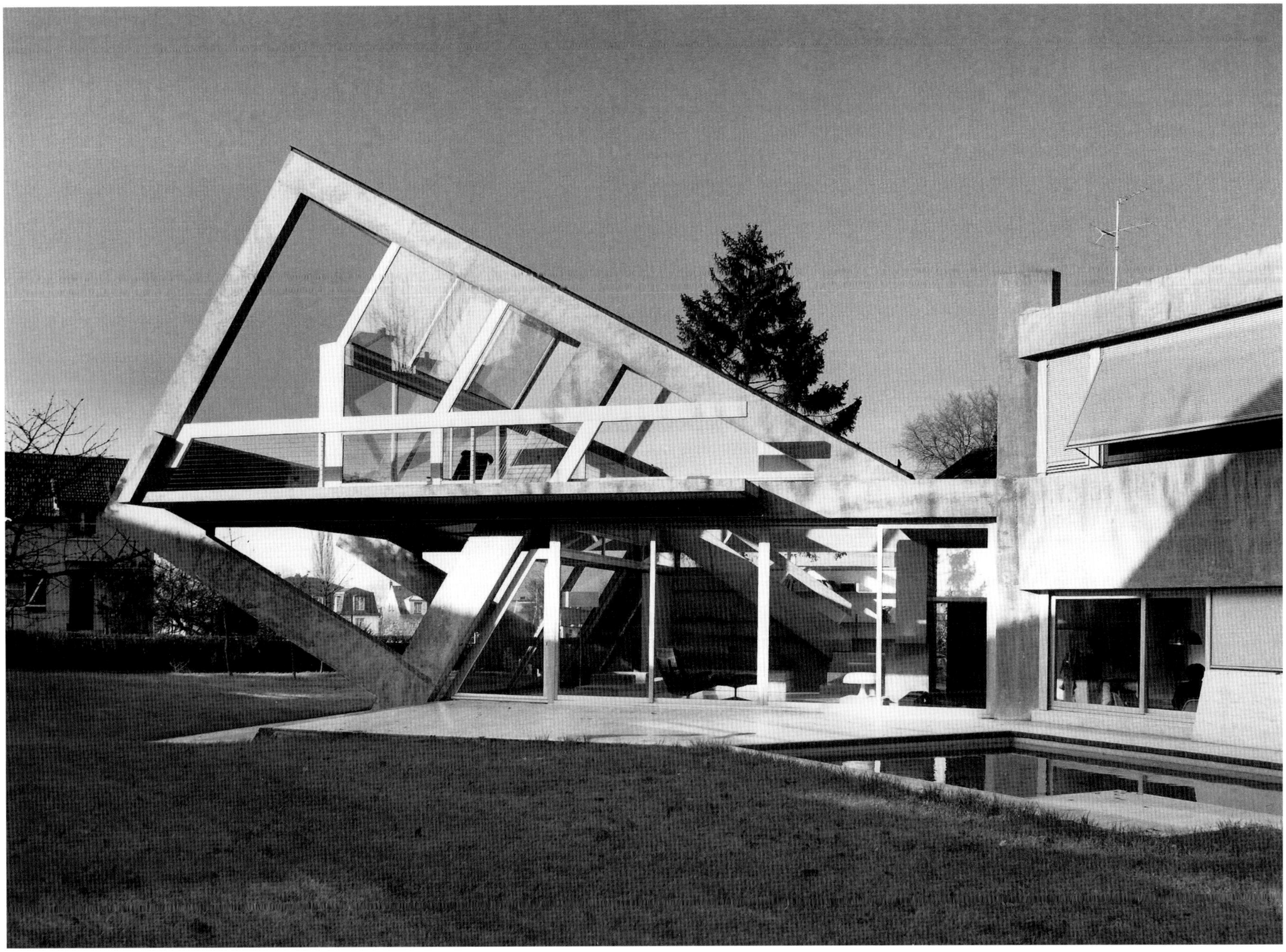

Maison Drush Claude Parent

The tilt of this Modernist, rectilinear house at a 120-degree angle is intended to blow apart the restrictions of straight-lined, static architecture. Designed in 1963, the Maison Drush was the first house built by the radical French architect Claude Parent, who, in his formative years, had worked with Le Corbusier. Parent advocated rejecting the conventional form of buildings to open up new freedoms: roofs tilted for walking over; walls only built in order to stop people walking into others who are sleeping. But the Maison Drush was also designed as a comfortable home for an engineer and his family, who originally wanted a traditional building. The house itself is composed of two separate parts, the tilted bedroom block anchored by the three-storey living accommodation block. Although the house itself is a pragmatic realization of an idea, the overwhelming impression of it falling over — with its suggested dynamism and instability — remains.

Maison Drush, Versailles, France, 1963–5. **Claude Parent**. **b** Neuilly-sur-Seine, France, 1923.

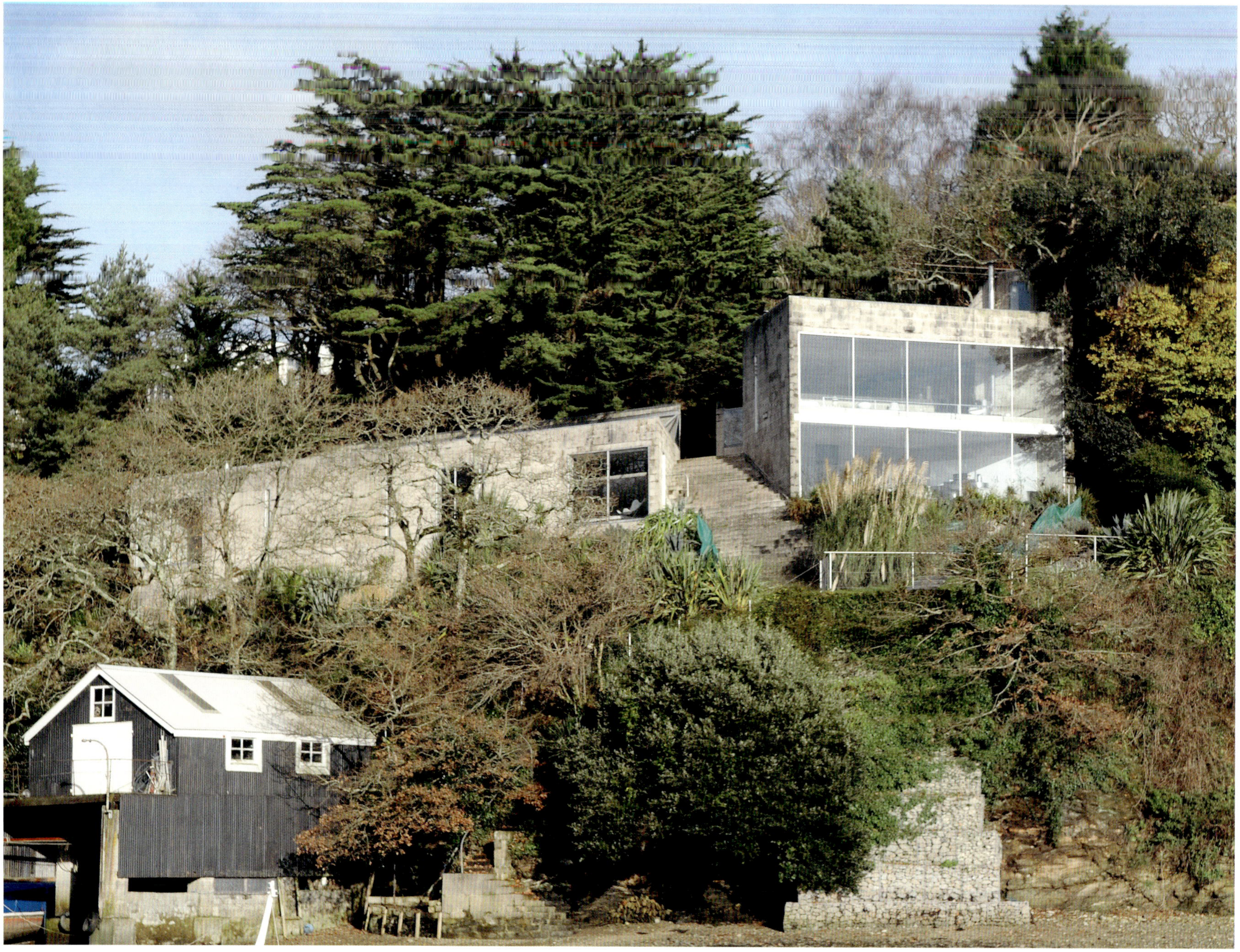

Creek Vean Team 4

Constructed from humble materials — predominately concrete blocks that are worked to an extraordinary level of precision — Creek Vean is a response to the steep and uneven landscape, and the particular requirements of the client. The central steps are a major organizational element in this seemingly simple house: they both separate and unite the two sleeping and living wings, while connecting the different levels and providing a static external space from which to enjoy the view. Team 4 comprised the young Richard Rogers and Norman Foster and their respective architect wives. It is said that the difficulty they had in achieving their required level of detail with the wet trades (concrete, mortar, plaster) used here, put them off working with traditional techniques. All their later work uses industrial prefabricated elements, a predominant feature of the uncompromising High-Tech architecture for which Richard Rogers and Norman Foster have both become known.

Creek Vean, Cornwall, UK, 1964–6. **Team 4**. **Norman Foster**. **b** Manchester, UK, 1935. **Wendy Foster**. **b** UK, 1935. **d** UK, 1989. **Richard Rogers**. **b** Florence, Italy, 1933. **Su Rogers**. **b** UK, 1940.

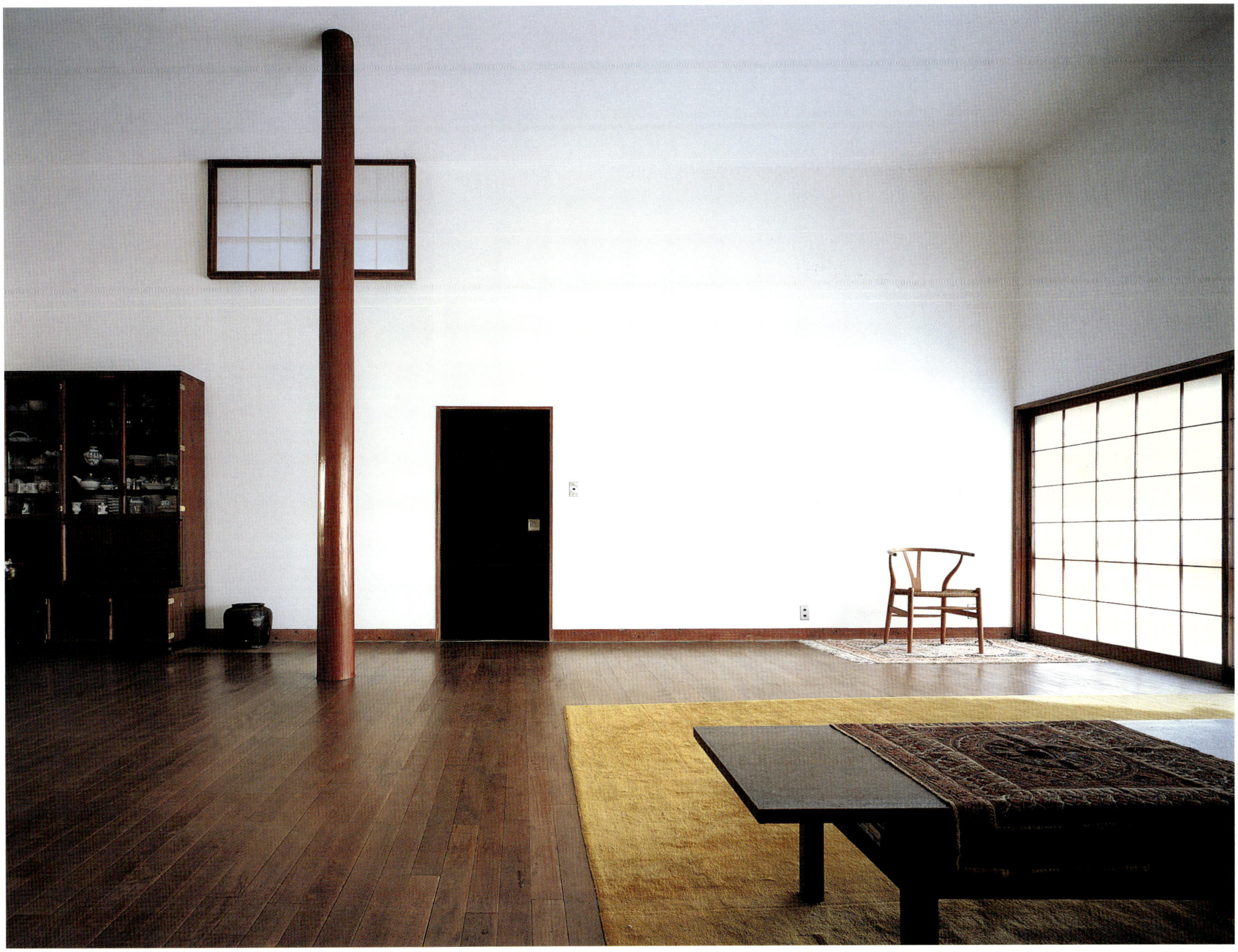

House in White Kazuo Shinohara

Space appears to expand horizontally and vertically within this square-plan, two-storey wooden house. With its double-height living area and compacted bedroom spaces stacked on top of each other, the house expresses Kazuo Shinohara's dual pursuit of abstraction and reinterpretation of traditional Japanese residential architecture. While the minimal elements of white walls, wooden floor and tile roof render abstract space, the central polished cedar column refers to quintessential, or almost mythic aspects of Japanese rural dwellings. Shinohara was completing a doctorate on the spatial composition of Japanese architecture at the Tokyo Institute of Technology under Kiyosi Seike at the time of this house's design, and went on to pursue further abstraction of space, both in residences and larger public works. His work has been profoundly influential on the 'Shinohara-school' architects, which include Toyo Ito and Itsuko Hasegawa.

House in White, Suginami Ward, Tokyo, Japan, 1966. **Kazuo Shinohara**. **b** Shizuoka, Japan, 1925. **d** Kawasaki City, Japan, 2006.

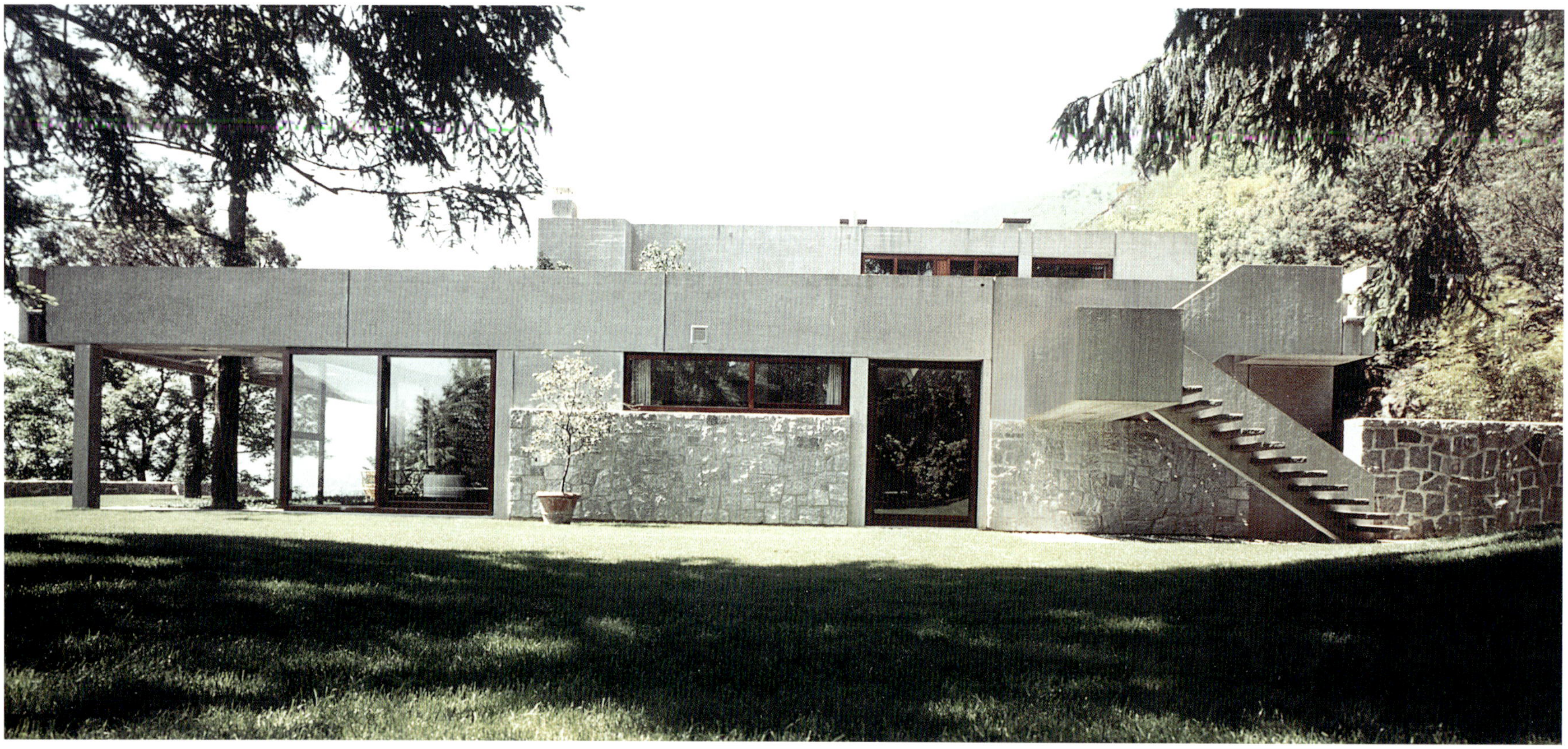

Koerfer House Marcel Breuer

The Koerfer House is one of Breuer's most ambitious and successful private homes. The architect's challenge was to design a house on a rugged hillside, terracing both house and land to provide usable outdoor areas and overcome the steep incline; to build on the hillside above the house a swimming pool pavilion opened to the sun by four large skylights; to emphasize the beautiful and sweeping view of the lake below. In 1972, the house received the prestigious Honor Award from the American Institute of Architects. The citation for the award reads: "this superb house commanded the unreserved admiration of the jury. The hand of a master is everywhere evident; in the elegant simplicity of plan and section; in the wonderful rapport between terraced volume and hillside site; in the subtle blend of openness and intimacy of space; and above all in the robust splendour of material and detail. This is everything that a great house should be — a work of art marvelously enriching the art of life."

Koerfer House, Ascona, Ticino, Switzerland, 1963–6. **Marcel Breuer**. **b** Pécs, Hungary, 1902. **d** New York, NY, USA, 1981.

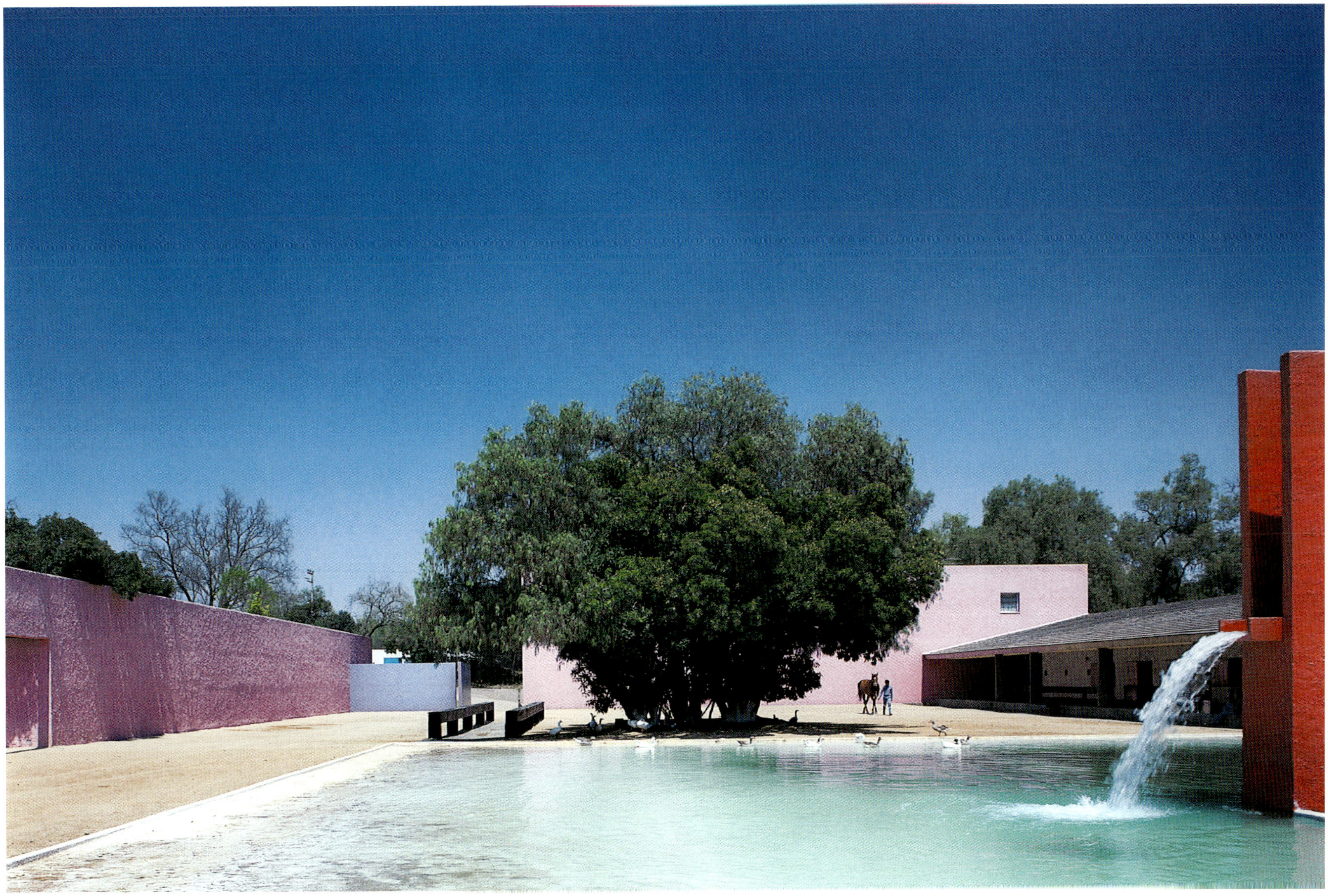

San Cristobal Luis Barragán

Luis Barragán's spare, planar compositional style is evident in this compound of family house with equestrian stables and a pool. The blue expanse of sky is reflected in the pool, juxtaposed with the solidity and texture of the pink walls behind; the ascetic stillness of the compound is complemented by the gushing water. Recalling the aqueducts of Barragán's own childhood village of Mazamitla, the troughed water is an example of how he drew inspiration from the vernacular of his native country. This complex, designed with his student, Andrés Casillas, is an interplay of human habitation and animal shelter, sunlight and shadow. Although the self-taught Barragán built relatively little, he has had an impact on three generations of Mexican architects as a revered mystic of architecture, and on minimalist architecture worldwide. As Barragán himself has summarized: 'Any work of architecture which does not express serenity is a mistake.'

San Cristobal, Egerstrom Residence and Stables, Los Clubes, Mexico City, Mexico, 1967–8. **Luis Barragán**. **b** Guadalajara, Mexico, 1902. **d** Mexico City, Mexico, 1988.

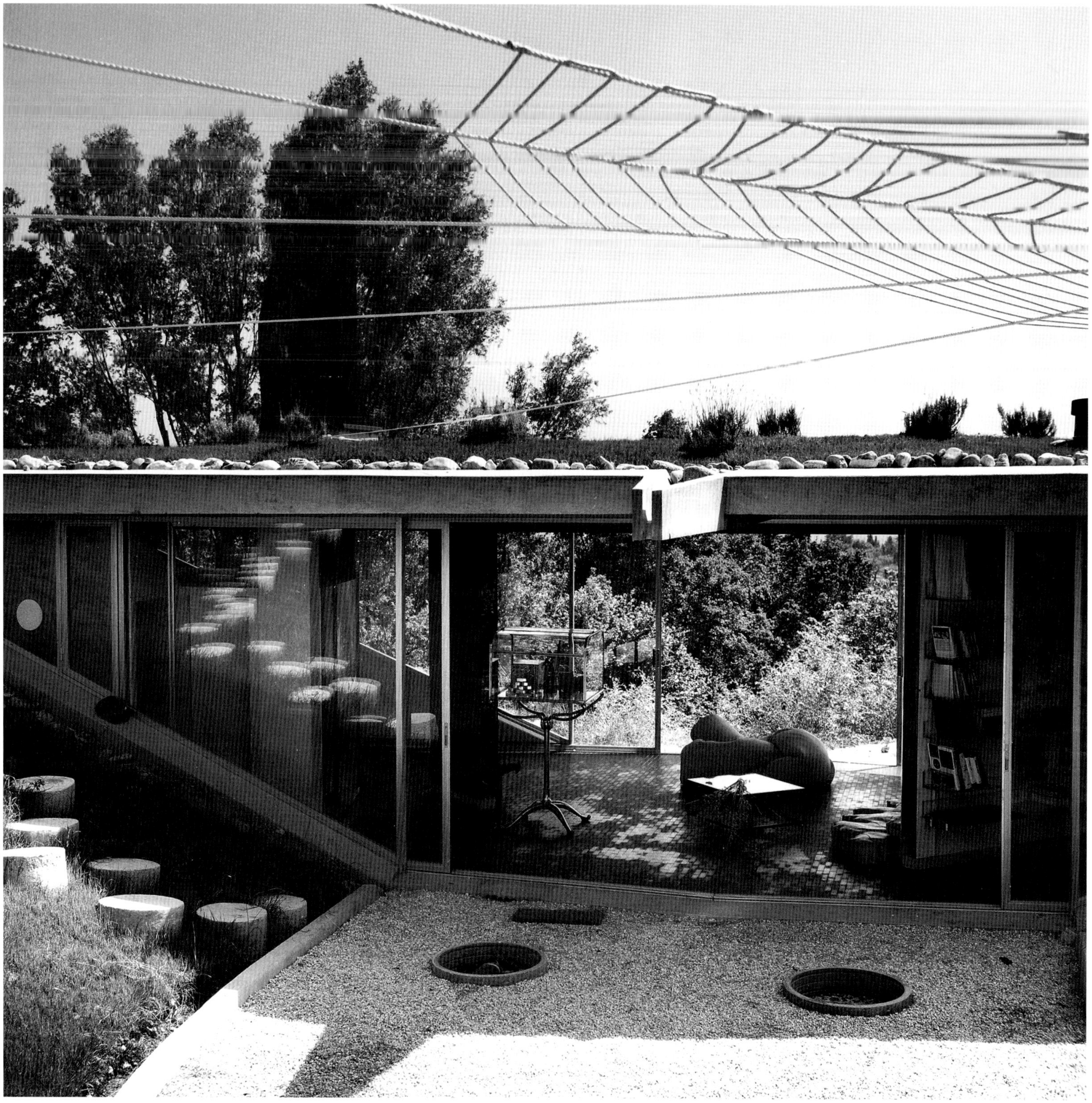

Arman House Guy Rottier

More a social philosopher and artist than an architect in the conventional sense, Guy Rottier has spent much of his career investigating the potential of buildings to express what he refers to as 'arTchitecture'. Many of his projects investigate temporary, environmentally considered structures that could be relocated or, in some cases, destroyed after use. The Arman House, designed for an artist as a living and studio space, is a built expression of some of these ideas, although without the budget or technical innovation to bring the ideal to full fruition. Following on from the theoretical Cable Village of 1965, in which temporary living pods were hung from a spider's web, the Arman House fits neatly into a small hollow, implying by its form that it has been dropped into place and could easily be removed. The nylon rope web suggests a structural capability, but is essentially a sculptural gesture in this dramatic and intriguing house.

Arman House, Vence, France, 1968. **Guy Rottier**. **b** Sumatra, Indonesia, 1922.

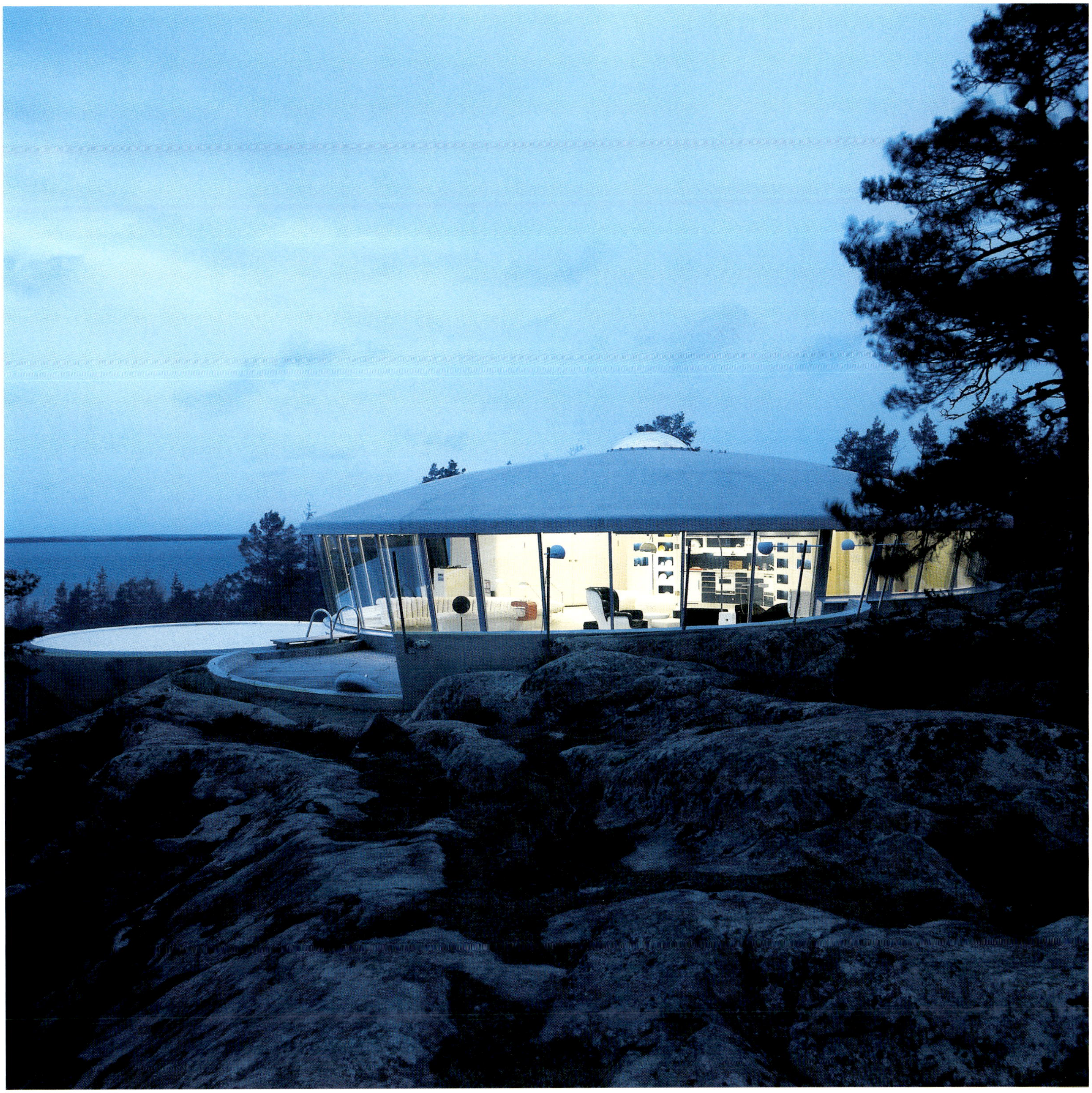

Villa Spies Staffan Berglund

Rising like an elegant hemispherical spacecraft above the dramatic rocky coastline, the Villa Spies is a summer house designed by Staffan Berglund for the wealthy Danish visionary and business genius, Simon Spies. The villa's futuristic features include a circular dining space, which rises out of the ground at the press of a button, sound-proofed walls, electric shutters, electronically controlled lighting and a heated outdoor swimming pool. With a band of windows in the place of an outer wall, the house has a 360-degree view to the sea and the archipelago that surrounds the city of Stockholm. Spies originally founded his business on tourism and set up a competition in 1967 to design an environment for leisure in the country that both visitors and residents could enjoy. Berglund's original entry won the 'Bubbles for Pleasure' competition, but it was never built; however, his ideas inspired Spies to commission this villa.

Villa Spies (Villa Fjolle), Torö, Sweden, 1969–70. **Staffan Berglund**. Active Sweden, mid-twentieth century to present day.

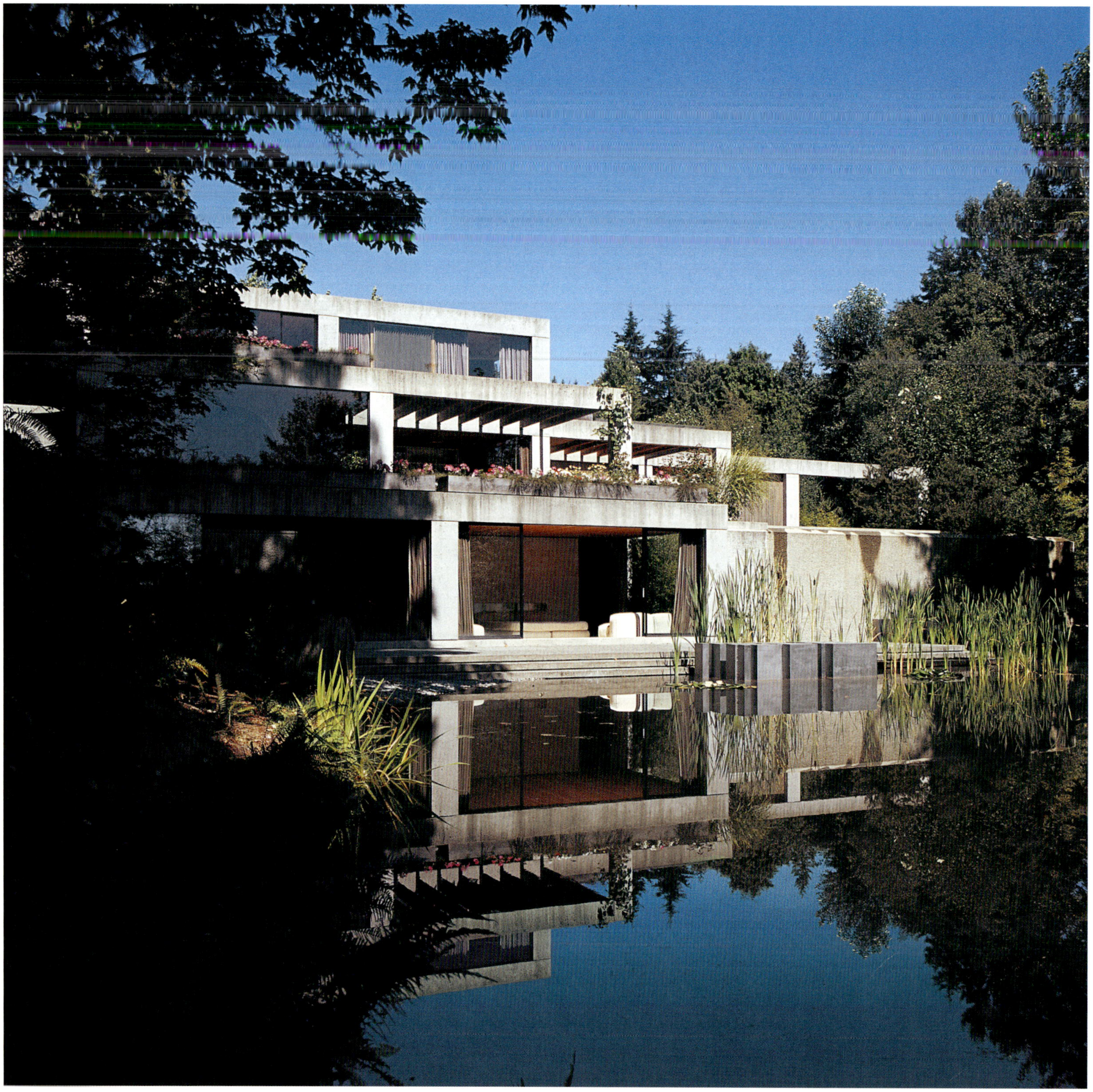

Helmut Eppich House Arthur Erickson

Despite the contrast between the structural geometry of this terraced concrete house and the fluidity of its natural surroundings, the ultimate unity achieved is perhaps the most distinctive characteristic of the Helmut Eppich House. Every element of its design — whether it be the overhang of its lowest level or the rhythm of its flying concrete beams — bears a sensitive relationship to the details and subtleties of its surroundings. The fluid dissolution of the distinction between man-made and natural — house and setting — is a trademark of Arthur Erickson's designs. Working at a time when Modern architecture was widely accepted, Erickson was free to endow his works with the deep appreciation for nature and experience he had accrued over his lifetime. This sensitivity both gained him an international reputation and characterized his seminal contribution to the creation of a North American 'West Coast' architectural style.

Helmut Eppich House, West Vancouver, BC, Canada, 1972. **Arthur Erickson**. **b** Vancouver, BC, Canada, 1924.

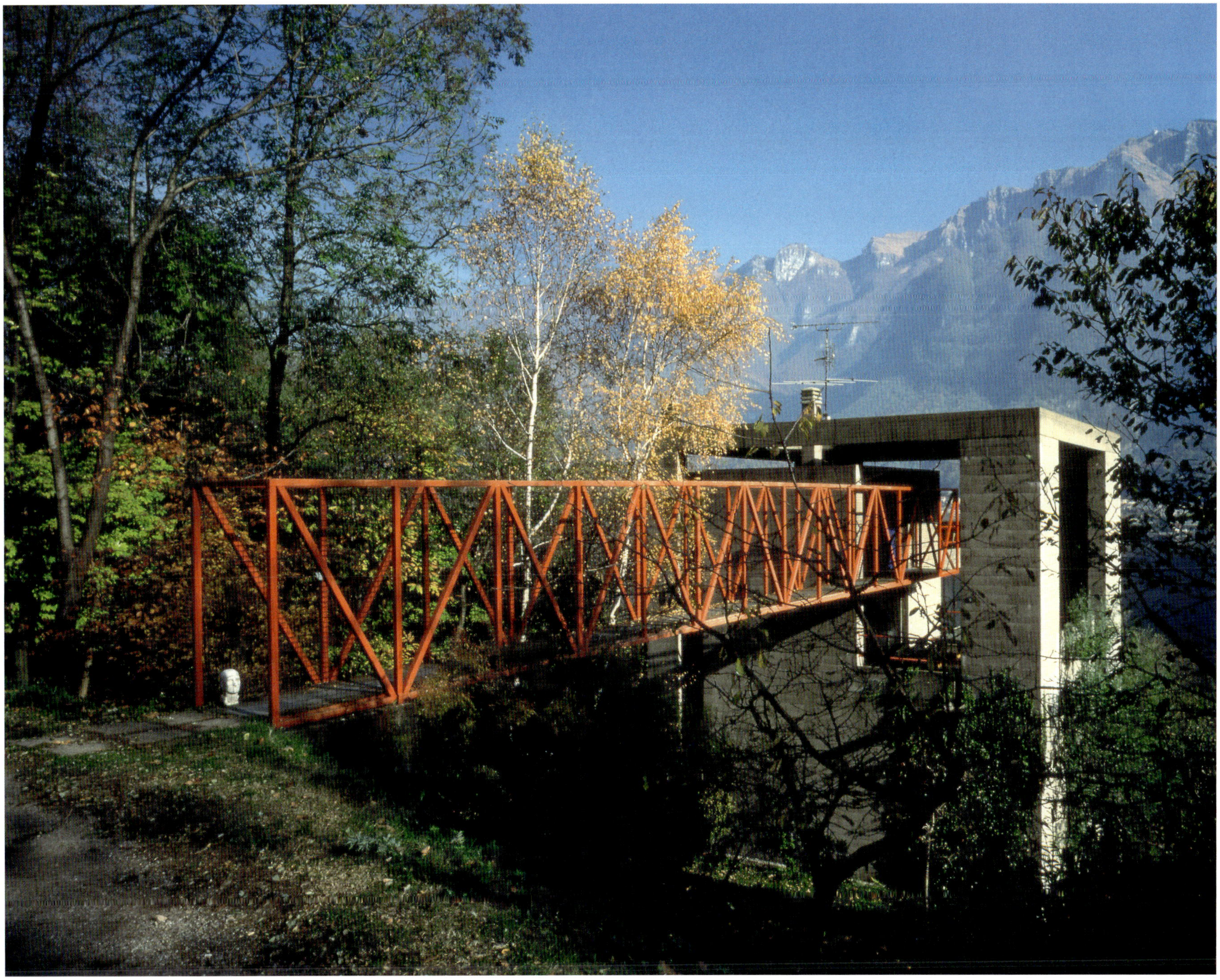

House at Riva San Vitale Mario Botta

The perilous-looking iron bridge emphasizes the isolation of this square-plan tower house, set on the hillside of Monte San Giorgio. Its pure form is typical of Mario Botta's interest in 'ideal' geometries, and he was one of a group of architects who looked back to the abstract forms of 1930s Italian Rationalism, seeking to create a contemporary monumentalism. His work is often based on the simple forms of cube and cylinder found in ancient architecture, rather than on specific historical references. The bridge penetrates the tower and leads to a studio on the top floor, where stairs lead down to the other levels. The austere, steep site does not permit the luxury of a garden, but there is a porch on the lowest level providing spectacular views over the snow-capped peaks above Lake Lugano. Other Swiss architects were influenced by Botta's 'interventionist' rather than contextual architecture, which also had its roots in *rocoli*, tower-like buildings traditional to the area.

House at Riva San Vitale, Ticino, Switzerland, 1971–3. **Mario Botta**. **b** Mendrisio, Switzerland, 1943.

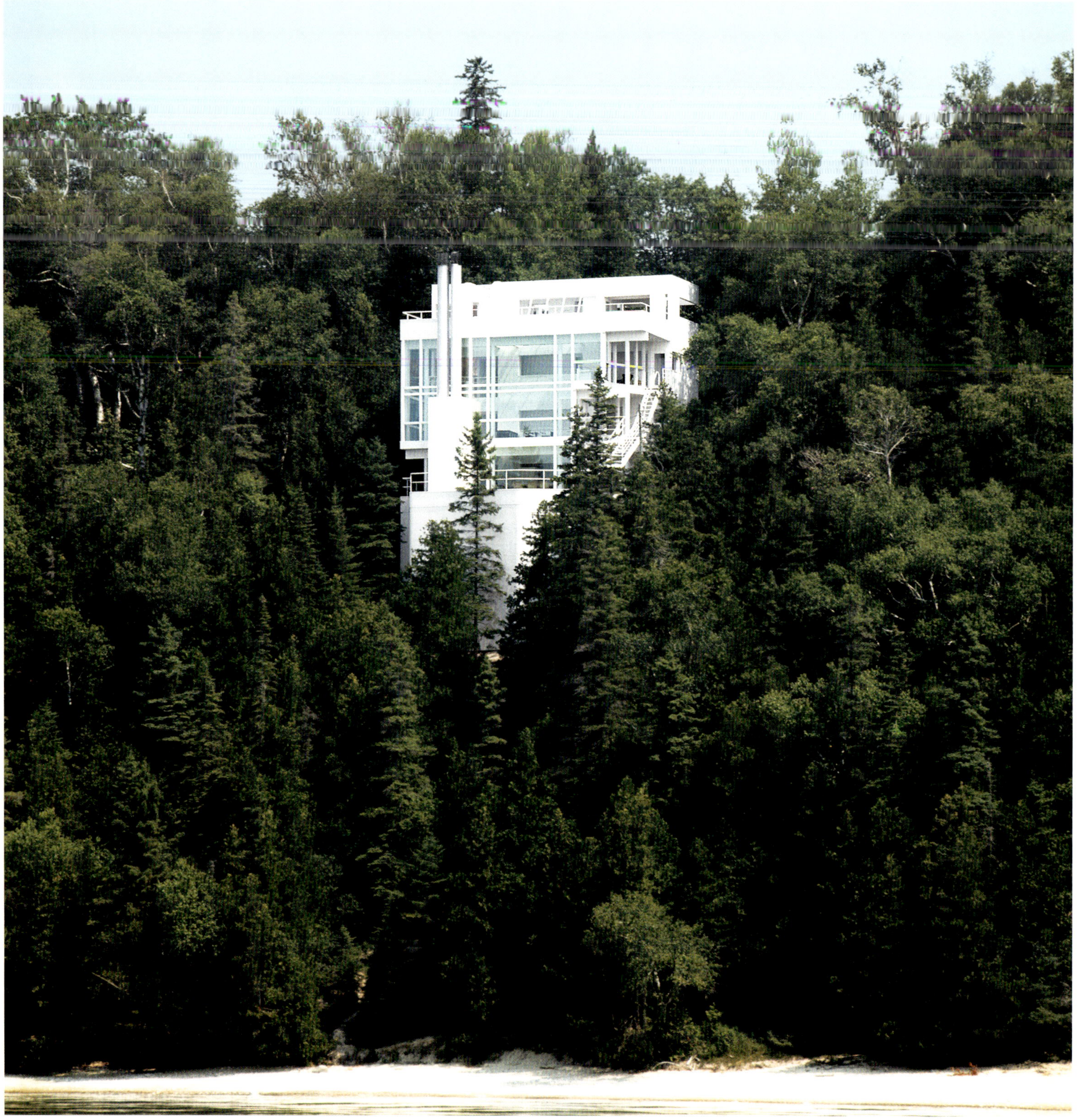

Douglas House Richard Meier

Douglas House is situated, almost precipitously, high above Lake Michigan on a steeply sloping site. Richard Meier designed this house early in his career, at a time when his ideas of form and colour (or the absence of colour, Meier's trademark), were drawn largely from his study of the purist work of Le Corbusier. Here, against the background of blue of the lake and sky and the green of the trees, Meier sought a 'dramatic dialogue' that would offer a contrast between the natural and the man-made, enhanced by the vivid whiteness of the house. Entered at roof level via a walkway, the house is arranged so that the lakeside view opens up as one descends to the living and dining areas, with the private spaces facing away from the lake. One of the New York Five group of architects, Meier's strength is in his consistency of an architectural philosophy, demonstrated in his early houses as well as his later public buildings, such as the Getty Museum in Los Angeles (1997).

Douglas House, Harbor Springs, MI, USA, 1971–3. **Richard Meier**. **b** Newark, NJ, USA, 1934.

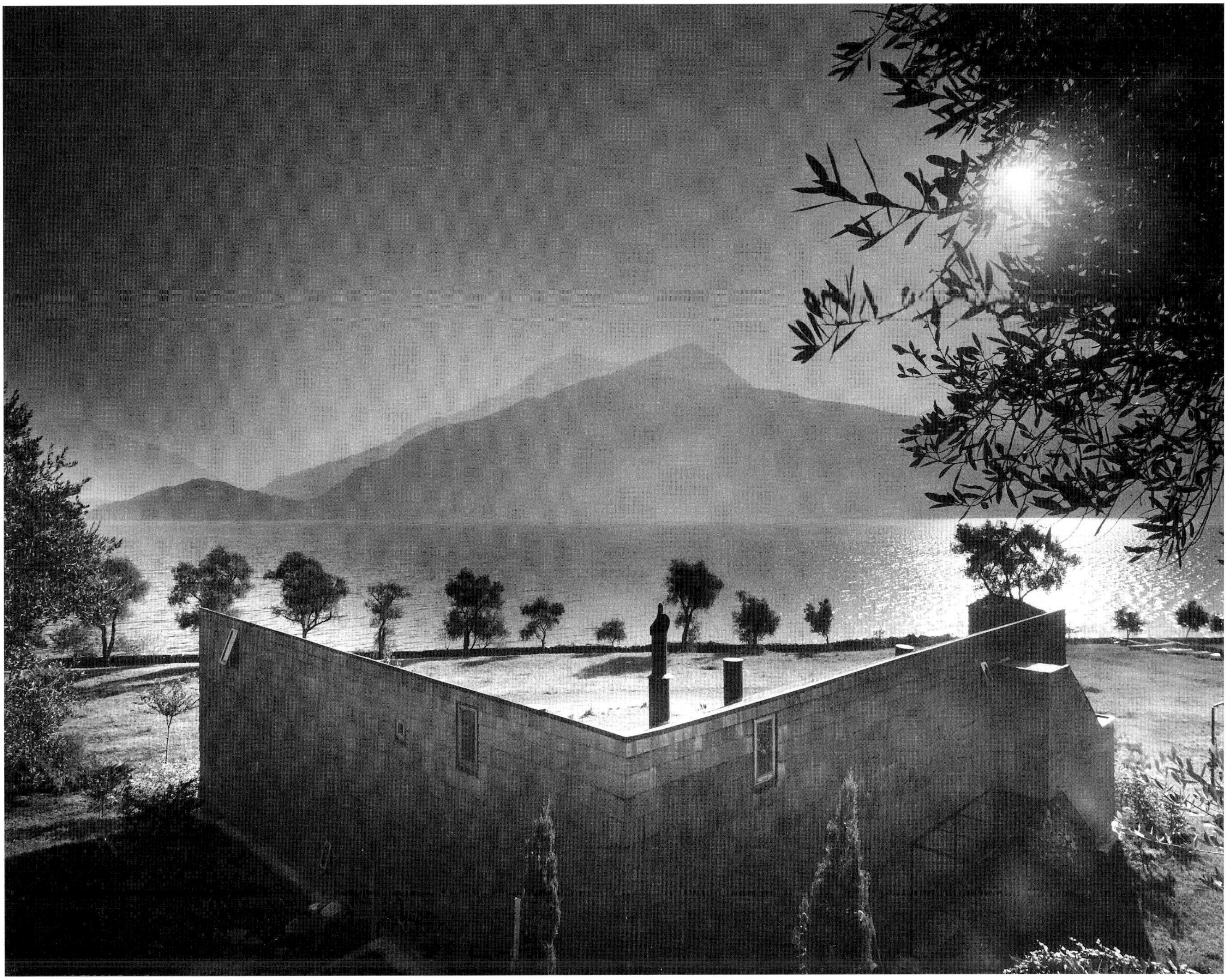

Zapper House Marco Zanuso

One side of this vacation house has only a few tiny windows punched in its walls, which form a crisp wedge that virtually mirrors the shape of the Alps directly across Lake Como. One of Marco Zanuso's priorities was siting and designing his buildings in harmony with their natural surroundings. Its appearance softened by wood-shingled siding, this steel-framed wedge discourages intrusions on privacy and focuses attention from within the house to the spectacular panorama. When the house is seen from the lake, however, it reveals a markedly different personality: a voluminous L-shaped dwelling with two, glass-enclosed wings under steeply pitched roofs. The wings, which are equal in size and provide separate accommodations for the children and their parents, embrace the nearby landscape and distant views. In the 'elbow' of this L-shaped house, Zanuso created an enclosed common room to provide a retreat from the glazed living areas.

Zapper House, Musso, Italy, 1972–3. **Marco Zanuso**. **b** Milan, Italy, 1916. **d** Milan, Italy, 2001.

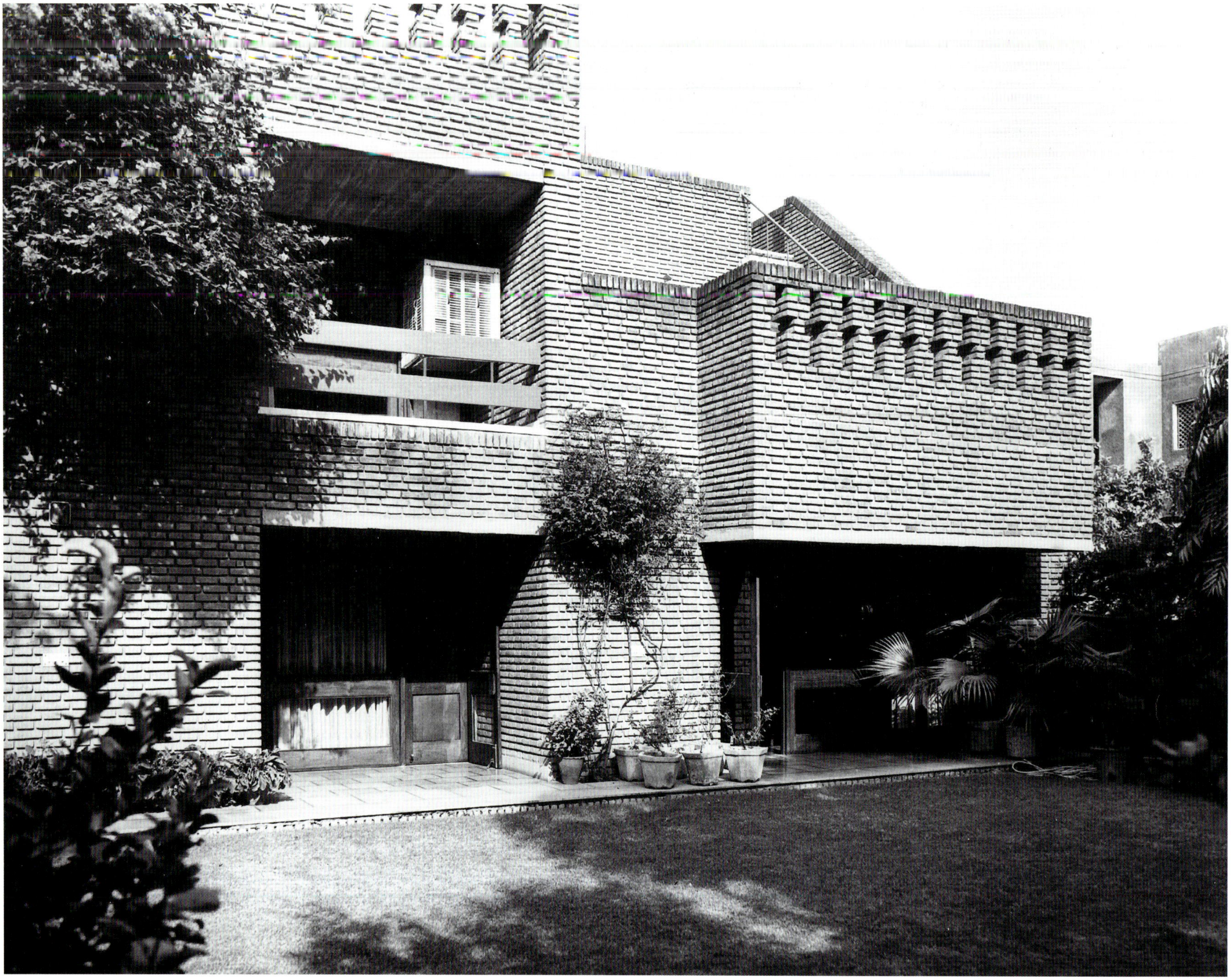

Sham Lal House Raj Rewal

Brickwork infuses this house with a complex texture. Raj Rewal's attention to detail and sensitivity to material are evident in the brick *jali* (lattice or screen work), which act as parapets for roof terraces, and the formwork marks left exposed on the balcony ceilings. Wall planes wrap around rooms and protect the deep-set windows from sun and rain. Vertical emphasis disappears in the fastidiously cornered brickwork, favouring the horizontality of the land. Brick-on-edge cornices, plastered fascias and an unobtrusive transition from floor to flora are gestures that reconcile house and garden. These finer details explain why such functionalism in brick — also seen in Rewal's houses for the painter, Satish Gujral, and for himself — was popular among Rewal's generation. Inspired by Pierre Jeanneret's Chandigarh and Le Corbusier's Primitivist *œuvre*, this fresh aesthetic happily marries Enlightenment-style Rationalism with India's labour-intensive building technologies.

Sham Lal House, New Delhi, India, 1973–5. **Raj Rewal**. **b** Hoshiarpur, India, 1934.

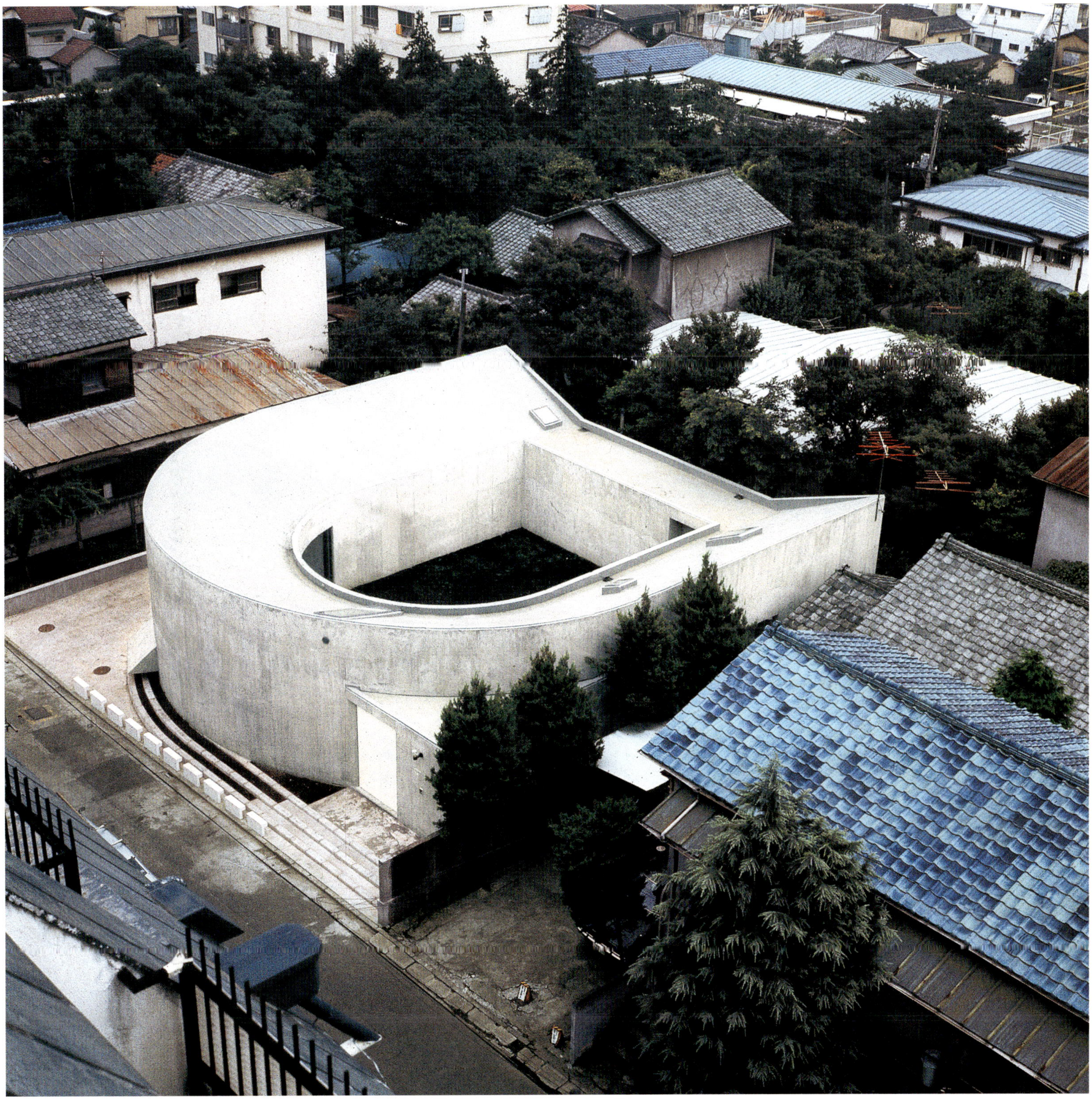

White 'U' House Toyo Ito

This house, as its name implies, consists of a continuous U-shaped volume with an inward-sloping roof and a rectangular volume connecting its two ends. The continuous 45 m (147 ft) interior space contains a minimal number of enclosed rooms, leaving the rest for circulation and an open living area. Toyo Ito intended the house's interior to be a fluid zone where light distribution, air movement and human activities would be perceived as in flow. In addition, he experimentally arranged the elements in the curved area — including skylights, fluorescent cove lights and furniture — with their own corresponding curves. The phenomenological experience which this generated was meant to express a physical sense of rhythm that the inhabitants might exhibit during the course of daily living. Ito's experimental design demonstrated that a house can significantly affect human experience and, at the same time, it challenged conventional designs for a dwelling.

White 'U' House, Nakano, Japan, 1976, demolished 1998. **Toyo Ito**. **b** Nagano, Japan, 1941.

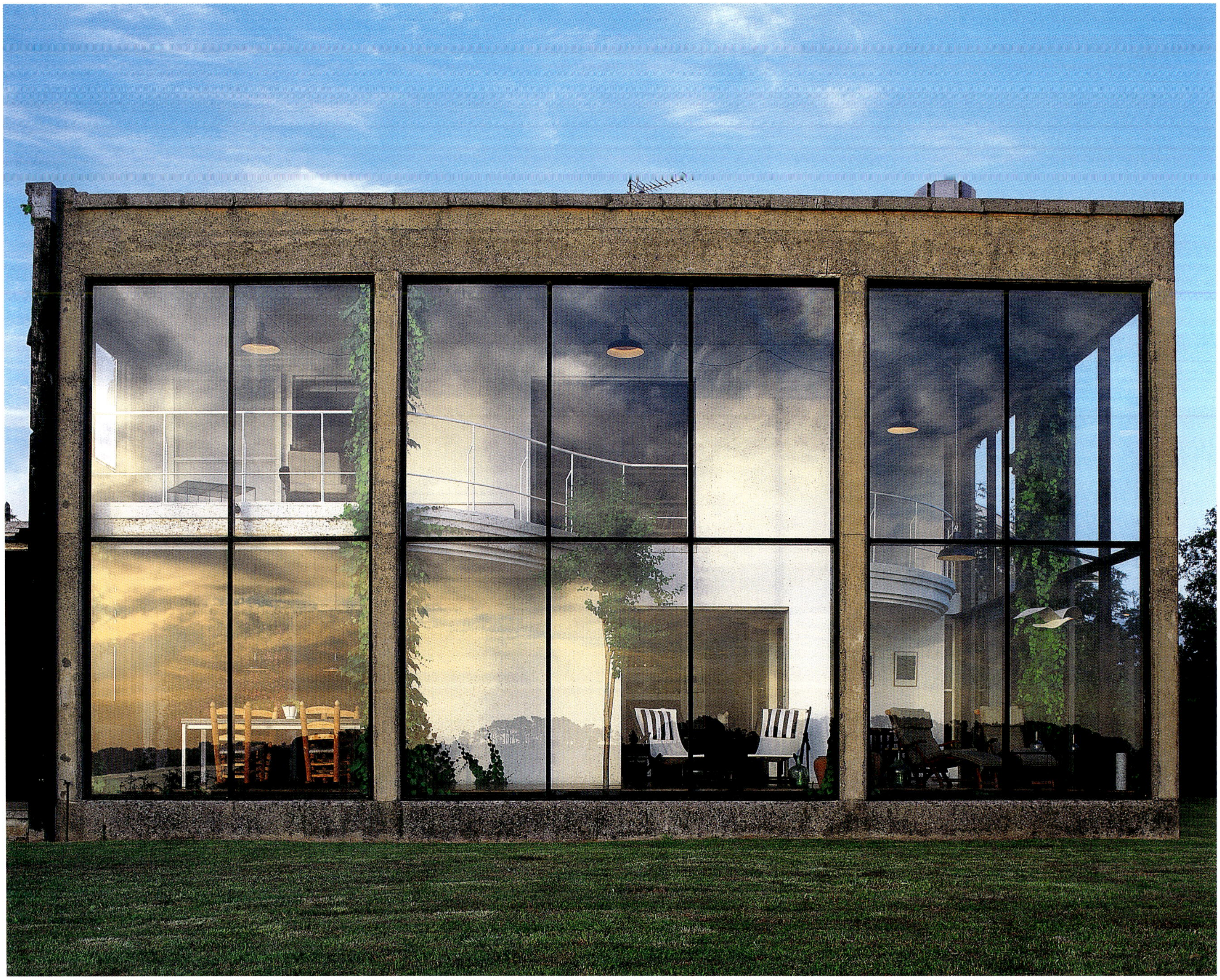

House at Santander Junquera & Pérez Pita

Sitting atop a flat rise, boldly overlooking the Santander port, this house design clearly embraces the International Style. Junquera & Pérez Pita have drawn their inspiration from the industrial glass building style developed by Mies van der Rohe, specifically from his Farnsworth House — the prototype for glass houses. The exterior expresses strict geometry in its modular component parts. Walls have been turned into window panels, thus exposing the traditionally private life of the home to the public. Virtually all structural and interior design elements are visible. The upper-level gallery floor undulates diagonally above the sitting room on the ground floor. The high ceilings and glass walls of the living room flood the home with light, and add to the open feel of the home. The architects have adapted what would traditionally be industrial building materials and design for this residential habitation.

House at Santander, Santander, Spain, 1982–3. **Jerónimo Junquera García del Diestro**. **b** Madrid, Spain, 1943. **Estanislao Pérez Pita**. **b** Madrid, Spain, 1943. **d** Madrid, Spain, 1999.

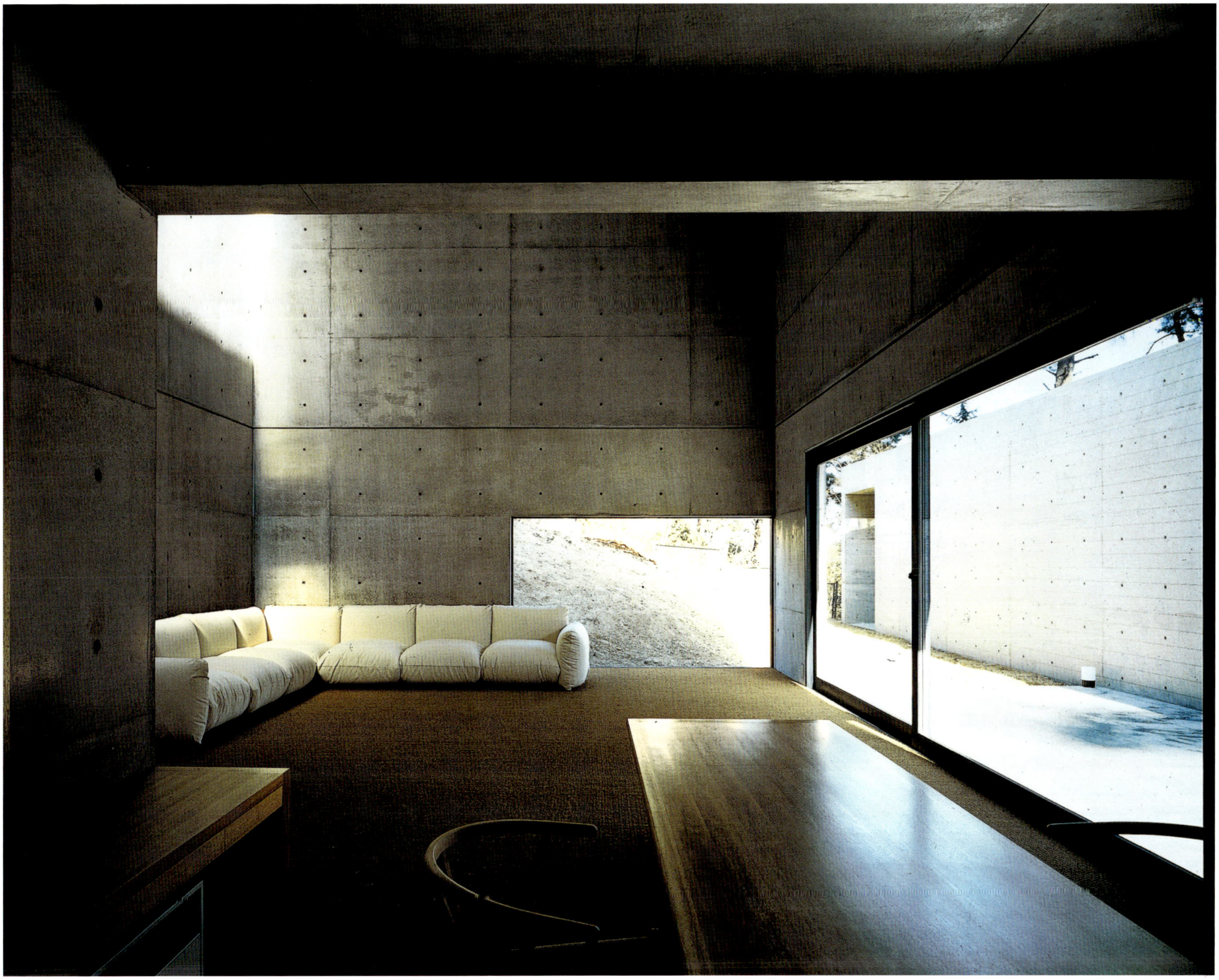

Koshino House Tadao Ando

This interior view of the main living area shows the extreme abstraction of this two-level house, composed of two concrete boxes embedded in a sloping site. Tadao Ando, one of the most renowned contemporary Japanese architects and a winner of the Pritzker Prize, challenges the emotions and the senses through a minimalism that, in many ways, alludes to the Zen tradition. He is concerned with the individual's confrontation with space and resistance to seduction through an attentiveness to the essential. The play of light and shadow and bare spatial asceticism, where the outside world and its distractions are erased, give a sense of psychological isolation and inward reflectiveness. This mood is emphasized by the blank window, which forces the observer to look deeper into one's relationship to the space. The house reflects the principles of the minimalist movement of the 1960s, and its reaction against commercial vulgarity and the commodification of culture.

Koshino House, Ashiya, Japan, 1979–81, with later additions, 1983–4. **Tadao Ando**. **b** Osaka, Japan, 1941.

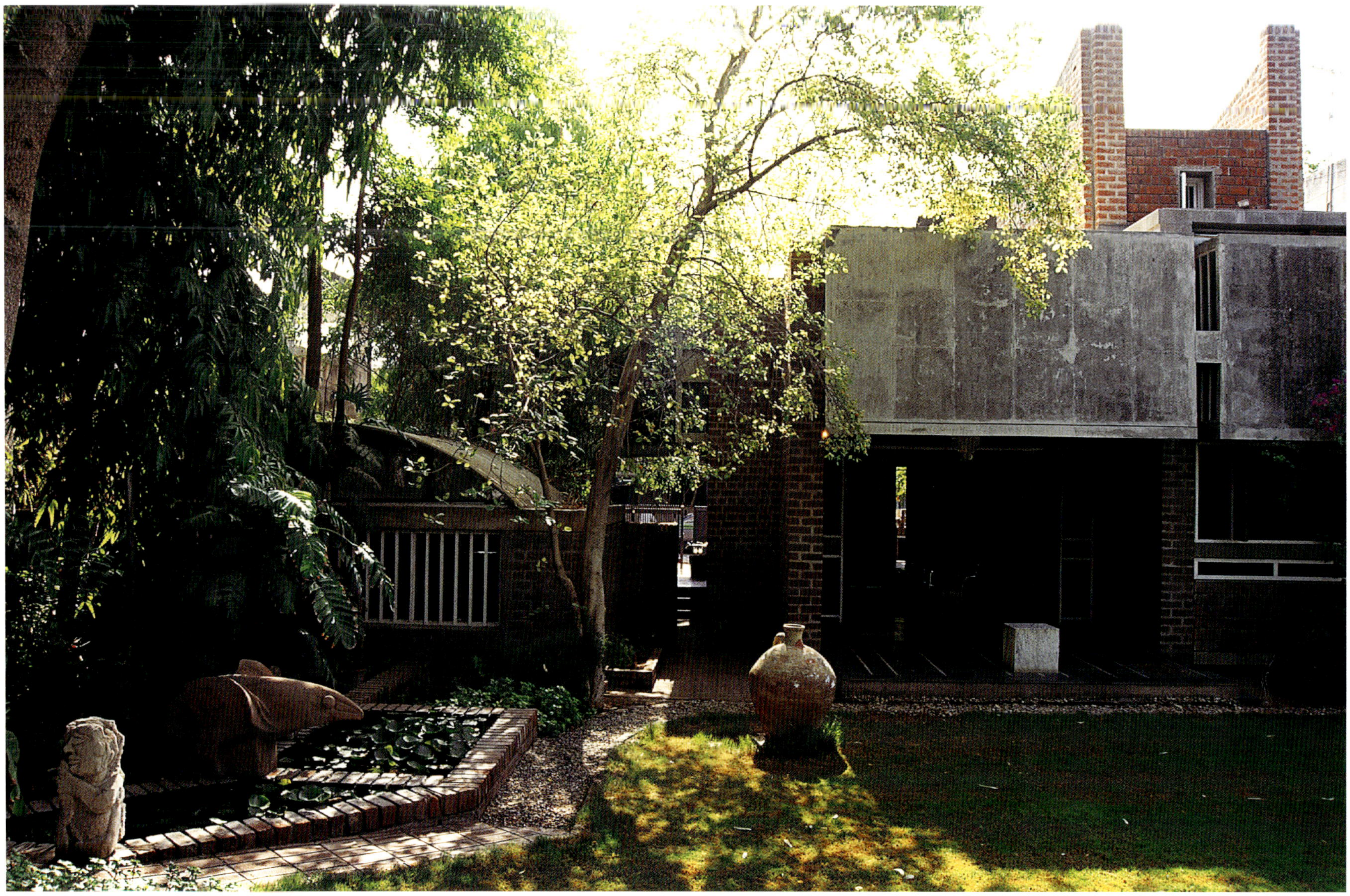

Doshi House Balkrishna Doshi

This Modernist house of exposed brick and concrete, inside as well as out, has an understated, almost austere presence which allows it to merge with its quiet surroundings. Yet, at the same time, it is designed to offer a rich, complex and dynamic living experience for the architect and his family, animated by distinctive contrasts in its spatial qualities, a lively visual and physical interaction of exterior and interior, and the use of stimulating colour schemes in the cool indoor areas. The house is characteristic of Balkrishna Doshi's work, which uses simple rectilinear geometries to build up complex building masses of open and closed spaces connected by a network of corridors, or ritual routes. Doshi worked in Paris for Le Corbusier on Le Corbusier's Indian projects of the 1950s, but subsequently, in his own practice, fused that rigorous Modernist vision with his own experience and reading of traditional Indian temple city architecture.

Doshi House, Ahmedabad, India, 1959–61, with later additions, 1985–7. **Balkrishna Vithaldas Doshi**. **b** Pune, Maharashtra, India, 1927.

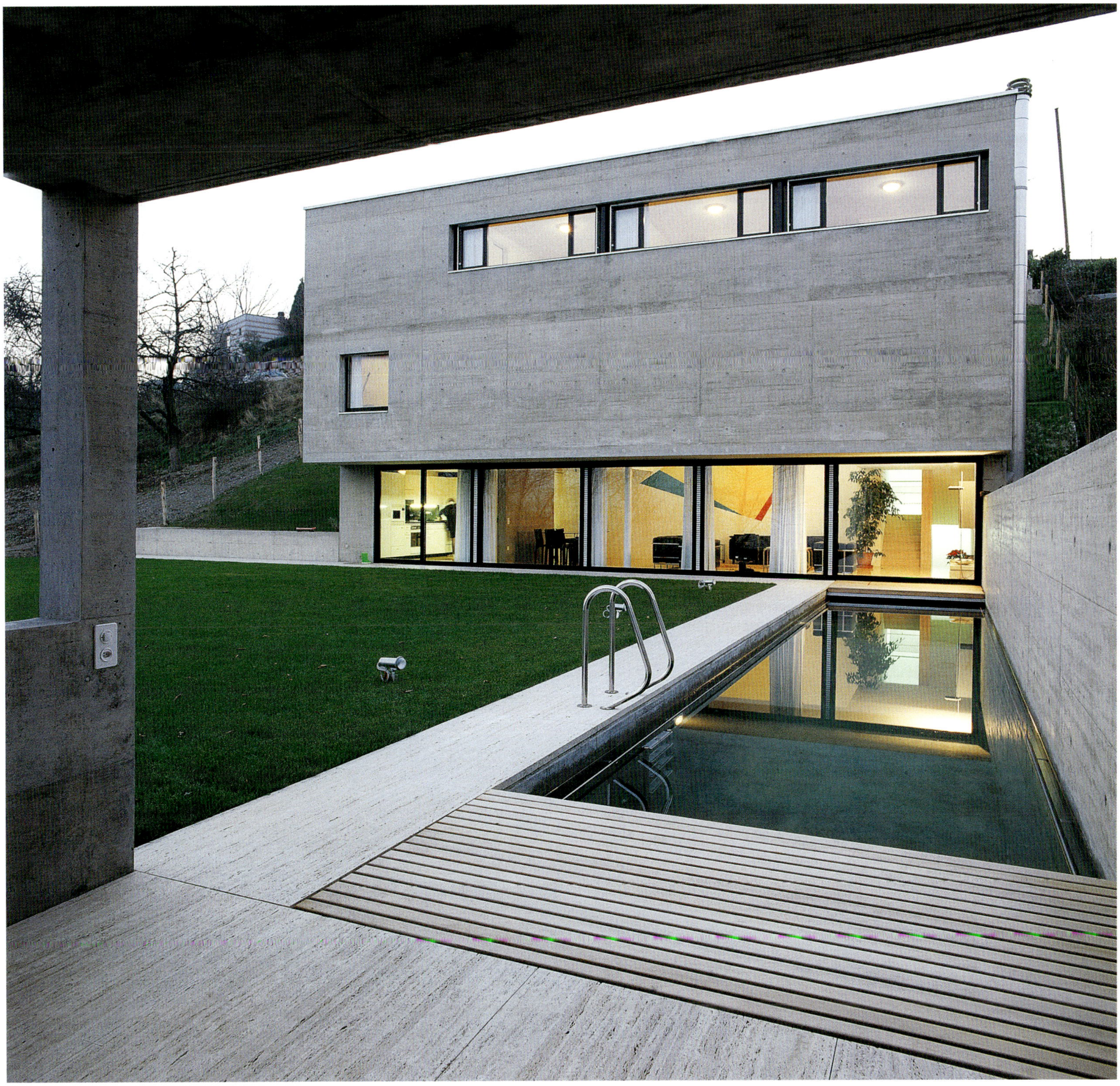

Casa Bernasconi Luigi Snozzi

Seen from the pergola, the house and garden of the Casa Bernasconi seem to converge: the green lawn transforms into the flat, blue surface of the swimming pool, which itself seems to be an extension of the skylit staircase, along the highly polished floor and through the large glass opening. It is built in the mountains of Italian-speaking Switzerland, Ticino, a famous enclave of Modern Rationalist architecture, of which Luigi Snozzi is a leading proponent. The house itself is a series of habitable terraces, set against its steep backdrop. It is entered at the top level, where the bedrooms are, via a long stair that cuts across the steeply sloping hill. The living room and kitchen are at pool level, with a pergola leading you still further down the hill. Snozzi's houses, always in exposed concrete and using the language of Modernism, draw on the elemental stone architecture of what was traditionally a poor region, but today is a popular tourist destination.

Casa Bernasconi, Carona, Ticino, Switzerland, 1989. **Luigi Snozzi**. **b** Mendrisio, Switzerland, 1932.

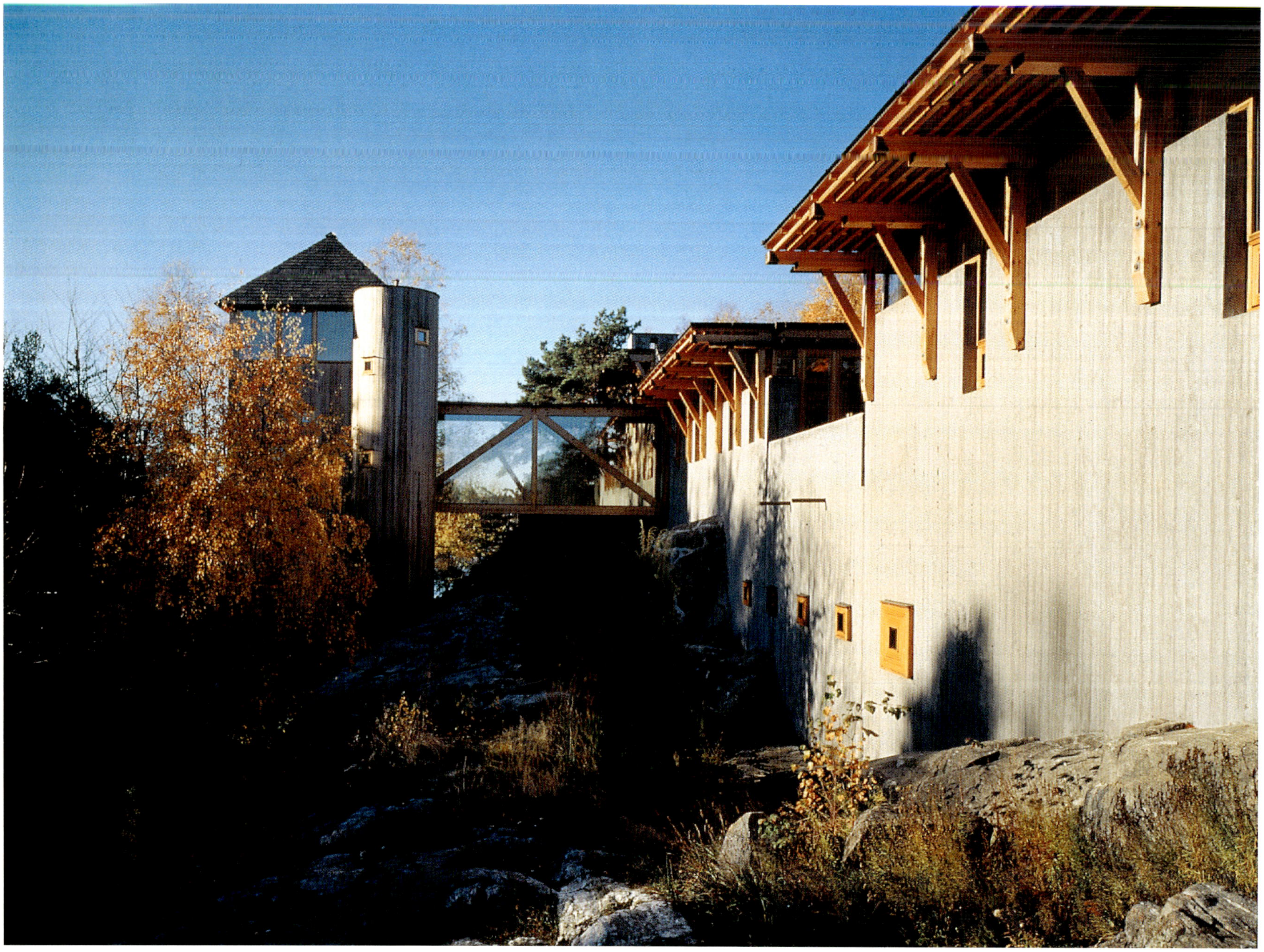

Villa Busk Sverre Fehn

Situated on rocky terrain along the Oslofjorden, the Villa Busk is anchored to the sloping ground with solid concrete walls, which give way to a lighter, timber-constructed roof. Sometimes called the 'poet of the straight line', Sverre Fehn plays on this theme in the rational plan of the house, built along the 'internal route' of a single corridor that runs its entire length. The adjoining four-storey tower, reached by an enclosed, glazed bridge, has children's rooms on the lower level and a study above, connected by a spiral stair. Avoiding a sensationalist 'signature' style, Fehn's thoughtful use of such materials as wood and concrete is similar to that of Louis Kahn, creating a tension with the natural setting by the undisguised human intervention. Noted as a regionalist architect, Fehn's work was cited by the 1997 Pritzker Prize jury for 'a fascinating and exciting combination of modern forms tempered by the Scandinavian tradition'.

Villa Busk, Bamble, Norway, 1987–90. **Sverre Fehn**. **b** Kongsberg, Norway, 1924.

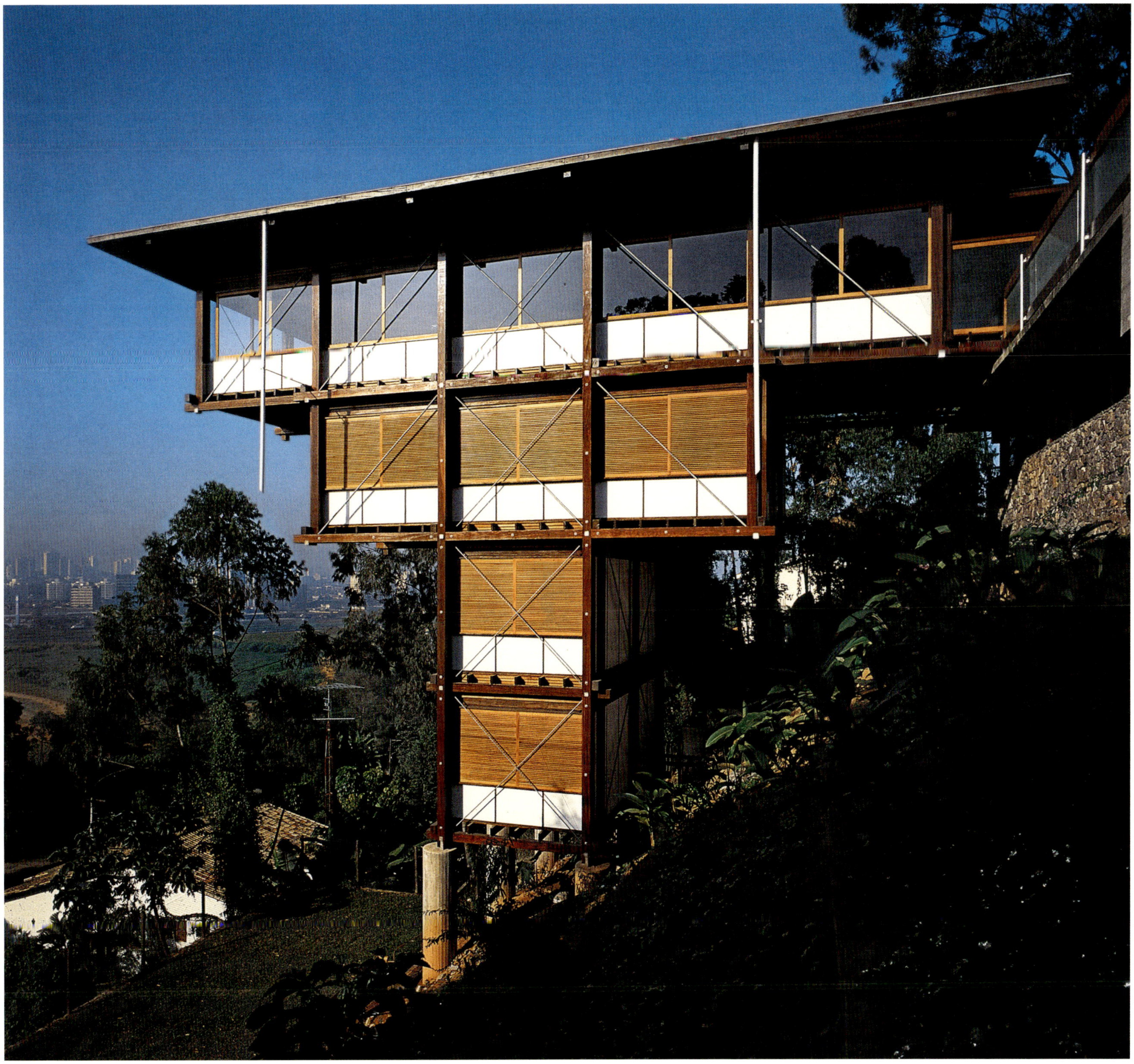

Residencia Olga Marcos Acayaba

A modern, inverted ziggurat forms the daring structure of the Residencia Olga. Built on a steeply sloping site, the project was conceived by Marcos Acayaba as a prototype of standardized housing for highly uneven hill sites common in Brazilian cities. Six concrete columns, sunk into the ground, provide the support for an industrialized wooden structure which is tied to the slope higher up for further stability. Three regular bays are divided into four levels of accommodation: the bottom three levels contain bedrooms, while the top level is an open-plan spacious living, dining and kitchen area. The house is entered from the top of the cliff at this level, giving an illusion of walking into open space, and the grounds here are landscaped with a swimming pool, terrace and garage. By using a modular system of bays, reinforced by cross-bracings, the cost and use of material is minimized, while the owners benefit from an uninterrupted view across the city.

Residencia Olga, São Paulo, Brazil, 1989–91. **Marcos Acayaba**. **b** São Paulo, Brazil, 1944.

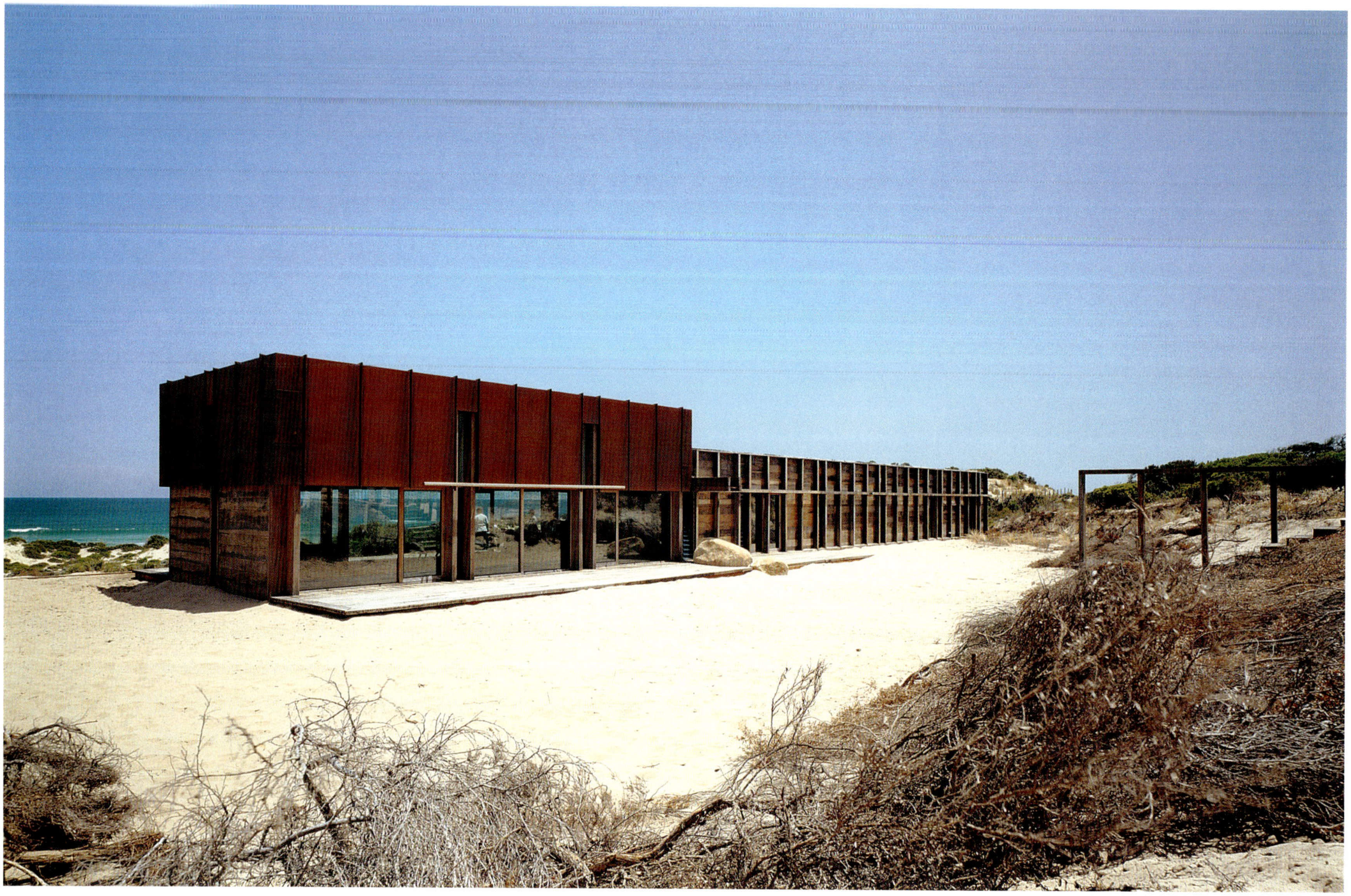

St Andrews House Nonda Katsalidis

More like a beached shipping container than a home, St Andrews House, says its architect, the acclaimed Australian designer Nonda Katsalidis, is a fusion of sentimental vernacular sources with the abstract traditions at the heart of Modernism. The house's rusty-looking, Corten steel and rough-hewn wood planking are reminiscent of traditional Australian building forms — the sort of rough-and-ready barns and outbuildings that you find in small settlements up and down the country. Yet here, Katsalidis has put them together with such knowing precision that they take on quite different connotations. The house has a straightforward arrangement: the heavy sections of recycled timber provide privacy for the bedroom wing; the living area is a large double-height space, glazed at ground-floor level, and clad above in Corten steel, the russet colour of which is echoed in the surrounding vegetation.

St Andrews House, St Andrews Beach, Mornington Peninsula, VIC, Australia, 1991. **Nonda Katsalidis**. **b** Athens, Greece, 1951.

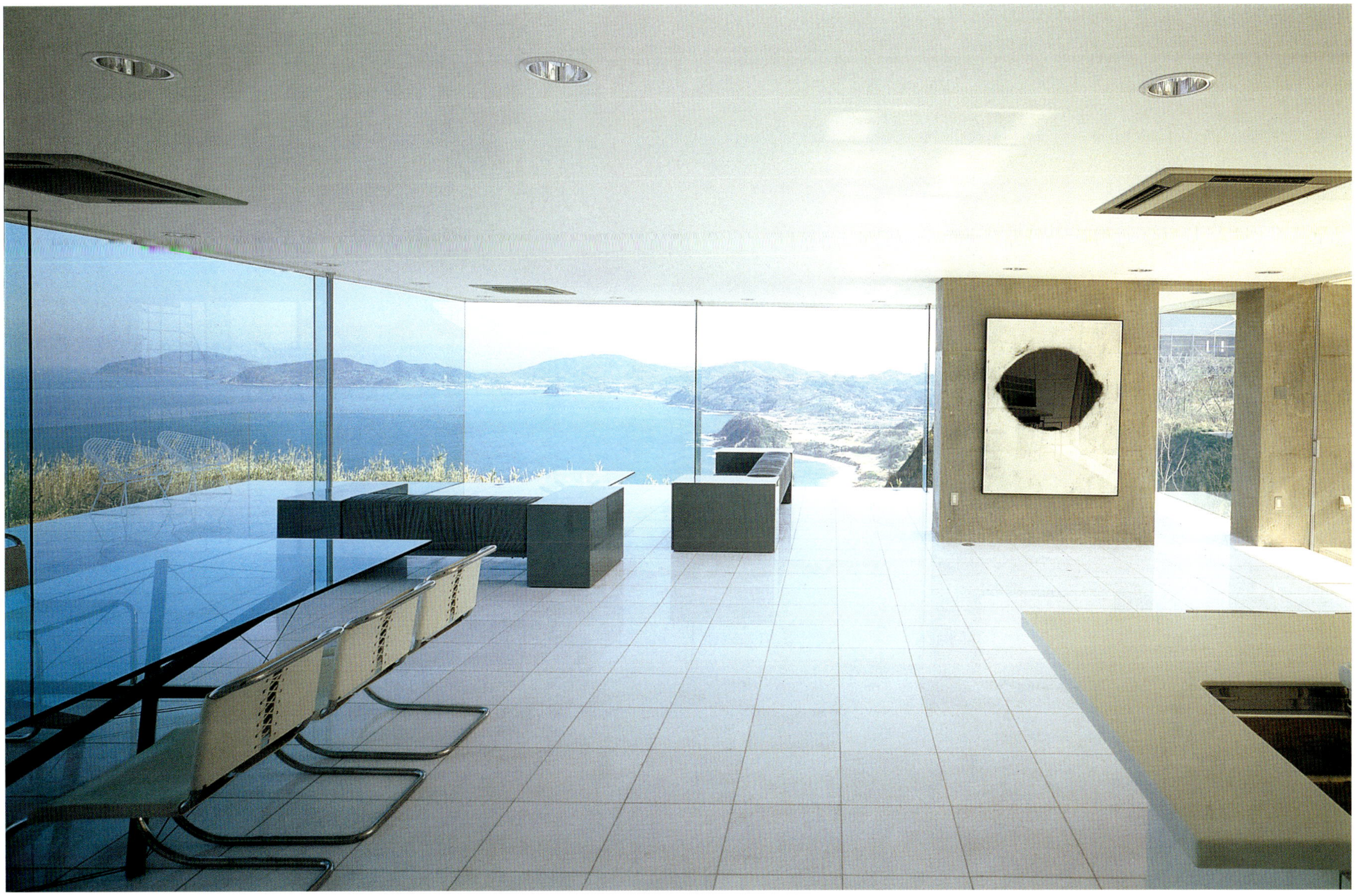

Another Glass House Between Sea and Sky Shoei Yoh

Parallel concrete walls set into the hillside support two cantilevered, shelf-like slabs between which enclosing glass walls define the interior space while providing maximum views. With this house, located on a steep hill site in Fukuoka overlooking the Sea of Japan, Shoei Yoh explores an idea of 'levitation' which he realizes by contrasting the apparent instability and lightness of the building with the solidity and weightiness of the site. With its vertical anchorage and horizontal cantilever, this structure can be understood not only as a technological innovation, but also as an expression of the unique relationship between the building and its surroundings. Yoh believes that the most beautiful structures are those which, deceptively, do not look strong, and he has produced many transparent designs, from furniture to museums. As a result, he is well known for his attention to light in his buildings, as perfectly demonstrated here.

Another Glass House Between Sea and Sky, Itoshima, Fukuoka, Japan, 1991. **Shoei Yoh**. **b** Kumamoto, Japan, 1940.

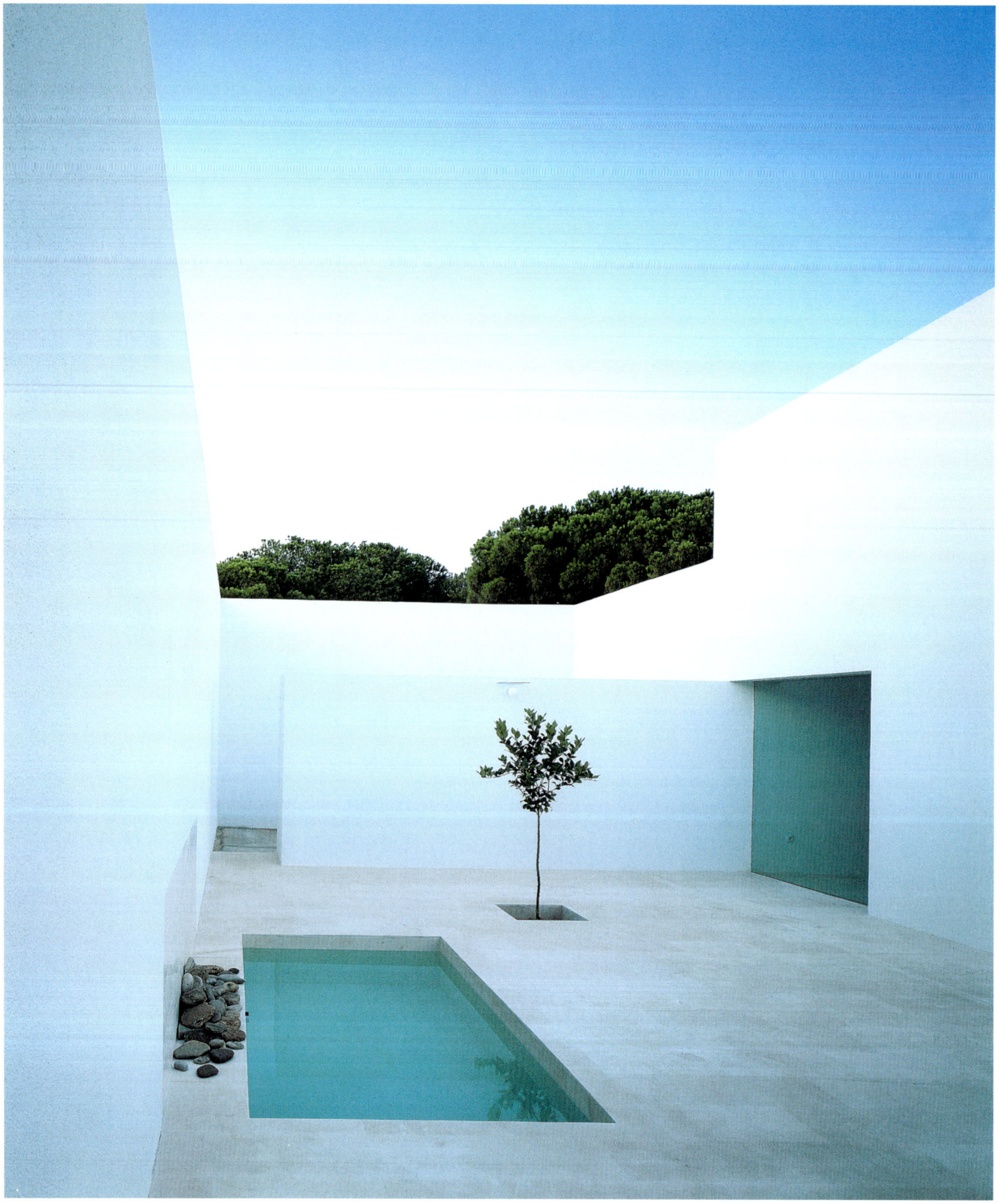

Casa Gaspar Alberto Campo Baeza

Casa Gaspar's high exterior walls, forming a perfect 18 m (60 ft) square, are unfenestrated despite its spectacular setting in an orange grove in southern Spain. The introspective plan is divided into three equal parts — two courtyards on either side of the central, generously proportioned house — all of which emphasize a deft control of direct and reflected light. Although the all-white planar architecture recalls the purist movement of the early twentieth century, the house's simple plan and stark geometry is indebted to Mies van der Rohe's courtyard house studies of the 1930s, as well as to the work of Luis Barragán. Campo Baeza's affinities with the sparse yet luxuriously detailed aesthetics of minimalism are evident, rather than an allegiance to the geometric gymnastics of his Spanish contemporaries, Torres & Lapeña. The Gaspar house sums up Campo Baeza's goal of 'achieving everything with almost nothing: more with less'.

Casa Gaspar, Cadiz, Spain, 1992. **Alberto Campo Baeza**. **b** Valladolid, Spain, 1946.

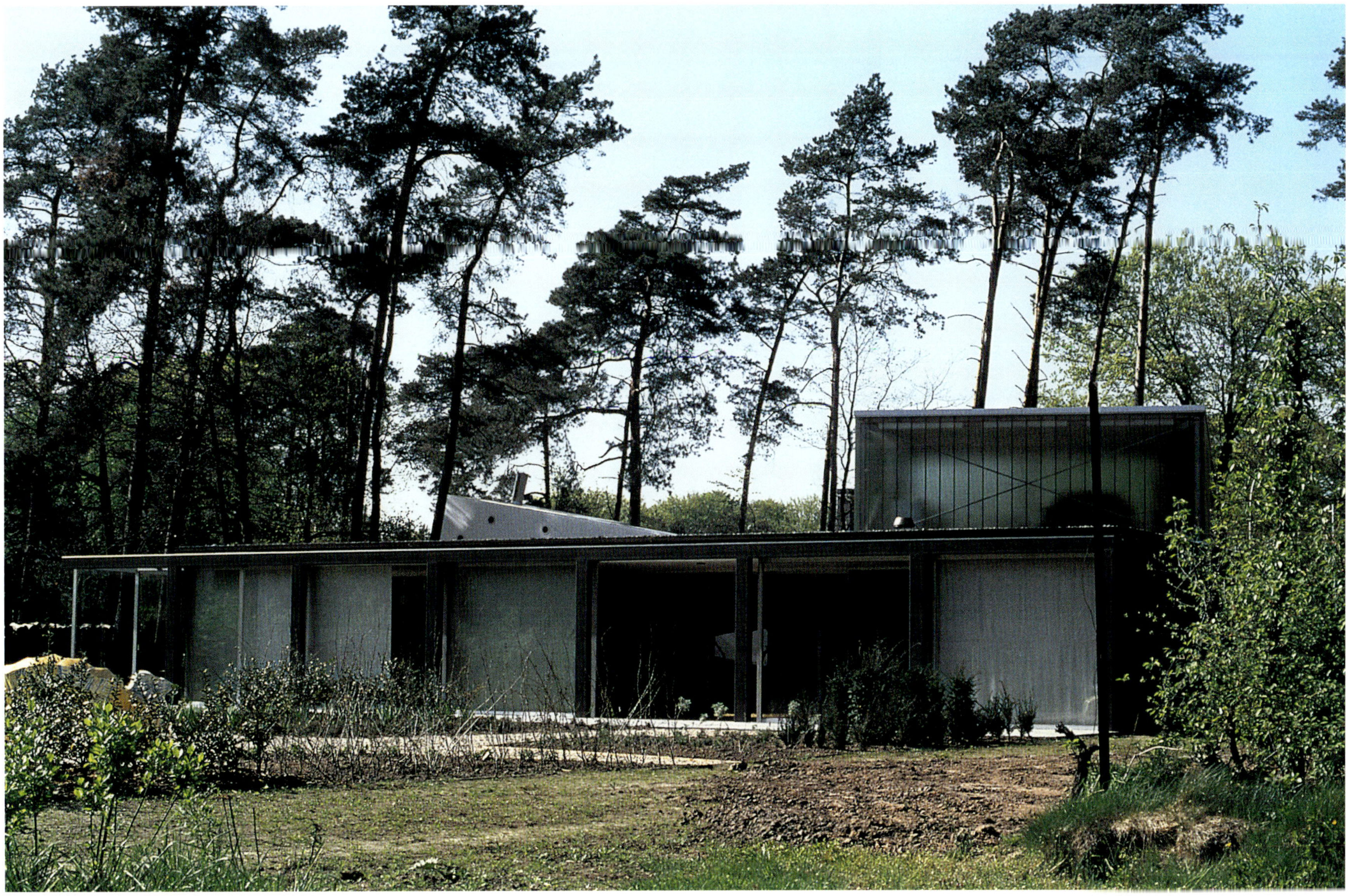

House in Brasschaat Xaveer de Geyter

Glass walls loosely defining living spaces that open onto enclosed courtyards belie the private nature of this ultra-modern villa. Taking advantage of a natural forested hill on this small suburban site, the architect buries the front of the structure into a dune, leaving only the canopy of the rooftop garage and entry exposed to its neighbours. Inverting the example of Le Corbusier's 'promenade architecturale', a ramp takes the visitor down towards the single-storey living quarters with their glass curtain walls. The ramp also acts as the divider between the private spaces, which open onto enclosed patios, and the communal living spaces, which open to the terrace and views of the garden beyond. The result is an open plan that still maintains a high level of privacy between the rooms. The architect successfully develops the concept of the airy Mies van der Rohe courtyard house, while gracefully overcoming the site's suburban constraints.

House in Brasschaat, Antwerp, Belgium, 1990–2. **Xaveer de Geyter**. **b** Doornik, Belgium, 1957.

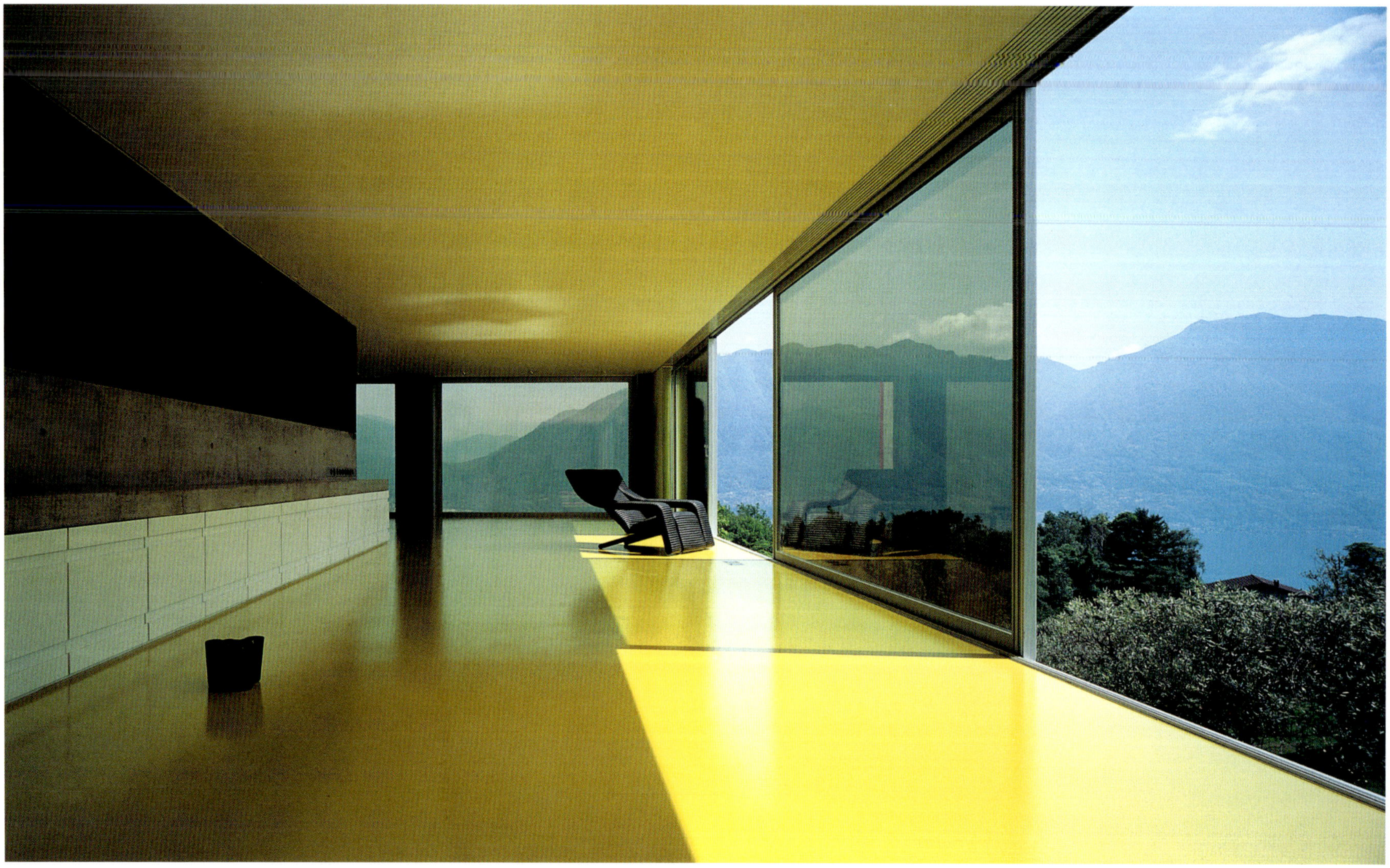

House at Tenero-Contra Livio Vacchini

Crisp geometries float against the mountain landscape, the full-height, sliding glass windows inviting you to step out into mid-air. But the shrill, stridently artificial yellow floor and raw concrete walls and roof bring you dramatically back to the reality of this house. The precast, reinforced concrete roof is supported by three columns (painted black) on the end elevations, giving the impression that this huge room has no vertical structure, but is rather sandwiched between the floor and the ceiling. The long concrete wall subdivides the rectangular space and screens the bathroom, kitchen and a dining alcove on the other side; these functions are not integral, but inserted like furniture. The building is trying to be a pure, uncompromising piece of architecture rather than fulfil a specific function, and is an almost rhetorical development of a classic Modernist building by Mies van der Rohe, the Farnsworth House.

House at Tenero-Contra, Ticino, Switzerland, 1991–2. **Livio Vacchini**. **b** Locarno, Ticino, Switzerland, 1933.

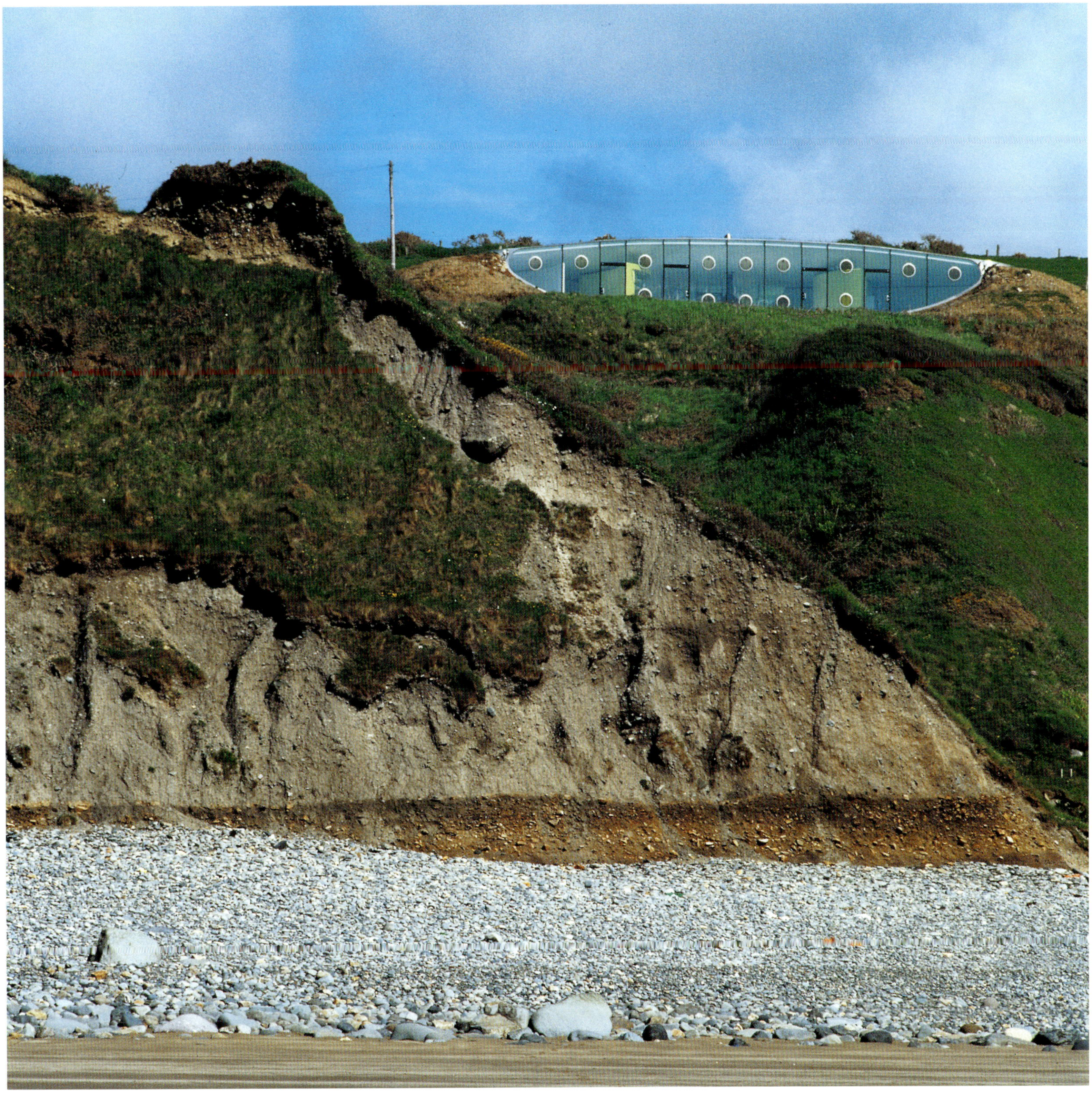

Project 222 Future Systems

This house is all but invisible; only the ellipse-shaped glazed facade orientated towards the sea gives away the fact of human presence on the site. The facade has been described as a lens, cut into the landscape above the cliffs on the Welsh coastline, trained on the magnificent view west which gives the house its *raison d'être*. The rest of the structure, consisting of an arc-shaped retaining wall banked up with earth, and a plywood roof laid on a steel ring-beam, is camouflaged with grass. Inside, a single space is divided by freestanding service pods, containing the bathroom and kitchen, and is dominated by a large circular sofa. The architects have built their reputation on innovation, pushing their designs to the aesthetic and technical limits. This house represents a development of the 'unique language of curvaceous forms' that characterizes most of their work, not least the Media Centre at Lord's Cricket Ground (1999) and Selfridges in Birmingham (2003).

Project 222, St Bride's Bay, Wales, UK, 1994. **Future Systems**. **Jan Kaplicky**. **b** Prague, Czech Republic, 1937. **d** Prague, Czech Republic, 2009. **Amanda Levette**. **b** Bridgend, UK, 1955.

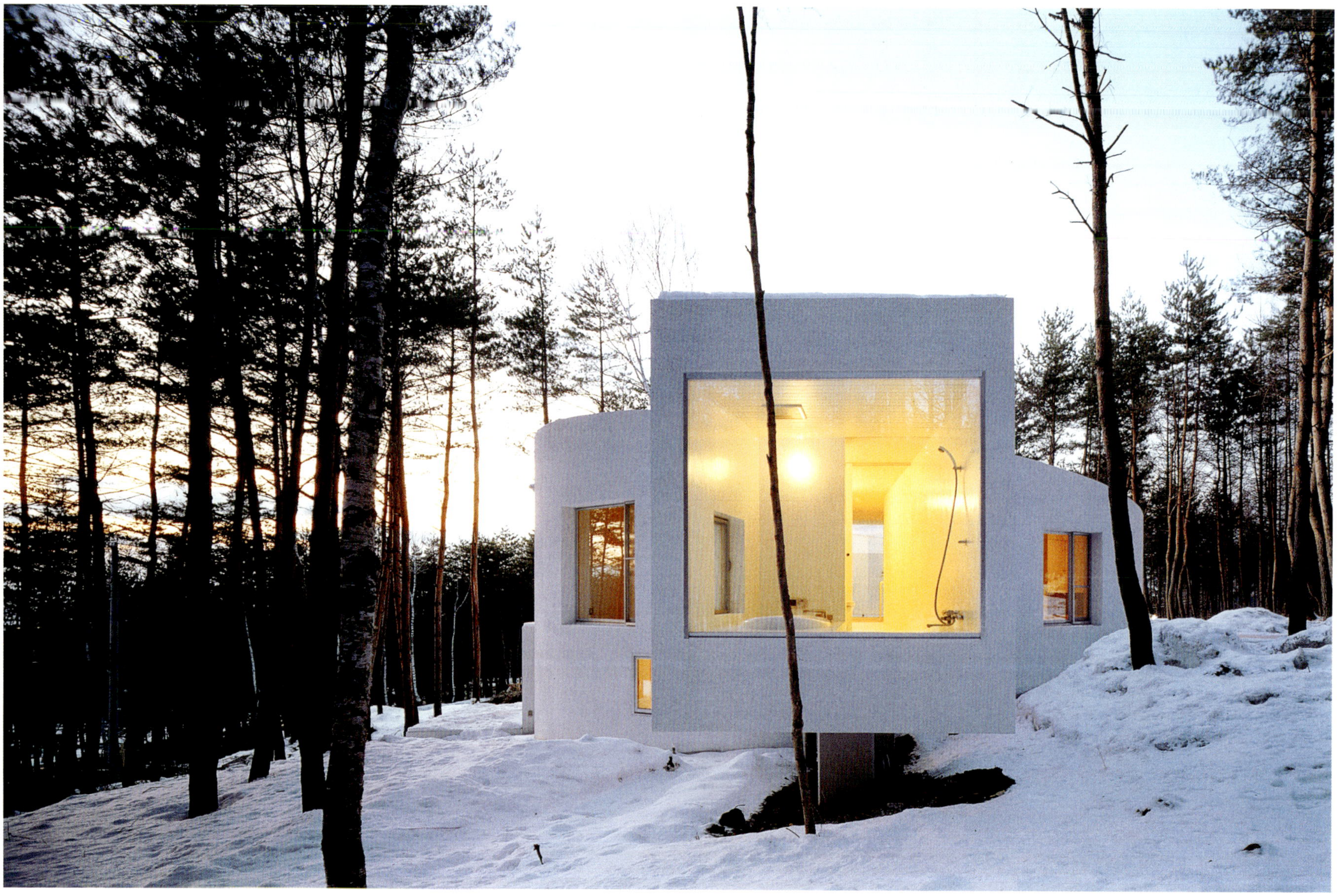

Villa in the Forest Kazuyo Sejima

The client of this house, a scientist who also deals in paintings, commissioned this as a second home to accommodate artists visiting from abroad. The house consists of two circular walls that each have different centres; the outer wall delineates a profile of the house while the inner wall divides the house into two parts, an atelier and a dwelling space. Due to its forest location in a cold climate, the house has a thick concrete perimeter wall. Kazuyo Sejima, whose earlier projects had emphasized a continuity between inside and outside, wanted to create a self-contained continuity within the building's substantial walls. The continuous space between the two eccentric circular walls gently diminishes and extends in width and height, demonstrating her almost obsessive preoccupation with circular movement. Here Sejima offers a simple yet evocative response to the demands of the forest environment and her client's practical requirements.

Villa in the Forest, Tateshina, Japan, 1994. **Kazuyo Sejima**. **b** Ibaraki, Japan, 1956.

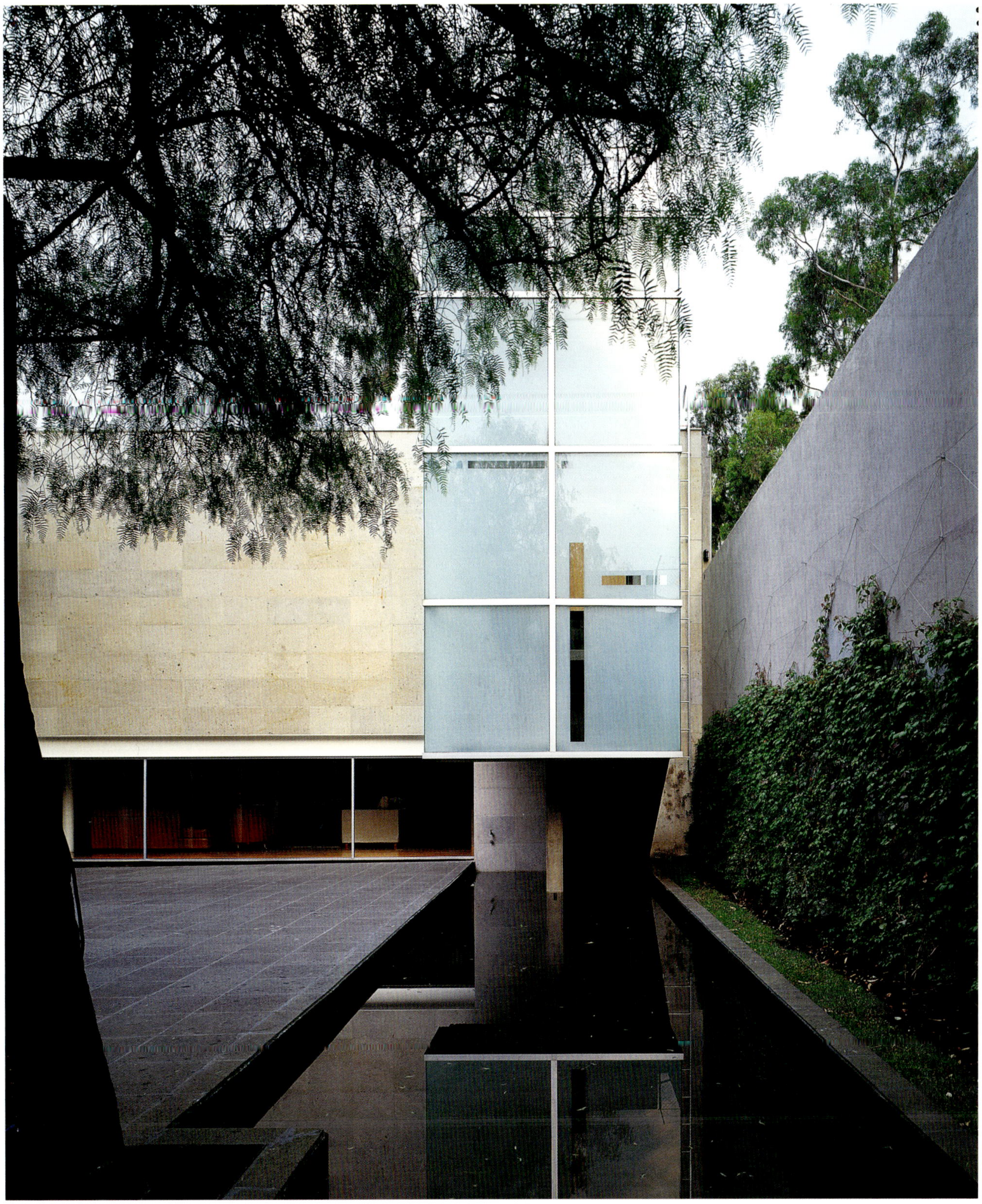

Casa RR TEN Arquitectos

The luminous, aquamarine glass stairtower, smooth stone wall and shimmering, reflecting pool of this courtyard house suggest a sleek townhouse. In fact, it is a suburban family home outside Mexico City that draws on the time-honoured courtyard house of colonial Latin America. Designed by local architect, Enrique Norten of TEN Arquitectos, who favours sophisticated forms and materials over historical ones, the house has an inwardly focused paved courtyard that screens out the surrounding neighbourhood. The stairs, encased in translucent glass that is incised with clear strips, lead to a catwalk that provides access to the bedrooms, screened by a smooth stone wall. Below the stone is a band of clear glass that looks into a double-height living room. With its composition of various masses and materials, the house suggests an abstract version of the individual buildings that ring Mexico's colourful *zócalos*, or public plazas.

Casa RR, Mexico City, Mexico, 1996. **TEN (Taller de Enrique Norten) Arquitectos**. **Enrique Norten**. **b** Mexico City, Mexico, 1954.

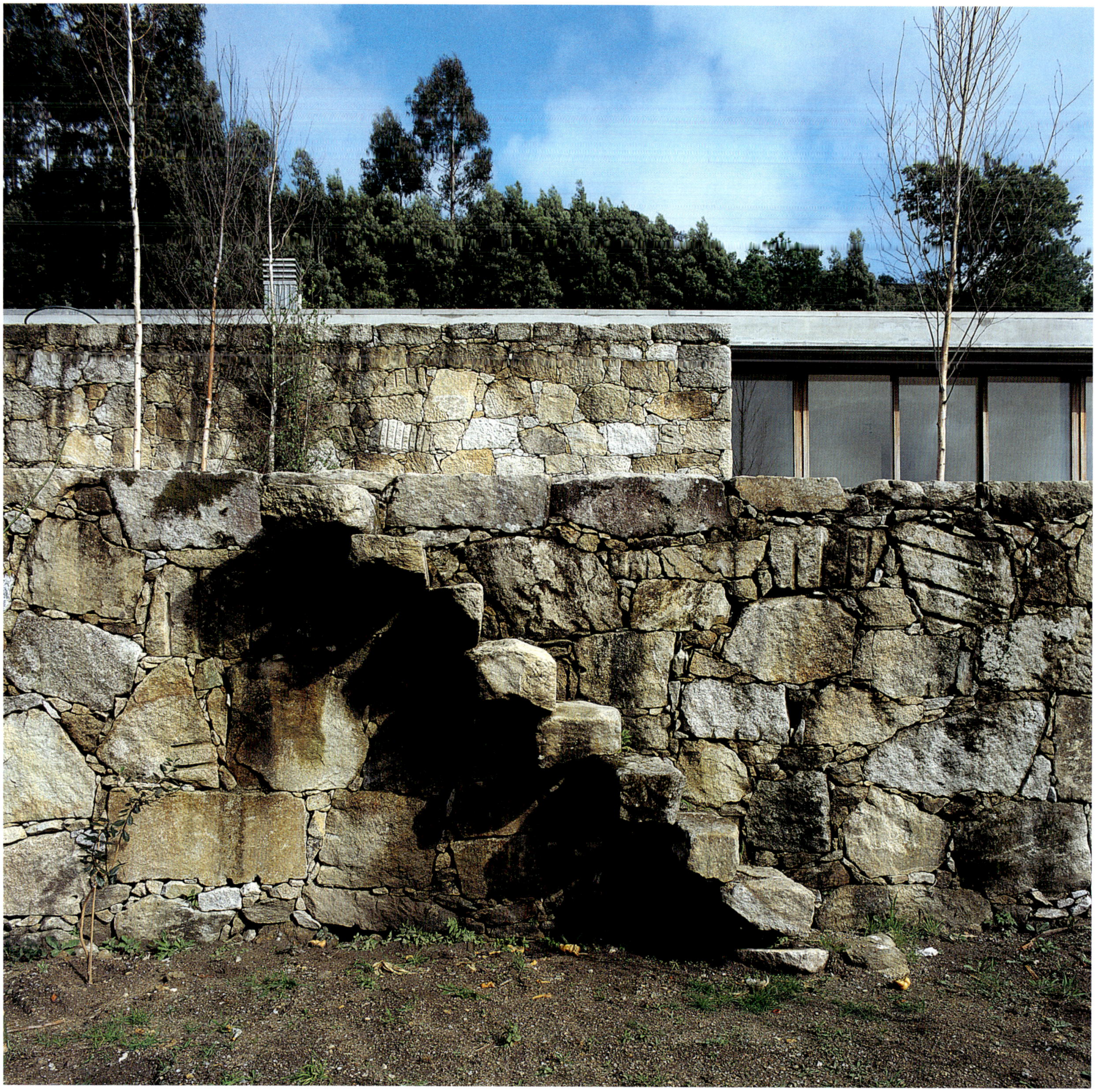

Casa Moledo Eduardo Souto de Moura

Architectural critics have identified a 'School of Oporto' — which includes Eduardo Souto de Moura and Álvaro Siza among others — united in a non-doctrinaire response to the complexities of a country in a sometimes difficult transition from its agricultural past. Here, granite walls, like those of the surrounding vineyards of northern Portugal, step up the hillside to form a series of flat terraces. Where the walls become higher, they split to reveal a simple house form — comprising a single row of rooms, glazed both front and back. The topmost terrace is a flat roof which appears almost to float above the live rock of the hillside. Beyond this is a spectacular view over the valley and towards the Atlantic Ocean. The Casa Moledo demonstrates a theme common in Souto de Moura's buildings: the fusion of traditional and modern, of using vernacular architecture without resorting to artifice. The simplest possible means are used, with the richest possible results.

Casa Moledo, Caminha, Portugal, 1998. **Eduardo Souto de Moura**. **b** Oporto, Portugal, 1952.

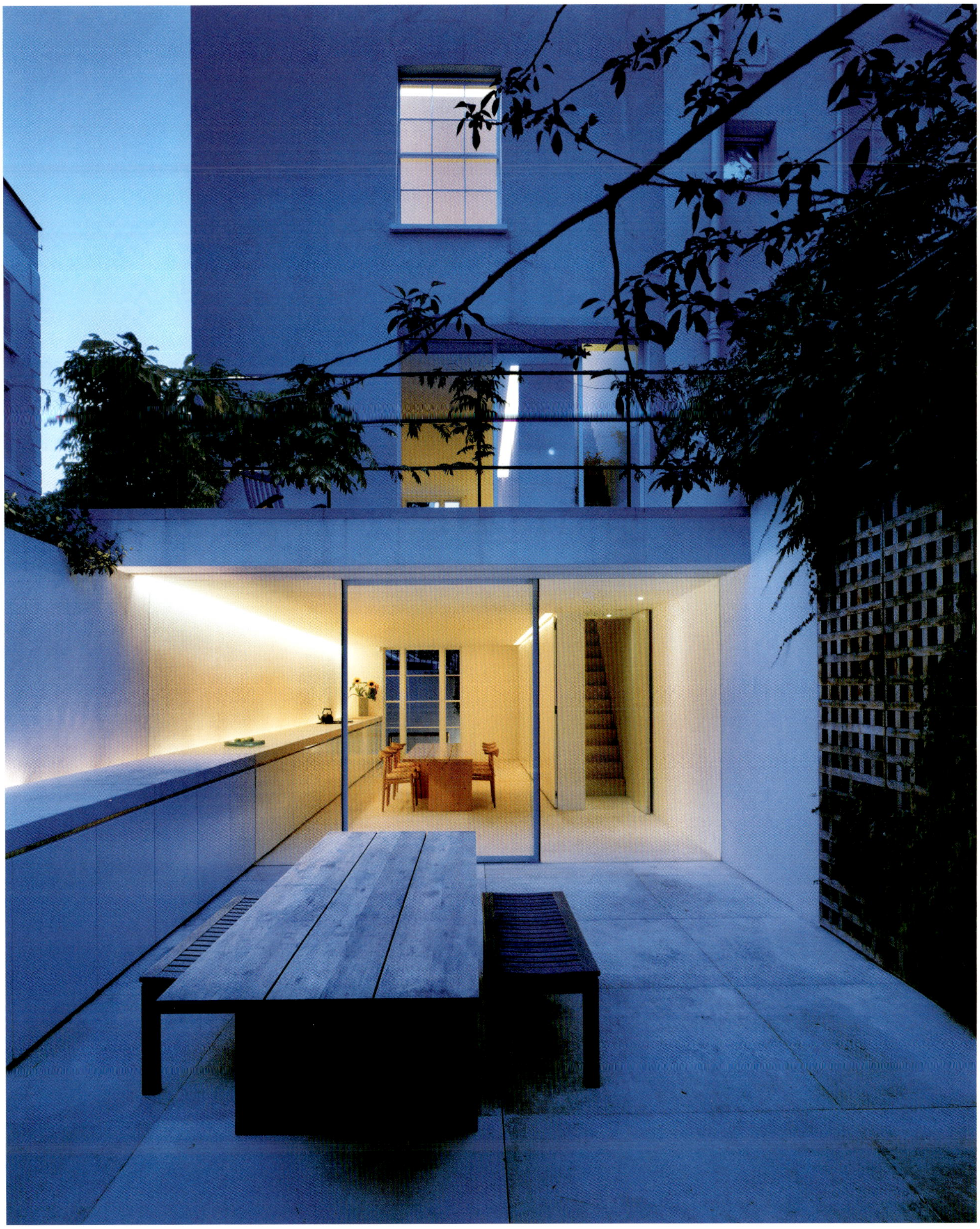

Pawson House John Pawson

If Modernism is a way of escaping decadence then minimalism must be its ultimate expression, stripping away any suggestion of ornamentation. John Pawson has been credited as the inventor of this architectural style and his home in west London is one of the finest examples of the minimalist aesthetic. The house is based on the shell of a Victorian terrace, the facade of which could not be altered due to planning restrictions. Inside however, the building has been completely transformed and the layout revised to create a large uninterrupted space furnished in high-quality materials. The open-plan living room is clad with Douglas Fir floorboards that stretch the depth of the house and beyond, forming the garden balcony outside. The focal point is the basement kitchen which extends out into the courtyard garden, interior and exterior divided only by a sliding glass wall. Pawson is primarily concerned with a lack of visual disorder and the house is virtually bare, affording it a starkly calm aesthetic.

Pawson House, London, UK, 1999. **John Pawson**. **b** Halifax, UK, 1949.

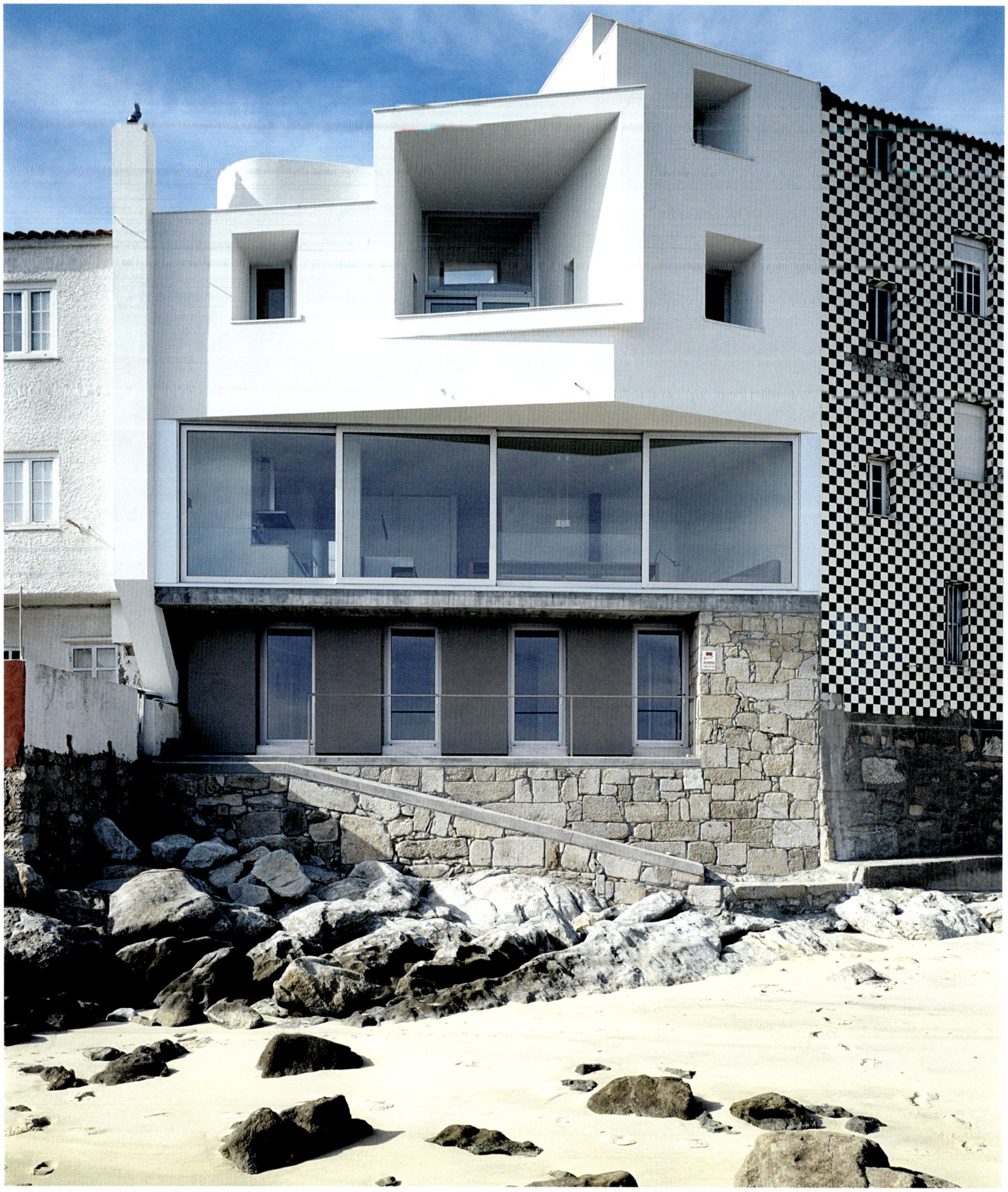

Private House in Corrubedo David Chipperfield

David Chipperfield's Spanish holiday home embodies the Modernist conviction that form should follow function. Defying local tradition, the house faces the sea rather than the busy road on its other side, using new technologies such as an aluminium facade system to combat the extreme Atlantic weather. Privacy is optimized by a minimum of window openings on the street elevation, concentrating light and space on the beach front with a huge glass wall that exploits the dramatic ocean vista. Above, a terrace protrudes towards the sea like the deck of a boat, a nautical feel accentuated by the cabin-like bedrooms below. The jutting geometric irregularity of the windows and roof reflect the shifting patterns of the sea's surface beyond. Although the unadorned modernity of the angular facade contrasts starkly with the surrounding vernacular architecture, Chipperfield attempts to unify the building with the existing terrace of houses by using matching colours and materials.

Private House in Corrubedo, Galicia, Spain, 1996–2002. **David Chipperfield**. **b** London, UK, 1953.

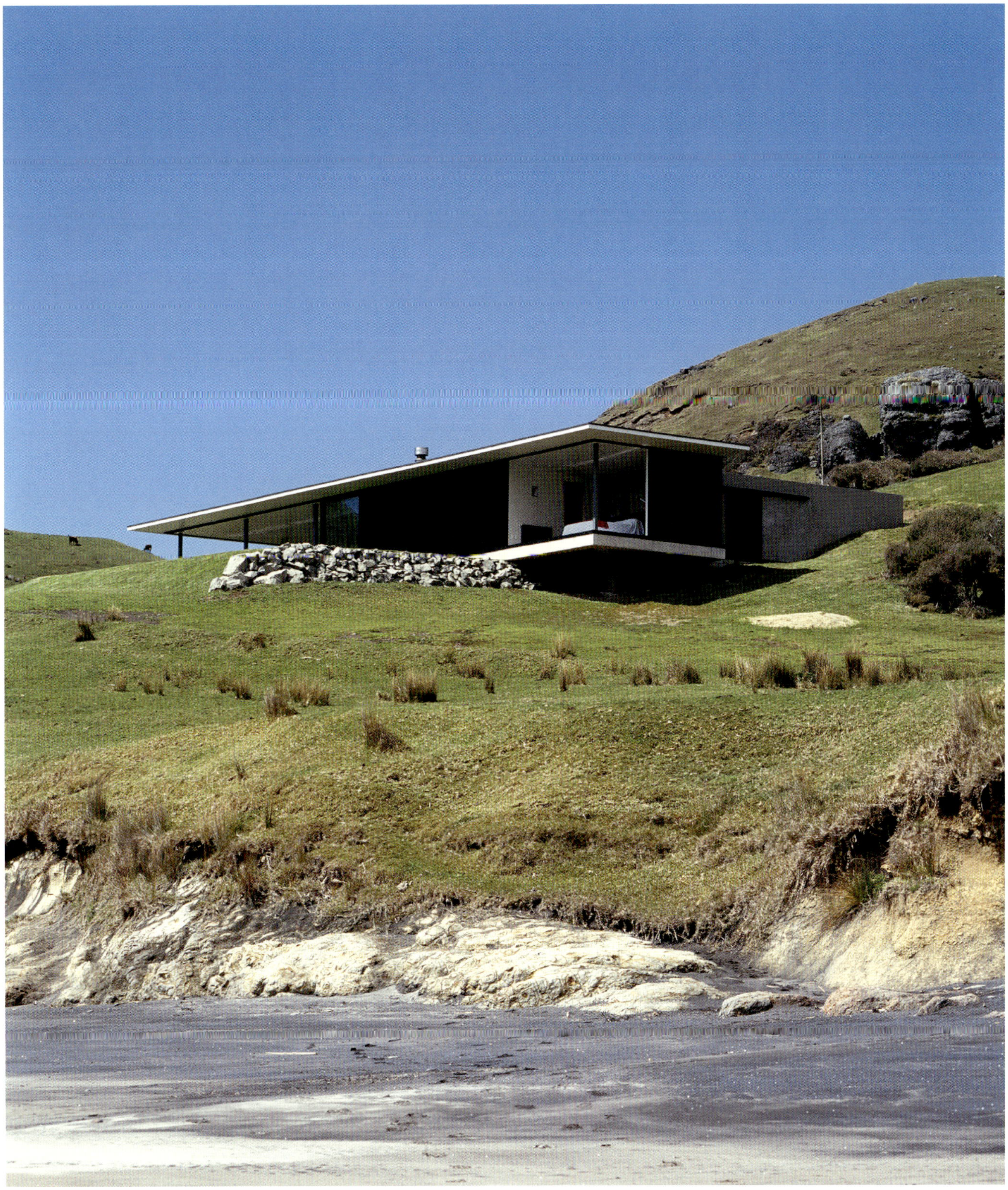

Shark Alley House Fearon Hay Architects

Nestled in an isolated cove of New Zealand's Great Barrier Island, Shark Alley House must be one of the remotest Modernist buildings in the world. The Auckland-based architects Fearon Hay are known for constructing minimal contemporary architecture amid diverse landscapes. Here the surroundings are beautiful but inhospitable and there is no electrical grid or public water supply. The single-storey house is a small yet quietly confident example of clean functional living. Such an unashamedly cosmopolitan design could seem incongruous when juxtaposed with the untamed environment but it has a simplicity of form that does not compete with the magnificence of its setting. Rather, the man-made embraces the natural as the glass exterior walls slide on tracks to open the house up to the elements, while aluminium shutters are available to protect against storms. Once the walls are removed, the interior becomes a viewing platform for the sea and sky, and only the skeleton of the structure remains.

Shark Alley House, Oruawharo Bay, Great Barrier Island, New Zealand, 2003. **Fearon Hay Architects**. **Jeff Fearon**. **b** Auckland, New Zealand, 1972. **Tim Hay**. **b** Auckland, New Zealand, 1973.

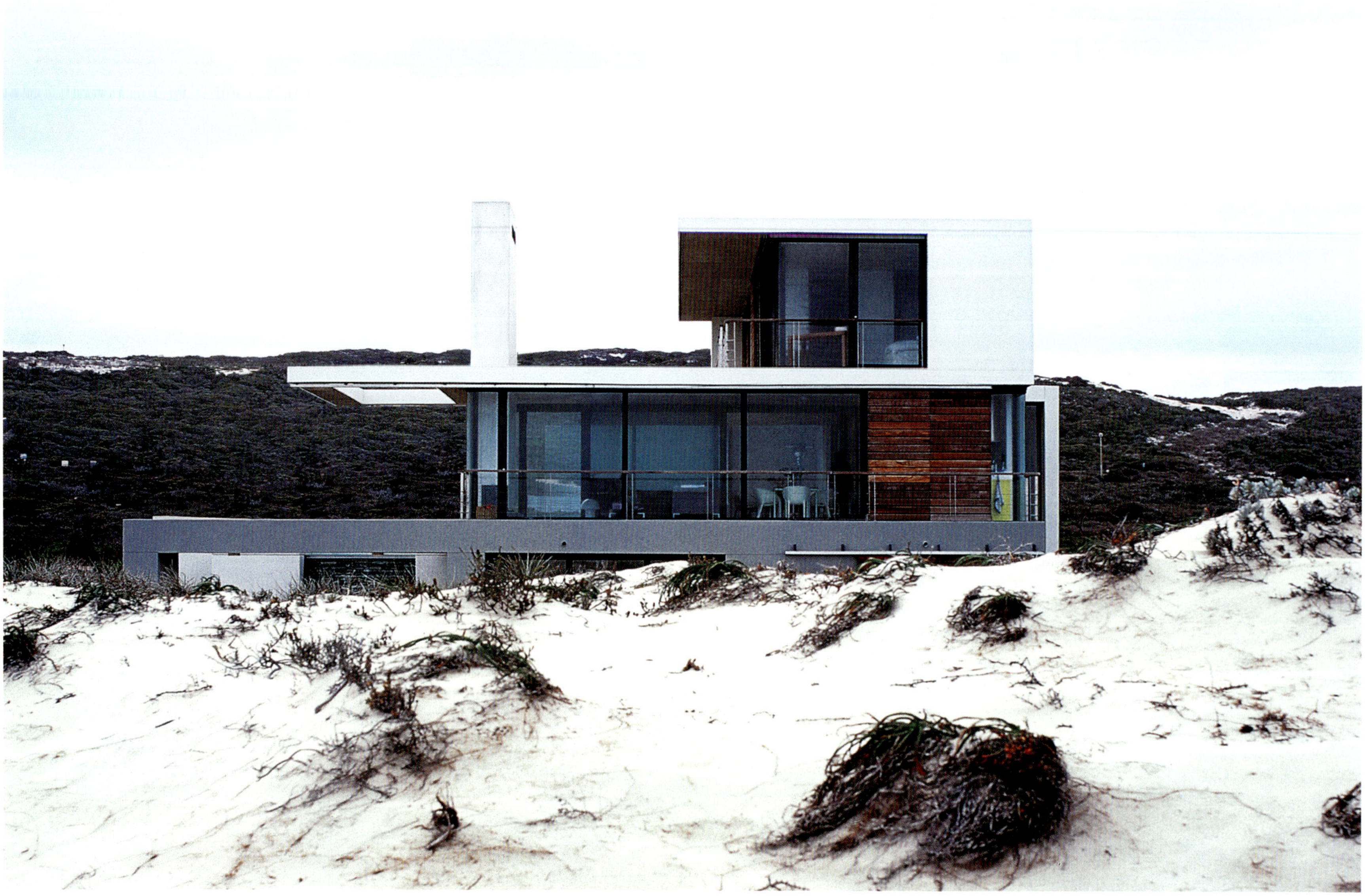

Yzerfontein House Stefan Antoni Olmesdahl Truen Architects

The South African architect Stefan Antoni has a reputation for tempering International Modernist stylistic traits, such as the employment of light and glass, with an understanding of local vernacular and natural materials. This two-bedroom vacation house for a Manhattan couple hovers over sand dunes in an undeveloped area of the coast. An L-shaped plan exploits the magnificent beach vista while creating a sheltered courtyard and pool area. Sliding glass walls allow the main living area to be opened up to the elements, while timber screens provide shade and privacy. A dramatic cantilevered staircase leads from the upper bedrooms and roof garden down to the basement studio. Antoni has used simple but high-quality materials: embossed concrete ceilings, polished cement floors and minimalist white plaster walls, eliminating unnecessary detail. The effect is sculptural, with a clean linearity and sophistication that contrasts pleasingly with the other more generic developments in the locality.

Yzerfontein House, Yzerfontein, South Africa, 2005. **Stefan Antoni Olmesdahl Truen Architects**. **Stefan Antoni**. **b** Cape Town, South Africa, 1963. **Richard Townsend**. **b** Cape Town, South Africa, 1966.

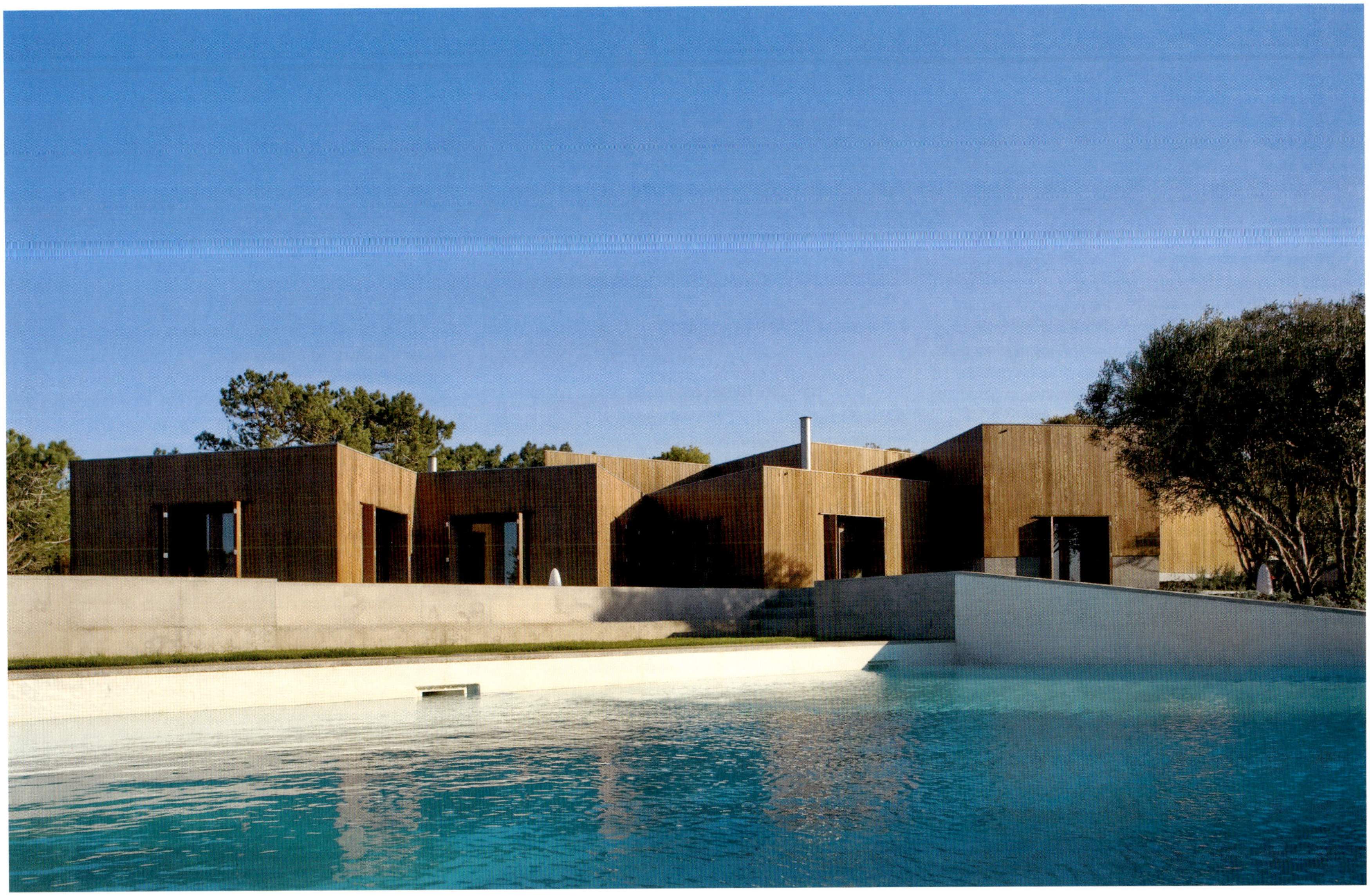

House in Pego Álvaro Siza

Álvaro Siza is known for his masterful, sculptural architecture. Functionality is a key priority in his work and elegant contemporary form invariably follows. His style is one of understated Modernism and there is a connection between his buildings and the natural environment. This single-storey house sprawls across the highest part of a sloping seafront site. The plan is an irregular, organic shape with the rooms running off a central circulation stem like the petals of a flower. This arrangement creates semi-private courtyard spaces between the rooms that enjoy stunning views and allow integration with the surrounding landscape. Light is used as an active architectural tool, not just as a means of illumination, and the connecting corridor has strategic viewing portals that create contemplative stopping points. The cubic structure is composed of simple materials: masonry clad in treated timber with a concrete roof covered with metal sheeting. Detail is kept to a minimum allowing the strength of the design to dominate.

House in Pego, Sintra, Portugal, 2002–7. **Álvaro Siza Vieira**. **b** Matosinhos, Portugal, 1933.

Moderne

A term used in the United States in the 1930s, synonymous with **Art Deco**.

Modernisme *see* Art Nouveau

Mullion

The vertical divisions between the glass panes in a window.

Neo-Rationalism

Neo-Rationalism (also called Tendenza) was a late twentieth-century movement that evolved in the 1960s after Italian architect, Aldo Rossi, published *L'Architettura della città* (Architecture of the City) in 1966. The movement favoured historical continuity and embraced Renaissance theories and **Classical** principles. Rejecting **Functionalism** and technology, Neo-Rationalists preferred the use of the old fabric of the city as a source of inspiration and reference, rather than the total reinvention of architecture as **Modernism** had advocated.

New York Five

A loose association of five architects whose work was exhibited at the Museum of Modern Art in New York in 1962 and was published in the 1972 book *Five Architects*. Also referred to as the 'Whites' (due to the absence of colour in their work), Peter Eisenman, Michael Graves, Charles Gwathmey, John Hejduk and Richard Meier all presented work that displayed a formal return to the **International Style** of the 1930s.
See page 78

Orders

Used in **Classical** architecture, an order is an assemblage of parts consisting principally of a column (base, shaft and capital) and an **entablature** (**architrave**, **frieze** and **cornice**), all proportioned and decorated according to one of the so-called Five Orders.
Doric: Characterized by a massive column placed on the ground without a base, terminating in a simple capital (crowning part of a column). The entablature consisted of a plain architrave and an ornamented frieze.
Ionic: The spreading scroll-shaped volute in the capital is the distinctive feature and the slender fluted shaft is used with a base. The entablature has a three-banded architrave and a frieze adorned with sculpture.
Corinthian: The most ornate of the Orders which, except for the distinctive capital decorated with acanthus leaves and volutes, is similar to the Ionic Order.
Tuscan: A simplified form of the Doric Order, the column has a simple base, and the capital and entablature above are stripped of ornament.
Composite: A variation of the Corinthian Order, the Composite Order is characterized by a capital which combines Corinthian foliage and Ionic volutes.

Organic Architecture

An elusive term that can and has been applied to widely diverse practices and forms. The early work of Frank Lloyd Wright and Alvar Aalto embodied a concept of organicism in which the parts of the building are inseparable from the whole, which in turn has an inseparable symbiotic relationship with nature. Conversely, architects in the late twentieth century have increasingly turned to scientific, mathematical and biological sources for inspiration, typically incorporating soft, flowing curvilinear shapes.
See pages 24, 44, 57 and 103

Pediment

A low-pitched gable front at the top of a Classical **Order**, often incorporating elaborate sculpture.

Piano nobile

The principal floor of a building, accommodating the reception, entertaining and living spaces. It is usually located above the ground floor and entered via a staircase in the entry hall. External facade treatments, such as large windows, indicate the importance given to the spaces within.
See page 36

Pilaster

A rectangular, non-structural projection with the appearance of a column, attached to the surface of a wall, which in **Classical** architecture conforms to one of the **Orders**.

Pilotis

A French word for columns that raise a building above the ground, creating an open space beneath. Used to great spatial and aesthetic effect by Le Corbusier and adopted by architects of the **Modern Movement** as a consistent motif.
See pages 25 and 62

Plan

An accurately scaled, two-dimensional drawing of a building seen from above, showing the arrangement of rooms and the thickness and composition of the walls. (See Elevation & Section)

Portico

A colonnaded roofed porch attached to the front of a building.

Post-Modern (also Post-Modernism)

A term used in the 1970s to refer to the work of architects who took a reactive stance against **Modernism** and the **Bauhaus**. Also known as POMO and P-M, Post-Modern architecture favoured a pluralist, eclectic aesthetic, often incorporating abstracted or simplistic references to **Classical** motifs, such as oversized columns, broken **pediments** and colourful mouldings.

Prairie Style (also Prairie School)

A style of architecture in the Midwestern United States between circa 1900 and 1916, named after designs by Frank Lloyd Wright — such as the Robie House in Chicago (1910) — which were inspired by the simple farm buildings of the American prairies. The style was characterized by low-pitched **roofs** with large overhanging eaves, a strong horizontal emphasis and the dominance of the hearth as the focus of the living spaces.
See pages 4 and 40

Prefabrication (also Prefabs)

A construction system in which the components of a building are manufactured and partly assembled in a factory before being transported and erected on site.
See pages 23, 51 and 58

Quoin

The external corner of a building, formed by placing alternating small and large stones in a vertical stack, raised from the surface of the wall to turn the corner.

Rationalism

A movement founded in Italy in 1926 by Gruppo 7 (Group of 7) and associated with the rise of Fascism in Italy. Italian architect Guiseppe Terragni was the key exponent; his Casa del Fascio building in Como (1932–6) is arguably the defining building of the movement. An essentially **Modernist** movement, Rationalism concerned itself with the pursuit of reason and encompassed a strong social, economic and political agenda, motivated by a desire to improve society through architecture.
See pages 35, 42, 77, 80 and 85

Render

A finish applied to a surface, usually a wall. Render is applied wet and can be worked to a smooth or textured finish. Typical materials are plaster, concrete, mud and pebble-dash.

Roof

The following examples represent a small number of the many types of roof.
Corbelled: Continuous layers of brick or masonry, where each course cantilevers over the one below to meet at the top, forming a rough vault or dome.
Gable or Pitched: The most common type, with sloping roof planes meeting at a top ridge and with gables at both ends.
Gambrel: In the United States, a gambrel roof is the same as a **mansard** roof. Elsewhere, it is a hipped roof with a gable end at the apex.
Hipped: A roof with sloping ends rather than flat gable ends.
Mansard: Devised by French architect François Mansard (1598–1666) and particularly associated with Second Empire, the mansard roof has a relatively flat top slope and a steeper lower slope on each side, allowing for a room, usually with **dormer** windows, within.

Section

An accurately scaled, two-dimensional drawing representing a vertical slice through a building to show the arrangement of spaces, walls, windows, doors and roofs. (See Plan & Elevation)

String course

A horizontal band of moulding, such as brick or stone, on a **facade**.

Stucco

Slow-setting plaster used in Roman and Renaissance architecture to achieve a very smooth finish and three-dimensional surface decoration. It was used in early nineteenth-century English houses as an economical alternative to **ashlar** and was a popular exterior finish on Spanish or Mission Style homes and churches in the United States.

Tatami

A straw floor mat of a standard size (approximately 1.8 x 1.9 m or 70 x 35 in) in Japanese domestic architecture. Used in multiples, *tatami* mats determine the size and proportions of rooms.
See pages 62 and 67

Taliesin

Frank Lloyd Wright began construction of a new home and studio in 1911 near Spring Green, Wisconsin, calling it Taliesin after an ancient Celtic poet. When the house burned down in 1914 and again in 1925 and 1927, Wright's commitment to the house only [illegible] Taliesin Fellowship, offering apprenticeships to young students to work in the Taliesin studio where they assisted with every aspect of the practice. From 1937 Wright decided to build a new home and studio in Paradise Valley, Arizona, called Taliesin West which became a permanent winter 'camp' for the Taliesin Fellowship. It was built over several years by Wright and his apprentices, and remained under construction until his death in 1959.
See page 44

Transome(e)

A horizontal bar dividing the panes of a **window**.

Truss

A timber frame placed at intervals to form the structural component of a roof.

Tuscan *see* Orders

Vernacular

A term for traditional building forms specific to a region or country, relying on indigenous building materials and methods of construction.

Volute

The scroll-shaped form found in the capital of the Ionic **Order**.

Weatherboard

External timber cladding made of overlapping horizontal boards.

Window

The following examples represent a small number of the many variations of window types.
Bay: A window projecting out from an external wall, forming a recess in a room.
Casement: A window where the framed glass is hung on hinges, and opens either inwards or outwards.
Dormer: A window projecting from the pitched surface of a roof, having its own roof which can be either flat or pitched.
Double-glazing: A modern window in which two planes of glass are separated by an air space for thermal or acoustic insulation.
French: A casement window carried down to the floor so as to open like doors.
Oriel: Similar to a bay window but located only on an upper floor, it can be **cantilevered** or **corbelled** out from the wall.
Sash: A double- or triple-hung window where the framed glass panes are raised and lowered vertically by cords with counter balancing weights.

Directory

House opening times may be subject to change and access may be limited during restoration work. It is advisable to check the times and dates of opening prior to visiting or making travel arrangements. Private houses are not listed, unless they are open to the public.

Australia

Rose Seidler House 1950
Clissold Road, Wahroonga, Sydney, NSW
Open Sun, 10am to 5pm, via the Historic Houses Trust
www.hht.net.au

Brazil

Canoas House 1954
Estrada das Canoas, São Conrado, Rio de Janeiro
Open Fri, 1pm to 5pm
www.niemeyer.org.br/canoas/canoas.htm

Czech Republic

Tugendhat House 1930
Cernopolní 45, Brno
Open Wed to Sun, 10am to 6pm
Guided tours available
www.tugendhat-villa.cz

Finland

Summer House 1953
Muuratsalo, Jyväskylä
Open daily, June to mid Sept
Advance reservations necessary
Guided tours available, Mon, Wed & Fri, 1.30pm to 3.30pm
www.alvaraalto.fi/info/experimentalhouse.htm

Villa Mairea 1939
Noormarkku
Open only by appointment
www.villamairea.fi

France

Maisons La Roche-Jeanneret 1925
8–10 square du Docteur Blanche, Paris
Open Mon, 1.30pm to 6pm; Tues, Wed & Thurs, 10am to 12.30pm & 1.30pm to 6pm; Fri, 10am to 12.30pm & 1.30pm to 5pm
www.fondationlecorbusier.asso.fr

Villa Noailles 1933
Montée de Noailles, Hyères
Open daily July to Sept (except Tues), 10am to 12pm & 4pm to 7.30pm; Jan to June & Oct to Dec (except Mon & Tues), 10am to 12.30pm & 2pm to 5.30pm
www.villanoailles-hyeres.com

Villa Savoye 1931
Chemin de Villiers, Poissy
Open daily except Mon, Mar to Apr & Sept to Oct, 10am to 5pm; May to Aug, 10am to 6pm; Nov to Feb, 10am to 1pm & 2pm to 5pm
Closed 1 Jan, 1 May, 1 & 11 Nov & 25 Dec
villa-savoye.monuments-nationaux.fr

Germany

Double House 1926
Ebertallee, Dessau
Open Tues to Sun, 10am to 6pm (summer) & 10am to 5pm (winter)
Guided tours available
www.bauhaus-dessau.de

Schminke House 1933
Kirschallee, Löbau
Open Tues to Sun, 10am to 5pm
Guided tours available
www.hausschminke.de

Mexico

Barragán House 1948
Open by appointment only, Mon to Fri, 10am to 2pm & 4pm to 6pm, Sat, 10am to 1pm
www.casaluisbarragan.org
www.barragan-foundation.org

The Netherlands

Rietveld Schröder House 1924
Prins Hendriklaan 50, Utrecht
Open Thurs, Fri, Sat & Sun
Reservations are strongly recommended via the Centraal Museum from where a special bus leaves at fixed times: 11.45am, 12.45pm, 1.45pm & 2.45pm
www.centraalmuseum.nl
www.rietveldschroderhuis.nl

USA

Eames House 1949
Chautauqua Boulevard, Pacific Palisades, CA
This is a private residence; however, self-guided visits to the exterior & grounds are available to the general public by appointment only
www.eamesfoundation.org

Eichler Home 1950s
Various locations in San Francisco Bay area & Marin County, CA
Tours of Eichler Homes operate annually and Eichler Homes can be purchased
www.eichlerforsale.com

Fallingwater 1939
Bear Run, PA
Open daily (except Wed), Mar to Thanksgiving weekend, Dec weekends, Christmas week and the first two weekends in Mar, 10am to 4pm; Easter Sunday, Memorial Day, 4 July, Labor Day, Columbus Day, Thanksgiving Friday, 1pm to 4pm; Closed Jan & Feb
Guided tours available
www.fallingwater.org

Farnsworth House 1950
River Road, Plano, IL
Open for tours, Apr to Oct, Tues to Sun, 10am to 3pm
Closed Mon, Easter, Labor Day & 4 July
Advance reservations are required for all admissions
www.farnsworthhouse.org

Glass House 1949
The Glass House Visitor Center, Elm Street, New Canaan, CT
Tours run annually from Apr to Oct
www.philipjohnsonglasshouse.org

J Irwin & Xenia Miller House & Garden 1957
5th Street, Columbus, IN
Open Apr to Sept; contact for details

Kings Road Studios 1922
Schindler House/MAK Center for Arts & Architecture, North Kings Road, Los Angeles, CA
Open Wed to Sun, 11am to 6pm
www.makcenter.org

Robie House 1910
5757 South Woodlawn Avenue
University of Chicago, IL
Open for guided tours only, Sat, 11am to 3pm, tours every hour
www.wrightplus.org/robiehouse

Umbrella House 1953
Lido Shores, Sarasota, FL
Visits by appointment; see website for details
www.umbrellahouse.com

Index

The entries in **bold** are the architects and houses featured in this book.

Acknowledgements

Texts written by Iona Baird, Raul Barreneche, Karla Britton, Catherine Croft, Talia Dorsey, Beth Dunlop, Kimberly Elman Zarecor, Martin Goalen, Sarah Jackson, Ann Jarmusch, Virginia McLeod, Clare Melhuish, Jeremy Melvin, Aulani Mulford, Dung Ngo, Ken Tadashi Oshima, Alan Powers, Anthony Quiney, Kester Rattenbury, Tsuto Sakamoto, Justine Sambrook, Torsten Schmiedneknecht, Jagan Shah, Steven Spier and Naomi Stungo.

Photographic Credits

© Akademie der Künste, Berlin, Luckhardt-Archiv: 18; AKG London/ Erich Lessing: 5; Ole Akhøj: 60; © Stefan Antoni: 102; Archipress/ Franck Eustache: 17, 20, 30; Archipress/Michel Moch: 57; Reproduced courtesy of the Architectural Review: 37; Luis Barragán/Armando Salas Portugal © 2009 Barragán Foundation, Birsfelden, Switzerland: 45; © CH Bastin & J Evrard: 39; Staffan Berglund Arkitektkontor AB: 75; Bildarchiv-Monheim.de/© Florian Monheim: 31; © Hélène Binet: 100; Arquivo Lina Bo Bardi/Arnaldo Pappalardo: 53; Canadian Centre for Architecture, Montréal/Collection Centre Canadien d'Architecture: 15, 21; Lluis Casals Fotografia: 97; Peter Cook: 40, 50; Richard Davies: 93; © Nick Dawe: 19, 33, 34; Orestis Doumanis: 65; Ezra Stoller © Esto: 56, 64, 78; Luis Ferreira Alves: 98; © FLC 2008: 25; © FLC 2009/Olivier Martin Gambier: 11; John Gollings: 88; Luis Gordoa: 95; Ian Graymore: 70; Fernando Guerra/FG+SG: 103; © Pedro E Guerrero: 46; Miguel de Guzman Garcia Monge: 82; Lars Hallén/Design Press: 41; Courtesy of the Frances Loeb Library, Harvard Graduate School of Design: 61; Hiroyuki Hirai/Hirai Photo Office: 35; Pierre Joly et Véra Cardot Photographes: 69, 74; © G.E. Kidder Smith/CORBIS: 4; Kitazawa Architects: 9; Nelson Kon: 87; Balthazar Korab Ltd: 48, 59; Mahatta Madan: 80; Mitsuo Matsuoka: 83; Kaneaki Monma: 67; Nacasa & Partners Inc.: 99; National Trust Photographic Library/Dennis Gilbert: 36; Collection Netherlands Architecture Institute, Rotterdam: 8, 22; Norsk Arkitekturmuseum/Jim Bengston: 26; Norsk Arkitekturmuseum/Jiri Havran: 86; Frank den Oudsten: 6, 10; John Panikar: 84; © Christine Pemberton/ Eye Ubiquitous/Hutchison: 42; Centre Pompidou: 58; Ramon Prat: 54; © Patrick Reynolds: 101; RIBA Library Photographs Collection: 32; Christian Richters: 12; Simo Rista: 55; © digital image (2007) The Museum of Modern Art/Scala, Florence: 16; Ben Schnall, New York: 72; © Simon Scott: 76; John Searle: 96; © Vaclav Sedy: 24, 28; Harry Seidler: 49; Shinkenchiku-sha: 29, 62, 71, 81, 89, 94; © J. Paul Getty Trust. Used with permission. Julius Shulman Photography Archive, Research Library at the Getty Research Institute: 23, 44, 51, 52, 63, 66; Filippo Simonetti: 85; Alison & Peter Smithson Archive: 13; Tim Street-Porter: 7, 47, 73; Hisao Suzuki: 90; UFSE, SAIF, 2009: 14; Nicos Valsamakis: 68; Kjeld Vindum: 38; Hans Werleman: 91; Claudio Williams: 43; Bertram D. Wolfe Collection/Hoover Institution Archives/ Stanford University: 27; Alo Zanetta: 77, 92; Courtesy of Marco Zanuso: 79.

Jacket front cover: Tim Street-Porter; back cover: © Adam Eastland/Alamy

All reasonable efforts have been made to trace the copyright holders of the photographs used in this book. We apologize to anyone that we have been unable to reach.

Phaidon Press Limited
Regent's Wharf
All Saints Street
London N1 9PA

Phaidon Press Inc.
180 Varick Street
New York, NY 10014

www.phaidon.com

First published as *The House Book* 2001
This edition abridged, revised and updated 2009

ISBN 978 0 7148 4968 3

A CIP catalogue record for this book is available from the British Library.

Designed by Susanne Olsson
Printed in China